Wisdom and Sound Advice from the Torah

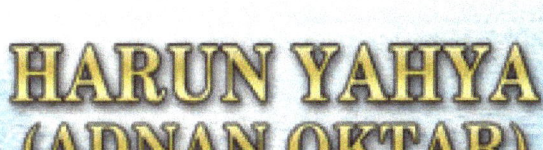

HARUN YAHYA
(ADNAN OKTAR)

About the Author

Now writing under the pen-name of HARUN YAHYA, Adnan Oktar was born in Ankara in 1956. Having completed his primary and secondary education in Ankara, he studied fine arts at Istanbul's Mimar Sinan University and philosophy at Istanbul University. Since the 1980s, he has published many books on political, scientific, and faith-related issues. Harun Yahya is well-known as the author of important works disclosing the imposture of evolutionists, their invalid claims, and the dark liaisons between Darwinism and such bloody ideologies as fascism and communism.

Harun Yahya's works, translated into 72 different languages, constitute a collection for a total of more than 55,000 pages with 40,000 illustrations.

His pen-name is a composite of the names Harun (Aaron) and Yahya (John), in memory of the two esteemed Prophets who fought against their peoples' lack of faith. The Prophet's seal on his books' covers is symbolic and is linked to their contents. It represents the Qur'an (the Final Scripture) and Prophet Muhammad (saas), last of the prophets. Under the guidance of the Qur'an and the Sunnah (teachings of the Prophet [saas]), the author makes it his purpose to disprove each fundamental tenet of irreligious ideologies and to have the "last word," so as to completely silence the objections raised against religion. He uses the seal of the final Prophet (saas), who attained ultimate wisdom and moral perfection, as a sign of his intention to offer the last word.

All of Harun Yahya's works share one single goal: to convey the Qur'an's message, encourage readers to consider basic faith-related issues such as Allah's existence and unity and the Hereafter; and to expose irreligious systems' feeble foundations and perverted ideologies.

Harun Yahya enjoys a wide readership in many countries, from India to America, England to Indonesia, Poland to Bosnia, Spain to Brazil, Malaysia to Italy, France to Bulgaria and Russia. Some of his books are available in English, French, German, Spanish, Italian, Portuguese, Urdu, Arabic, Albanian, Chinese, Swahili, Hausa, Dhivehi (spoken in Maldives), Russian, Serbo-Croat (Bosnian), Polish, Malay, Uighur Turkish, Indonesian, Bengali, Danish and Swedish.

Greatly appreciated all around the world, these works have been instrumental in many people recovering faith in Allah and gaining deeper insights into their faith. His books' wisdom and sincerity, together with a distinct style that's easy to understand, directly affect anyone who reads them. Those who seriously consider these books, can no longer advocate atheism or any other perverted ideology or materialistic philosophy, since these books are characterized by rapid effectiveness, definite results, and irrefutability. Even if they continue to do so, it will be only a sentimental insistence, since these books refute such ideologies from their very foundations. All contemporary movements of denial are now ideologically defeated, by means of the books written by Harun Yahya.

This is no doubt a result of the Qur'an's wisdom and lucidity. The author modestly intends to serve as a means in humanity's search for Allah's right path. No material gain is sought in the publication of these works.

Those who encourage others to read these books, to open their minds and hearts and guide them to become more devoted servants of Allah, render an invaluable service.

Meanwhile, it would only be a waste of time and energy to propagate other books that create confusion in people's minds, lead them into ideological confusion, and that clearly have no strong and precise effects in removing the doubts in people's hearts, as also verified from previous experience. It is impossible for books devised to emphasize the author's literary power rather than the noble goal of saving people from loss of faith, to have such a great effect. Those who doubt this can readily see that the sole aim of Harun Yahya's books is to overcome disbelief and to disseminate the Qur'an's moral values. The success and impact of this service are manifested in the readers' conviction.

One point should be kept in mind: The main reason for the continuing cruelty, conflict, and other ordeals endured by the vast majority of people is the ideological prevalence of disbelief. This can be ended only with the ideological defeat of disbelief and by conveying the wonders of creation and Qur'anic morality so that people can live by it. Considering the state of the world today, leading into a downward spiral of violence, corruption and conflict, clearly this service must be provided speedily and effectively, or it may be too late.

In this effort, the books of Harun Yahya assume a leading role. By the will of Allah, these books will be a means through which people in the twenty-first century will attain the peace, justice, and happiness promised in the Qur'an.

TO THE READER

• A special chapter is assigned to the collapse of the theory of evolution because this theory constitutes the basis of all anti-spiritual philosophies. Since Darwinism rejects the fact of creation—and therefore, Allah's existence—over the last 150 years it has caused many people to abandon their faith or fall into doubt. It is therefore an imperative service, a very important duty to show everyone that this theory is a deception. Since some readers may find the opportunity to read only one of our books, we think it appropriate to devote a chapter to summarize this subject.

• All the author's books explain faith-related issues in light of Qur'anic verses, and invite readers to learn Allah's words and to live by them. All the subjects concerning Allah's verses are explained so as to leave no doubt or room for questions in the reader's mind. The books' sincere, plain, and fluent style ensures that everyone of every age and from every social group can easily understand them. Due to their effective, lucid narrative, they can be read at one sitting. Even those who rigorously reject spirituality are influenced by the facts these books document and cannot refute the truthfulness of their contents.

• This and all the other books by the author can be read individually, or discussed in a group. Readers eager to profit from the books will find discussion very useful, letting them relate their reflections and experiences to one another.

• In addition, it will be a great service to Islam to contribute to the publication and reading of these books, written solely for the pleasure of Allah. The author's books are all extremely convincing. For this reason, to communicate true religion to others, one of the most effective methods is encouraging them to read these books.

• We hope the reader will look through the reviews of his other books at the back of this book. His rich source material on faith-related issues is very useful, and a pleasure to read.

• In these books, unlike some other books, you will not find the author's personal views, explanations based on dubious sources, styles that are unobservant of the respect and reverence due to sacred subjects, nor hopeless, pessimistic arguments that create doubts in the mind and deviations in the heart.

HARUN YAHYA
(ADNAN OKTAR)

Wisdom and Sound Advice from the Torah

CONTENTS

**VERSES FROM THE QUR'AN ABOUT
THE TORAH SENT TO THE JEWISH PEOPLE** 16

LOVE OF GOD ACCORDING TO THE TORAH 18

FEAR OF GOD ACCORDING TO THE TORAH 21

**CLOSENESS TO GOD AND DEPTH OF FAITH
ACCORDING TO THE TORAH** 31
  Closeness to God 31
  Devotion and Loyalty to God 35
  Showing Respect for God 37
  The Excitement and Joy of Faith................... 38
  The Importance of Deep Thinking 47
  Passages from the Torah Encouraging Examination
  of the Signs Leading to Faith 49
  Statements from the Torah Regarding the Transient
  Nature of This World 54

**THE ATTRIBUTES OF GOD
ACCORDING TO THE TORAH** 60
  The Oneness of God 60
  God's Being Eternal and Infinite 63
  God the Creator of All Things 64
  God the All-seeing, All-Hearing and Omniscient 70

God the Only Power and Will 72
God's Bestowal of the Human Soul 74
God the Infinitely Just 76
God the Loving, Compassionate and All-Forgiving 79
God's Being Omnipresent 84
God the Provider of Sustenance 85
God the All-Encompassing Ruler 87
God's Being Free From All Imperfection 89

BELIEF IN THE HEREAFTER
ACCORDING TO THE TORAH 90
Resurrection 90
The Last Day 91
The Day of Judgment 94
Hell 95
Paradise 99
The Prophet Adam (pbuh) and the Garden of Eden 101

THE OBLIGATIONS OF FAITH
ACCORDING TO THE TORAH 102
Faith in God Without Idolatry 102
Gratitude to God 105
Submission to God 109
Obedience to God's Commandments 119
Heeding the Conscience 129
Timelessness and Belief in Destiny 130
The Importance of Prayer 133
Belief in Angels 140

**MORAL VIRTUES RECOMMENDED
IN THE TORAH** 144
    Humility: Avoiding Pride and Arrogance 144
    Overcoming Anger 153
    Forgiveness 154
    Compassion and Affection 155
    Ruling with Justice and Defending the Truth 159
    Helping Others 167
    Doing Good and Turning from Evil 170
    Truthfulness and Honesty 172
    Patience 176
    Loyalty 176
    Avoiding Despotism 179
    The Importance of Peace and Friendship 181
    The Importance of Reason and Wisdom 186
    Generosity and Avoiding Parsimony 198
    Trusting in God, not in Material Power 200
    Avoiding Unfair Earnings 202
    Industry and Avoiding Sloth 205
    Avoiding Mockery 207
    Avoiding Despair and Finding Peace Through
    Faith in God 209
    Spiritual Cleanliness 212
    The Servants Promised Happiness by God 215

**THE IMPORTANCE OF REMEMBERING GOD AND SAYING
GOOD WORDS ACCORDING TO THE TORAH** 218
    Speaking of God 218
    Speaking the Truth 221
    Speaking Wisely and Concisely 225

Avoiding Evil Words and Speaking Truthfully 226

Preaching Goodness and Forbidding Evil 228

Avoiding Idle Talk 229

Avoiding Gossip 230

Other Forms of Speech Recommended 230

THE COMMANDMENTS AND PROHIBITIONS ACCORDING TO THE TORAH THAT ARE COMPATIBLE WITH THOSE IN THE QUR'AN 232

Lying Is Prohibited 232

Theft Is Prohibited 233

Eating Pork Is Prohibited 234

Earning Interest Is Prohibited 234

Distractions Such As Astrology and Fortune-Telling
Are Prohibited 235

Taking Bribes Is Prohibited 236

Cheating Is Prohibited 237

Murdering Is Prohibited 238

Adultery Is Prohibited 238

Homosexuality Is Prohibited 239

Eating Blood Products Is Prohibited 239

Eating the Flesh of Dead Animals Is Prohibited 240

RELIGIOUS OBSERVANCES ACCORDING TO THE TORAH THAT ARE COMPATIBLE WITH THE QUR'AN 241

Daily Prayer (Salat) 241

Fasting 245

Giving Alms (Zakat) 246

Ablution (Wudu) 248

**SOME OF THE BEAUTIES CREATED BY GOD THAT ARE
REFERRED TO IN THE TORAH** 250

    The Beauty of God 250

    The Beauty in Objects..................................... 251

    Beautiful Plants.. 251

    Beautiful Foods.. 252

    Beautiful Places... 253

    Beautiful Scents... 254

    Beautiful Words 256

**THE ORDER IN THE UNIVERSE AND CREATION
ACCORDING TO THE TORAH** 257

    The Creation of the Heavens and the Earth............... 257

    The Creation of Light...................................... 258

    The Creation of Night and Day 259

    The Creation of Celestial Bodies 259

    The Creation of the Heavens Within an Order 260

    The Earth's Position in Space 260

    The Course of the Sun 260

    The Movement of the Winds Within an Order 260

    The Order and Cycle in the Waters....................... 261

    The Protective Nature of the Atmosphere 261

    The Creation of Animals.................................. 262

    The Creation of Plants 262

    The Creation of Man 263

    The Heretical Darwinist Idea of "Mother Nature" 264

    The Positive Effect on Health of Moral Virtue 265

ART AND ARCHITECTURE
ACCORDING TO THE TORAH 266
   Gold Veneer 266
   Timber Panelling 268
   The Art of Carving and Relief Work 269
   The Use of Decorative Plant Motifs 270
   Decorative Gold Objects 273
   The Use of Silver 277
   Thick Beams 278
   Decorated Baths 278
   Windows 280
   Ivory Decorations 280
   Columns 281
   Courtyards 283
   Curtains 283
   Embroidered Garments 285
   Decoration with Precious Stones 288
   An Understanding of Art and Beauty
   as a Blessing from God 289

SIMILAR PASSAGES FROM THE QUR'AN AND
THE TORAH 290
   Everything Is Written in a Book 290
   God Is Always with Believers 291
   Even if the Faithful are Few in Numbers,
   They Will Still Emerge Victorious 291
   A Thousand Years is Like One Day in the Sight of God .. 291
   Sinners Can Be Known from Their Faces 292
   Human Beings Are Tested 292

Unbelievers' Mockery of the Messengers 292
God Is Close to Believers and Answers Prayers 292
People's True Duty Is to Serve God 293
The Hardening of Hearts 294
How Unbelievers Killed Prophets.......................... 294
Believers Think Deeply About God's Creation 295
Nobody Can Alter God's Laws 295
Worldly Riches Are of No Avail in the Hereafter........... 295
How the Number of God's Blessings
Cannot Be Counted 296
God Elevates or Lowers Whomsoever He Chooses 296
People Are Punished for Their Own Evil Deeds.............. 297
How the Morally Corrupt Communicate by Means of
Ignorant Facial Expressions 297
Unbelievers' Eyes and Ears Are Insensitive................ 297
Believers' Responding to Evil with Good................... 298
It Is God Who Bestows Sustenance 298
Those Who Do Good and Evil Will Be Recompensed 299
Nothing Can Be Hidden from God 299
Nobody Can Assume Responsibility for Another's Sins 300
If the Guilty Were Punished At Once, There
Would Be Nobody Left on Earth 301
An Example of Those Who Do not Put Their
Trust in God 301
The Oneness of God....................................... 301
God Being the Generous and Loving 302
God Leads Those on His Path to Success................... 302
God is the Creator of the Earth and
the Heavens and All Between 302

Believers' Placing Their Hopes in God 303
He is the Creator of Ears and Eyes 303
Everything Being Simultaneously Under God's Command . . . 304
It is God Who Leads to Salvation 304
God is He in Whom Shelter is Sought 304
How the Earth will Be Flattened on the Judgment Day 305
It is God Who Bestows Life and Kills 305
How God Gives All Living Things to Man
as a Blessing 305
God Raises, Lowers and Bestows Goods on
Whom He Pleases. 306
Believers' Fearing None Other Than God 307
How God Shapes Man. 308
The Order in the Heavens. 308

**PRACTICES IN THE TORAH COMPATIBLE
WITH THE SUNNAH OF THE PROPHET MUHAMMAD
(May God Bless Him and Grant Him Peace) 309**
Forms of Dress Recommended According to the Torah 311
The Importance Attached to Cleanliness
According to the Torah 316
Foods and Drinks Noted in the Torah 325
Other Practices in the Torah Compatible with the Sunnah of
the Prophet Muhammad (May God Bless Him
and Grant Him Peace) 335

PASSAGES FROM THE PSALMS AND THE PROVERBS 338

THE DECEPTION OF EVOLUTION 434

VERSES FROM THE QUR'AN ABOUT THE TORAH[1] SENT TO THE JEWISH PEOPLE

We sent down the Torah containing guidance and light, and the Prophets who had submitted themselves gave judgement by it for the Jews—as did their scholars [Rabaniyun] and their rabbis [Ahbar]—by what they had been allowed to preserve of Allah's Book to which they were witnesses... (Surat al-Ma'ida, 44)

Then **We gave Moses the Book, complete and perfect for him** who does good, elucidating everything, and a guidance and a mercy, so that hopefully they believe in their encounter with their Lord. (Surat al-An'am, 154)

But before it **there was the Book of Moses as a model [imam] and a mercy**. And this is a corroborating Book in the Arabic tongue so that you may warn those who do wrong, and as good news for the good-doers. (Surat al-Ahqaf, 12)

We sent Moses with Our signs: **"Bring your people from the darkness to the light, and remind them of the Days of Allah."** There are certainly signs in that for everyone who is steadfast, thankful. (Surah Ibrahim, 5)

He [Allah] said, "Moses, I have chosen you over all mankind for My message and My word. Take what I have given you and be among the thankful." **We wrote about everything for him on the Tablets as an admonition and making all things clear**. "Seize hold of it vigorously and command your people to adopt the best in it. I will show you the home of the deviators!" (Surat al-A'raf, 144-145)

When Moses's anger abated he picked up the Tablets and in their inscription was **guidance and mercy for all of them who feared their Lord.** (Surat al-A'raf, 154)

We gave Moses the Book -be in no doubt about the meeting with him- and **made it a guidance** for the tribe of Israel. (Surat as-Sajda, 23)

Say, "We believe in Allah and what has been sent down to us and what was sent down to Abraham and Ishmael and Isaac and Jacob and the Tribes, and what Moses and Jesus were given, and what all the Prophets were given by their Lord. We do not differentiate between any of them. We are Muslims submitted to Him." (Surat al-Baqara, 136)

He has laid down the same religion for you as He enjoined on Noah: that which We have revealed to you and which We enjoined on Abraham, Moses and Jesus: "Establish the religion and do not make divisions in it."... (Surat al-Shura, 13)

Allah has bought from the believers their selves and their wealth in return for the Garden. They fight in the way of Allah and they kill and are killed. It is a promise binding on Him in the Torah, the Gospel and the Qur'an and who is truer to his contract than Allah? Rejoice then in the bargain you have made. That is the great victory. (Surat at-Tawba, 111)

1- The term 'Torah' relates in this book to all the books of the Hebrew Bible, held holy by the Jews.

LOVE OF GOD ACCORDING TO THE TORAH

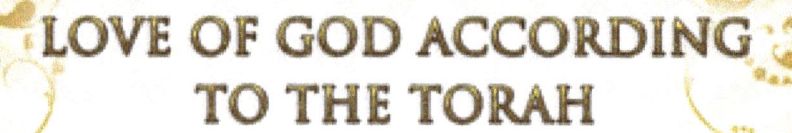

Love the Lord your God with all your heart and with all your soul and with all your strength. (Deuteronomy, 6:5)

... **The Lord your God is testing you to find out whether you love Him with all your heart and with all your soul.** (Deuteronomy, 13:3)

... **What does the Lord your God ask of you** but to fear the Lord your God, to walk in all His ways, **to love Him,** to serve the Lord your God with all your heart and with all your soul, and to observe the Lord's commands and decrees that I am giving you today for your own good? (Deuteronomy, 10:12-13)

Love the Lord your God and keep His requirements, His decrees, His laws and His commands always. (Deuteronomy, 11:1)

I love those who love Me... (Proverbs, 8:17)

[The Lord] ... **showing love to a thousand generations of those who love Me** and keep My commandments. (Deuteronomy, 5:10)

... **Love the Lord your God**... (Deuteronomy, 30:20)

... **Love the Lord your God,** to walk in all His ways, to obey His commands, to hold fast to Him and to serve Him with all your heart and all your soul. (Joshua, 22:5)

Know therefore that the Lord your God is God; He is the faithful God, keeping His covenant of love to... **those who love Him** and keep His commands. (Deuteronomy, 7:9)

So **if you faithfully obey the commands I am giving you today—to love the Lord your God** and to serve Him with all your heart and with all your soul—then I will send rain on your land in its season, both autumn and spring rains... (Deuteronomy, 11:13-14)

O Lord, God of Heaven, the great and awesome God, **Who keeps His covenant of love with those who love Him** and obey His commands. (Nehemiah, 1:5)

I love... O Lord, the place where Your glory dwells. (Psalms, 26:8)

How lovely is Your dwelling place, O Lord Almighty!... for the courts of the Lord; my heart and my flesh cry out for the living God. (Psalms, 84:1-2)

So **be very careful to love the Lord your God**. (Joshua, 23:11)

Love the Lord your God and keep His requirements, His decrees, His laws and His commands always. (Deuteronomy, 11:1)

... **You may love Him [God] with all your heart and with all your soul, and live**. (Deuteronomy, 30:6)

WISDOM AND SOUND ADVICE FROM THE TORAH

Love the Lord, all His saints! The Lord preserves the faithful... (Psalms, 31:23)

I love you, O Lord, my strength. (Psalms, 18:1)

I love the Lord... I will call on Him as long as I live. (Psalms, 116:1-2)

"Because he loves Me," says the Lord, "I will rescue him..." (Psalms, 91:14)

Let **those who love the Lord** hate evil, for He guards the lives of His faithful ones and delivers them from the hand of the wicked. (Psalms, 97:10)

For **I command you today to love the Lord your God**, to walk in His ways, and to keep His commands, decrees and laws... and the Lord your God will bless you... (Deuteronomy, 30:16)

... You carefully follow all these laws I command you today— **to love the Lord your God** and to walk always in His ways... (Deuteronomy, 19:9)

If you carefully observe all these commands I am giving you to follow—**to love the Lord your God**, to walk in all His ways and to hold fast to Him- (Deuteronomy, 11:22)

But let all who take refuge in You be glad; ... those who love Your name may rejoice in You. (Psalms, 5:11)

The Lord watches over all who love Him... (Psalms, 145:20)

FEAR OF GOD ACCORDING TO THE TORAH

But from **everlasting to everlasting the Lord's love is with those who fear Him**... (Psalms, 103:17)

The fear of the Lord is the beginning of wisdom; all who follow His precepts have good understanding. (Psalms, 111:10)

Serve the Lord with fear and rejoice with trembling. (Psalms, 2:11)

Blessed are all who fear the Lord, who walk in His ways. You will eat the fruit of your labor; blessings and prosperity will be yours. **Thus is the man blessed who fears the Lord.** (Psalms, 128:1-2-4)

The fear of the Lord leads to life: Then one rests content, untouched by trouble. (Proverbs, 19:23)

Do not be wise in your own eyes; **fear the Lord** and shun evil. **This will bring health to your body and nourishment** to your bones. (Proverbs, 3:7-8)

He who fears the Lord has a secure fortress... The fear of the Lord is a fountain of life ... (Proverbs, 14:26-27)

... **Through the fear of the Lord a man avoids evil.** (Proverbs, 16:6)

... **Always be zealous for the fear of the Lord**. There is surely a future hope for you, and your hope will not be cut off. (Proverbs, 23:17-18)

... **What does the Lord your God ask of you but to fear the Lord your God,** to walk in all His ways, to love Him, to serve the Lord your God with all your heart and with all your soul, and to observe the Lord's commands and decrees that I am giving you today for your own good? (Deuteronomy, 10:12-13)

It is the Lord your God you must follow, and **Him you must revere.** Keep His commands and obey Him; serve Him and hold fast to Him. (Deuteronomy, 13:4)

The fear of the Lord is pure, enduring forever. (Psalms, 19:9)

Moses said to the people "... God has come to test you, so that **the fear of God will be with you to keep you from sinning.**" (Exodus, 20:20)

He will be the sure foundation for your times, a rich store of salvation and wisdom and knowledge; **the fear of the Lord is the key to this treasure.** (Isaiah, 33:6)

If you do not carefully follow all the words of this law, which are written in this book, and do not **revere this glorious and awesome name—the Lord your God—**the Lord will send fearful plagues on you and your descendants, harsh and prolonged disasters, and severe and lingering illnesses. (Deuteronomy, 28:58-59)

The fear of the Lord teaches a man wisdom, and humility comes before honor. (Proverbs, 15:33)

Now **fear the Lord** and serve Him with all faithfulness. (Joshua, 24:14)

The Lord Almighty is the One you are to regard as holy, **He is the One you are to fear,** He is the One you are to dread. (Isaiah, 8:13)

Fear the Lord your God and serve Him. Hold fast to Him and take your oaths in His name. (Deuteronomy, 10:20)

Observe the commands of the Lord your God, walking in His ways and **revering Him.** (Deuteronomy, 8:6)

... so that you, your children and their children after them may **fear the Lord your God** as long as you live by keeping all His decrees and commands that I give you, and so that you may enjoy long life. (Deuteronomy, 6:2)

Praise the Lord. **Blessed is the man who fears the Lord,** who finds great delight in His commands. (Psalms, 112:1)

You who fear the Lord, praise Him! (Psalms, 22:23)

In the council of the holy ones God is greatly feared. He is more awesome than all who surround Him. (Psalms, 89:7)

To fear the Lord is to hate evil... (Proverbs, 8:13)

I am a friend to all who fear You, to all who follow Your precepts. (Psalms, 119:63)

Oh, **that their hearts would be inclined to fear Me** and keep all My commands always, so that it might go well with them and their children forever! (Deuteronomy, 5:29)

The midwives, however, **feared God...** and **because the midwives feared God,** He gave them families of their own. (Exodus, 1:17, 21)

In the land of Uz there lived a man whose name was **Job**. This man was blameless and upright; **he feared God** and shunned evil. (Job, 1:1)

The mountains quake before Him and the hills melt away. The earth trembles at His presence, the world and all who live in it. (Nahum, 1:5)

I issue a decree that in every part of my kingdom people **must fear and reverence the God** of Daniel... (Daniel, 6:26)

Who, then, is **the man that fears the Lord**? He will instruct him in the way chosen for him. He will spend his days in prosperity... (Psalms, 25:12-14)

... **You must serve** faithfully and wholeheartedly **in the fear of the Lord.** (2 Chronicles, 19:9)

The fear of the Lord is the beginning of knowledge... (Proverbs, 1:7)

Do not take advantage of each other, but **fear your God**. I am the Lord your God. (Leviticus, 25:17)

If you fear the Lord and serve and obey Him and do not rebel against His commands... But **be sure to fear the Lord** and serve Him faithfully with all your heart; consider what great things He has done for you. (1 Samuel, 12:14, 24)

Assemble the people—men, women and children, and the aliens living in your towns—so they can listen and **learn to fear the Lord your God a**nd follow carefully all the words of this law... **[They must] learn to fear the Lord your God** as long as you live in the land... (Deuteronomy, 31:12-13)

The Lord is near to all who call on Him, to all who call on Him in truth. **He fulfills the desires of those who fear Him**... (Psalms, 145:18-19)

Let all the earth fear the Lord; let all the people of the world revere Him. For He spoke, and it came to be; He commanded, and it stood firm. (Psalms, 33:8-9)

Fear the Lord your God, serve Him only and take your oaths in His name. Do not follow other gods, the gods of the peoples around you. (Deuteronomy, 6:13-14)

Do not curse the deaf or put a stumbling block in front of the blind, **but fear your God.** I am the Lord. (Leviticus, 19:14)

... Show respect for the elderly and **you will fear the Lord your God**. I am the Lord. (Leviticus, 19:32)

My son, if you accept My words and store up My commands within you, turning your ear to wisdom and applying your heart to understanding, and if you call out for insight and cry aloud for understanding, and if you look for it as for silver and search for it as for hidden treasure, then **you will under-**

WISDOM AND SOUND ADVICE FROM THE TORAH

stand the fear of the Lord and find the knowledge of God. For the Lord gives wisdom... (Proverbs, 2:1-6)

Instruct a wise man and he will be wiser still; teach a righteous man and he will add to his learning. **The fear of the Lord is the beginning of wisdom,** and knowledge of the Holy One [God] is understanding. (Proverbs, 9:9-10)

The Lord is compassionate and gracious... **so great is His love for those who fear Him... so the Lord has compassion on those who fear Him.** (Psalms, 103:8, 11,13)

The fear of the Lord adds length to life, but the years of the wicked are cut short. (Proverbs, 10:27)

He whose walk is upright fears the Lord... (Proverbs, 14:2)

The angel of the Lord encamps around those who fear Him, and He delivers them... **Fear the Lord... for those who fear Him lack nothing.** (Psalms, 34:7-9)

For You are great and do marvelous deeds; You alone are God. Teach me Your way, O Lord, and I will walk in Your truth; **give me an undivided heart, that I may fear Your Name.** (Psalms, 86:10-11)

You who fear Him, trust in the Lord—He is their help and shield [protector]... **He will bless those who fear the Lord** small and great alike. (Psalms, 115:11-13)

Give thanks to the Lord, for He is good; His love endures forever... **Let those who fear the Lord say: "His love endures forever."** (Psalms, 118:1-4)

... You who fear Him, praise the Lord. (Psalms, 135:20)

The Lord delights in those who fear Him, who put their hope in His unfailing love. (Psalms, 147:11)

A wise man fears the Lord and shuns evil... (Proverbs, 14:16)

Better a little with **the fear of the Lord** than great wealth with turmoil. (Proverbs, 15:16)

Humility and **the fear of the Lord** bring wealth and honor and life. (Proverbs, 22:4)

He whose walk is blameless and who does what is righteous, who speaks the truth from his heart... **honors those who fear the Lord...** (Psalms, 15:2-4)

Then the Lord said... "Have you considered My servant **Job**? ... He is blameless and upright, **a man who fears God** and shuns evil..." (Job, 2:3)

How great is Your goodness, which You have stored up **for those who fear You...** (Psalms, 31:19)

But **the eyes of the Lord are on those who fear Him**, on those whose hope is in His unfailing love. (Psalms, 33:18)

Come, my children, listen to me; **I will teach you the fear of the Lord.** Whoever of you loves life and desires to see many good days, keep your tongue from evil and your lips from speaking lies. Turn from evil and do good; seek peace and pursue it. (Psalms, 34:11-14)

Come and listen, **all you who fear God**; let me tell you what He [God] has done for me. (Psalms, 66:16)

Teach them the decrees and laws, and show them the way to live and the duties they are to perform. But **select capable men from all the people—men who fear God**, trustworthy men who hate dishonest gain... (Exodus, 18:20-21)

May the peoples praise You, O God; may all the peoples praise You... **and all the ends of the earth will fear Him.** (Psalms, 67:5-7)

If your brother becomes poor and is unable to support himself among you, help him as you would a stranger or a temporary resident, so he can continue to live among you. Do not take interest of any kind from him, **but fear your God**, so that your brother may continue to live among you... Do not rule over them with rigor, but **fear your God.** (Leviticus, 25:35-36, 43)

You [My Lord] alone are to be feared... (Psalms, 76:7)

He promises peace to His people, His saints—but let them not return to folly. Surely **His salvation is near those who fear Him...** (Psalms, 85:8-9)

... **The people feared the Lord** and put their trust in Him and in Moses His servant. (Exodus, 14:31)

It [a copy of this law] is to be with him, and he is to read it all the days of his life so that he may **learn to fear the Lord his God** and follow carefully all the words of this law and these decrees and not consider himself better than his brothers and turn from the law to the right or to the left. Then he and his descendants will reign a long time over his kingdom in Israel. (Deuteronomy, 17:19-20)

For the fear of God kept me back, and because of His power I might not do such things. (Job, 31:23)

Is not your fear of God your confidence, you're your upright way of life your hope? (Job, 4:6)

The Lord commanded us to obey all these decrees and **to fear the Lord our God**, so that we might always prosper... (Deuteronomy, 6:24)

But the earlier governors—those preceding me—placed a heavy burden on the people... Their assistants also lorded it over the people. But I did not so **because of the fear of God**. (Nehemiah, 5:15)

Now let the fear of the Lord be upon you. Judge carefully, for with the Lord our God there is no injustice or partiality or bribery... Jehoshaphat... gave them these orders: "You must serve faithfully and wholeheartedly in the fear of the Lord." (2 Chronicles 19:7-9)

WISDOM AND SOUND ADVICE FROM THE TORAH

Although a wicked man commits a hundred crimes and still lives a long time, I know that **it will go better with God-fearing men, who are reverent before God.** Yet because the wicked do not fear God, it will not go well with them... (Ecclesiastes, 8:12-13)

Listen!... **to fear Your [God's] name is wisdom**... (Micah, 6:9)

Did He not **fear the Lord** and seek his favor?... (Jeremiah, 26:19)

You are great, and Your name is mighty in power. **Who should not fear You...** (Jeremiah, 10:6-7)

... so that **they will fear You** and walk in Your ways all the time they live... so that **all the peoples of the earth** may know Your name and **fear You...** (2 Chronicles, 6:31-33)

CLOSENESS TO GOD AND DEPTH OF FAITH ACCORDING TO THE TORAH

Closeness to God

The Lord is near to all who call on Him, to all who call on Him in truth. (Psalms, 145:18)

Find rest, O my soul, **in God alone;** my hope comes from Him. (Psalms, 62:5)

To You, O Lord, **I lift up my soul.** (Psalms, 25:1)

But your hearts must be fully committed to the Lord our God, to live by His decrees and obey His commands, as at this time. (1 Kings, 8:61)

I love those who love Me, and **those who seek Me find Me.** (Proverbs, 8:17)

... and that you may love the Lord your God, listen to His voice, and **hold fast to Him. For the Lord is your life**... (Deuteronomy, 30:20)

Be careful that you do not forget the Lord your God, failing to observe His commands, His laws and His decrees that I am giving you this day. (Deuteronomy, 8:11)

But you are to hold fast to the Lord your God, as you have until now. (Joshua, 23:8)

Circumcise your hearts, therefore, and do not be stiff-necked any longer. (Deuteronomy, 10:16)

Seek the Lord while He may be found; **call on Him** while He is near. (Isaiah, 55:6)

My soul finds rest in God alone... (Psalms, 62:1)

The Lord is near to all who call on Him, to all who call on Him in truth. He fulfills the desires of those who fear Him; He hears their cry and saves them. The Lord watches over all who love Him... (Psalms, 145:18-20)

And you, my son Solomon, acknowledge the God of your father, and **serve Him with wholehearted devotion and with a willing mind,** for the Lord searches every heart and understands every motive behind the thoughts. **If you seek Him, He will be found by you;** but if you forsake Him, He will reject you forever. (1 Chronicles, 28:9)

Now fear the Lord and serve Him with all faithfulness. Throw away the deities your forefathers worshiped... and serve the Lord. (Joshua, 24:14)

Beware that **you do not forget the Lord your God**... (Deuteronomy, 8:14)

... What does the Lord your God ask of you but to fear the Lord your God, to walk in all His ways, to love Him, to **serve the Lord your God with all your heart and with all your soul.** (Deuteronomy, 10:12)

Fear the Lord your God and serve Him. **Hold fast to Him** and take your oaths in His name. (Deuteronomy, 10:20)

So if you faithfully obey the commands I am giving you today—**to love the Lord your God and to serve Him with all your heart and with all your soul.** (Deuteronomy, 11:13)

It is the Lord your God you must follow, and Him you must revere. Keep His commands and obey Him; serve Him and hold fast to Him. (Deuteronomy, 13:4)

But You are a shield around me, O Lord; You bestow glory on me and lift up my head. (Psalms, 3:3)

My shield is God Most High, Who saves the upright in heart. (Psalms, 7:10)

I will lie down and sleep in peace, **for You alone, O Lord, make me dwell in safety.** (Psalms, 4:8)

... for **I hide myself in You**. Teach me to do Your will, for You are my God... (Psalms, 143:9-10)

Let us acknowledge the Lord; let us press on to acknowledge Him. (Hosea, 6:3)

The Lord says: "These people come near to Me with their mouth and honor Me with their lips, **but their hearts are far from Me....**" (Isaiah, 29:13)

This is what the Lord says: "Cursed is the one who trusts in man, who depends on flesh for his strength and whose heart turns away from the Lord. He will be like a bush in the wastelands; he will not see prosperity when it comes..." (Jeremiah, 17:5-6)

WISDOM AND SOUND ADVICE FROM THE TORAH

... I have kept the ways of the Lord; **I have not done evil by turning from my God.** (Psalms, 18:21)

Sow for yourselves righteousness, reap the fruit of unfailing love... for **it is time to seek the Lord**... (Hosea, 10:12)

But **you must return to your God**; maintain love and justice, and wait for your God always. (Hosea, 12:6)

Return... to the Lord your God. Take words with you and **return to the Lord**. Say to Him: "Forgive all our sins and receive us graciously..." (Hosea, 14:1-2)

Let the wicked forsake his way and the evil man his thoughts. **Let him turn to the Lord**, and He will have mercy on him, and to our God, for He will freely pardon. (Isaiah, 55:7)

Rend your heart and not your garments. **Return to the Lord your God,** for He is gracious and compassionate... abounding in love... (Joel, 2:13)

Devotion and Loyalty to God

Fear the Lord your God and serve Him. **To Him you will cleave** and take your oaths in His name. (Deuteronomy, 10:20)

If you carefully observe all these commands I am giving you to follow—to love the Lord your God, to walk in all His ways and **cleave to Him**... There will be no man be able to stand before you... (Deuteronomy, 11:20-25)

For I delight in loving kindness, not sacrifice, **and acknowledgment of God** rather than burnt offerings. (Hosea, 6:6)

It is the Lord your God you must follow, and Him you must fear. Keep His commands and obey Him; serve Him and **cleave to Him.** (Deuteronomy, 13:4)

Love the Lord, **all His saints**! The Lord preserves the faithful... Be strong and take heart, **all you who hope in the Lord**. (Psalms, 31:23-24)

Solomon answered, "You have shown great kindness to Your servant, my father David, because **he was faithful to You** and righteous and upright in heart..." (1 Kings, 3:6)

... to love the Lord your God, to walk in all His ways, to obey His commands, **to cleave unto Him** and to serve Him with all your heart and all your soul. (Joshua, 22:5)

He cleaved to the Lord and did not cease to follow Him; he kept the commands the Lord had given Moses. (2 King, 18:6)

But **all of you who kept faith with the Lord your God** are still alive today. See, I have taught you decrees and laws as the

Lord my God commanded me, so that you may follow them in the land you are entering to take possession of it. Observe them carefully... (Deuteronomy, 4:4-6)

But **cleave to the Lord your God,** as you have been till this day. (Joshua, 23:8)

Let us examine our ways and test them, and **let us return to the Lord.** (Lamentations, 3:40)

Because Abraham obeyed Me and **kept My requirements, My commands, My decrees and My laws.** (Genesis, 26:5)

He will guard the feet of **His saints**, but the wicked will be silenced in darkness. It is not by strength that one prevails. (1 Samuel, 2:9)

To the faithful You show Yourself faithful. With the perfect man you will show yourself perfect. (2 Samuel, 22:26)

"O Lord... You Who keep Your covenant of love with **Your servants who continue wholeheartedly in Your way**." (1 Kings, 8:23)

... May **Your priests,** O Lord God, be clothed with salvation, may **Your saints rejoice in Your goodness**. (2 Chronicles, 6:41)

Let those who love the Lord hate evil, for He guards the lives of **His faithful ones** and delivers them from the hand of the wicked. (Psalms, 97:10)

Now fear the Lord and **serve Him with all faithfulness**. (Joshua, 24:14)

Showing Respect for God

Now all has been heard; here is the conclusion of the matter: **Revere God** and keep His commandments, for this is the whole duty of man. (Ecclesiastes, 12:13)

Let all the earth fear the Lord; **let all the people of the world revere Him**. For He spoke, and it came to be; He commanded, and it stood firm. (Psalms, 33:8-9)

Therefore **stand in awe of God**. (Ecclesiastes, 5:7)

You who fear the Lord, praise Him! ...honor Him! Revere Him...! (Psalms, 22:23)

For I delight in Your commands because I love them. **I lift up my hands to Your commands**, which I love, and I meditate on your decrees. (Psalms, 119:47-48)

Have awe of the Lord... my son, and do not join with the rebellious. (Proverbs, 24:21)

... I know that it will go better with **God-fearing men, who are reverent before God**. (Ecclesiastes, 8:12)

I know that everything God does will endure forever; nothing can be added to it and nothing taken from it. **God does it so that men will revere Him**. (Ecclesiastes, 3:14)

The Excitement and Joy of Faith

Be glad... rejoice in the Lord your God. (Joel, 2:23)

... I desire to do Your will, O my God; **Your law is within my heart.** (Psalms, 40:8)

I rejoice in following Your statutes as one rejoices in great riches. I meditate on Your precepts and consider Your ways. **I delight in Your decrees;** I will not neglect Your word. (Psalms, 119:14-16)

... The Lord your God is testing you to find out whether you love Him with all your heart and with all your soul. (Deuteronomy, 13:3)

Many are the woes of the wicked, but the Lord's unfailing love surrounds the man who trusts in Him. **Rejoice in the Lord and be glad, you righteous; sing, all you who are upright in heart!** (Psalms, 32:10-11)

... I **keep Your precepts with all my heart**. Their hearts are callous and unfeeling, but **I delight in Your law**... The law from Your mouth is more precious to me than thousands of pieces of silver and gold. (Psalms, 119:69-72)

Love the Lord your God with all your heart and with all your soul and with all your strength. (Deuteronomy, 6:5)

Blessed is the man who does not walk in the counsel of the wicked or stand in the way of sinners or sit in the seat of mockers. But **his delight is in the law of the Lord,** and on His law he meditates day and night. (Psalms, 1:1-2)

Then Hannah prayed and said: **"My heart rejoices in the Lord;** in the Lord my horn is lifted high. My mouth boasts over my enemies, for **I delight in Your deliverance.** There is no one holy like the Lord; there is no one besides You; there is no strength like our God." (1 Samuel, 2:1-2)

... for I delight in Your commands because I love them. I lift up my hands to Your commands, which I love, and I meditate on your decrees. (Psalms, 119:47-48)

Trouble and distress have come upon me, but Your commands are my delight. Your statutes are forever right; give me understanding that I may live. (Psalms, 119:143-144)

Great peace have they who love Your law, and nothing can make them stumble. I wait for Your salvation, O Lord, and I follow Your commands. **I obey Your statutes, for I love them greatly.** (Psalms, 119:165-167)

The law of the Lord is perfect, reviving the soul. The statutes of the Lord are trustworthy, making wise the simple. **The precepts of the Lord are right, giving joy to the heart.** The commands of the Lord are radiant, **giving light to the eyes.** The fear of the Lord is pure, enduring forever. The ordinances of the Lord are sure and altogether righteous. **They are more precious than gold, than much pure gold; they are sweeter than honey, than honey from the comb.** (Psalms, 19:7-10)

WISDOM AND SOUND ADVICE FROM THE TORAH

Great are the **works of the Lord;** they are pondered by all who **delight in them.** (Psalms, 111:2)

Though rulers sit together and slander me, Your servant will meditate on Your decrees. **Your statutes are my delight;** they are my counselors. (Psalms, 119:23-24)

Teach me, O Lord, to follow Your decrees; then I will keep them to the end. Give me understanding, and I will keep Your law and **obey it with all my heart.** Direct me in the path of Your commands, **for there I find delight.** (Psalms, 119:33-35)

May **Your unfailing love be my comfort,** according to Your promise to Your servant. Let Your compassion come to me that I may live, for **Your law is my delight.** (Psalms, 119:76-77)

But if from there you seek the Lord your God, you will find Him if you **look for Him with all your heart and with all your soul.** (Deuteronomy, 4:29)

Then I was... at His side. I was filled with delight day after day, rejoicing always in His presence, rejoicing in His whole world and delighting in mankind. (Proverbs, 8:30-31)

If Your law had not been my delight, I would have perished in my affliction. I will never forget Your precepts, for by them You have preserved my life. (Psalms, 119:92-93)

May my lips overflow with praise, for You teach me Your decrees. May my tongue sing of Your word, for all Your commands are righteous... I long for Your salvation, O Lord, and **Your law is my delight.** Let me live that I may praise You, and may Your laws sustain me. (Psalms, 119:171-175)

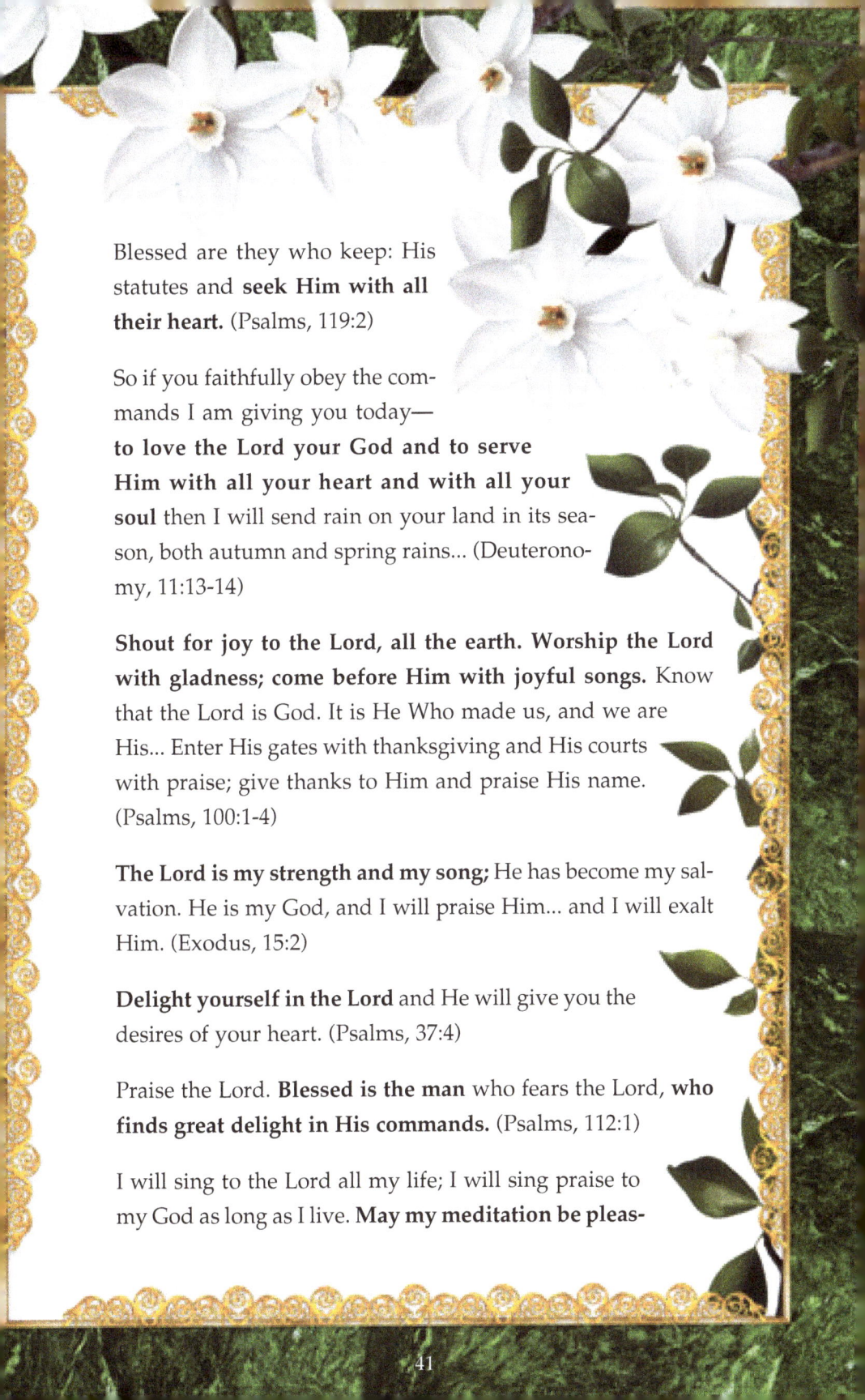

Blessed are they who keep: His statutes and **seek Him with all their heart.** (Psalms, 119:2)

So if you faithfully obey the commands I am giving you today— **to love the Lord your God and to serve Him with all your heart and with all your soul** then I will send rain on your land in its season, both autumn and spring rains... (Deuteronomy, 11:13-14)

Shout for joy to the Lord, all the earth. Worship the Lord with gladness; come before Him with joyful songs. Know that the Lord is God. It is He Who made us, and we are His... Enter His gates with thanksgiving and His courts with praise; give thanks to Him and praise His name. (Psalms, 100:1-4)

The Lord is my strength and my song; He has become my salvation. He is my God, and I will praise Him... and I will exalt Him. (Exodus, 15:2)

Delight yourself in the Lord and He will give you the desires of your heart. (Psalms, 37:4)

Praise the Lord. **Blessed is the man** who fears the Lord, **who finds great delight in His commands.** (Psalms, 112:1)

I will sing to the Lord all my life; I will sing praise to my God as long as I live. **May my meditation be pleas-**

ing to Him, as I rejoice in the Lord... Praise the Lord, O my soul. Praise the Lord. (Psalms, 104:33-35)

Blessed are those who have learned to acclaim You, who walk in the light of Your presence, O Lord. **They rejoice in Your name all day long;** they exult in Your righteousness. **For You are their glory and strength, and** by Your favor You exalt the strength. (Psalms, 89:15-17)

But may all who seek You rejoice and be glad in You; may those who love Your salvation always say, "The Lord be exalted!" (Psalms, 40:16; Psalms, 70:4)

Then will I go to the altar of God, **to God, my joy and my delight.** I will praise You with the harp, O God, my God. (Psalms, 43:4)

When Your words came, **I ate them; they were my joy and my heart's delight,** for I bear Your name, O Lord God Almighty. (Jeremiah, 15:16)

But may the righteous be glad and **rejoice before God; may they be happy and joyful. Sing to God, sing praise to His name...** (Psalms, 68:3-4)

Accept, O Lord, the willing praise of my mouth, and teach me Your laws... **Your statutes** are my heritage forever; **they are the joy of my heart.** (Psalms, 119:108, 111)

I know, my God, that You test the heart and are pleased with integrity. **All these things have I given willingly and with honest intent.** And now I have seen with joy how willingly Your people who are here have given to You. O Lord... keep

this desire in the hearts of Your people forever, and keep their hearts loyal to You. And give my son Solomon **the wholehearted devotion to keep Your commands, requirements** and decrees and to do everything to build the palatial structure for which I have provided. (1 Chronicles, 29:17-19)

Sing for joy to God our strength; shout aloud to the God of Jacob! Begin the music, strike the tambourine, play the melodious harp and lyre. (Psalms, 81:1-2)

Create in me a pure heart, O God, and renew a steadfast spirit within me... **Restore to me the joy of Your salvation** and **grant me a willing spirit,** to sustain me...and **my tongue will sing of Your righteousness.** O Lord, open my lips, and my mouth will declare Your praise. (Psalms, 51:10-15)

But be glad and rejoice forever in what I will create... (Isaiah, 65:18)

Your statutes are wonderful; therefore I obey them. The unfolding of Your words gives light; it gives understanding to the simple. **I open my mouth and pant, longing for Your commands.** (Psalms, 119:129-131)

I will praise You with the harp for Your faithfulness, O my God; **I will sing praise to You with the lyre... My lips will shout for joy when I sing praise to You**—I, whom You have redeemed. My tongue will tell of Your righteous acts all day long... (Psalms, 71:22-24)

... So **they sang praises with gladness** and bowed their heads and worshipped. (2 Chronicles, 29:30)

With praise and thanksgiving they sang to the Lord... And all the people gave a great shout of praise to the Lord... (Ezra, 3:11)

... But Hezekiah prayed for them, saying, **"May the Lord, Who is good, pardon everyone who sets his heart on seeking God**—the Lord, the God of his fathers—even if he is not clean according to the rules of the house." (2 Chronicles, 30:19)

My words come from an upright heart; my lips sincerely speak what I know. The Spirit of God has made me; **the breath of the Almighty gives me life.** (Job, 33:3-4)

The people rejoiced at the willing response of their leaders, **for they had given freely and wholeheartedly to the Lord.** David the king also rejoiced. (1 Chronicles, 29:9)

... and **everyone who was willing and whose heart moved him** came and brought an offering to the Lord for the work on the Tent of Meeting, for all its service, and for the sacred garments. **All who were willing,** men and women alike, came... (Exodus, 35:21-22)

... [They] brought to the Lord **freewill offerings** for all the work the Lord through Moses had commanded them to do. (Exodus, 35:29)

Oh, that their hearts would be inclined to fear Me and **keep all My commands always,** so that it might go well with them and their children forever! (Deuteronomy, 5:29)

O Lord, let Your ear be attentive to the prayer of this Your servant and to the prayer of Your servants **who delight in revering Your name. Give Your servant success today...** (Nehemiah, 1:11)

... You made him glad with the joy of Your presence. For the king trusts in the Lord; through the unfailing love of the Most High he will not be shaken. (Psalms, 21:6-7)

The trumpeters and singers joined in unison, as with one voice, to give praise and thanks to the Lord. Accompanied by trumpets, cymbals and other instruments, **they raised their voices in praise to the Lord and sang**: "He is good; His love endures forever." (2 Chronicles, 5:13)

I will praise You as long as I live, and in Your name I will lift up my hands. **My soul will be satisfied as with the richest of foods; with singing lips my mouth will praise You.** (Psalms, 63:4-5)

Sing the glory of His name; make His praise glorious! (Psalms, 66:2)

Be exalted, O Lord, in Your strength; **we will sing and praise Your might.** (Psalms, 21:13)

... They rejoice before You as people rejoice at the harvest, as men rejoice when dividing the plunder. (Isaiah, 9:3)

... Levites and priests **sang to the Lord every day,** accompanied by the Lord's instruments of praise. (2 Chronicles, 30:21)

Glorify the Lord with me; let us exalt His name together. (Psalms, 34:3)

Let the **saints rejoice in this honor and sing for joy** on their beds. (Psalms, 149:5)

My servants will sing out of the joy of their hearts, but you will cry out from anguish of heart and wail in brokenness of spirit. (Isaiah, 65:14)

Because you did not **serve the Lord your God joyfully and gladly** in the time of prosperity, therefore in hunger and thirst, in nakedness and dire poverty, you will serve the enemies the Lord sends against you. (Deuteronomy, 28:47-48)

"... Do not grieve, **for the joy of the Lord is your strength**." (Nehemiah, 8:10)

... to love the Lord your God, to walk in all His ways,

to obey His commands, to hold fast to Him and to **serve Him with all your heart and all your soul.** (Joshua, 22:5)

The Importance of Deep Thinking

On my bed I remember You; **I think of You through the watches of the night.** (Psalms, 63:6)

But his delight is in the law of the Lord, and **on His law he meditates day and night.** (Psalms, 1:2)

I will remember the deeds of the Lord; yes, I will remember Your miracles of long ago. **I will meditate on all Your works** and consider all Your mighty deeds. (Psalms, 77:11-12)

Though rulers sit together and slander me, **Your servant will meditate on Your decrees.** Your statutes are my delight; they are my counselors. (Psalms, 119:23-24)

Oh, how I love Your law! **I meditate on it all day long.** Your commands make me wiser than my enemies, **for they are ever with me.** I have more insight than all my teachers, **for I meditate on Your statutes.** (Psalms, 119:97-99)

I rise before dawn and cry for help; I have put my hope in Your word. **My eyes stay open through the watches of the night, that I may meditate on Your promises.** (Psalms, 119:147-148)

I applied my heart to what I observed and learned a lesson from what I saw. (Proverbs, 24:32)

Consider what God has done: Who can straighten what He has made crooked? When times are good, be happy; **but when times are bad, consider...** (Ecclesiastes 7:13-14)

... I rejoice in following Your statutes as one rejoices in great riches. **I meditate on Your precepts and consider Your ways.** I delight in Your decrees; I will not neglect Your word. (Psalms, 119:13-16)

Listen to this, Job; **stop and consider God's wonders.** (Job, 37:14)

Do not let this Book of the Law depart from your mouth; **meditate on it day and night,** so that you may be careful to do everything written in it. Then you will be prosperous and successful. (Joshua, 1:8)

I remember the days of long ago; **I meditate on all Your works and consider...** I spread out my hands to You; my soul thirsts for You like a parched land. (Psalms, 143:5-6)

Great are the works of the Lord; they are pondered by all who delight in them. (Psalms, 111:2)

But be sure to fear the Lord and serve Him faithfully with all your heart; **consider what great things He has done for you.** (1 Samuel, 12:24)

... for I delight in Your commands because I love them. I lift up my hands to Your commands, which I love, **and I meditate on Your decrees.** (Psalms, 119:47-48)

My heart grew hot within me, and **as I meditated,** the fire burned; then I spoke with my tongue: "Show me, O Lord, my life's end and the number of my days; let me know how fleeting is my life." (Psalms, 39:3-4)

One generation will commend Your works to another; they will tell of Your mighty acts. They will speak of the glorious splendor of Your majesty, and **I will meditate on Your wonderful works,** they will tell of the power of Your awesome works. (Psalms, 145:4-5)

Now this is what the Lord Almighty says: **"Give careful thought to your ways."** (Haggai, 1:5)

"Now give careful thought to this from this day on... I struck all the work of your hands with blight, mildew and hail, yet you did not turn to Me," declares the Lord. **"... Give careful thought."** (Haggai, 2:15-18)

So **I reflected on all this** and concluded that the righteous and the wise and what they do are in God's hands. (Ecclesiastes, 9:1)

... When **I think of all this**, I fear Him. (Job, 23:15)

Passages from the Torah Encouraging Examination of the Signs Leading to Faith

For You created my inmost being; You knit me together in my mother's womb. I praise You because I am fearfully and

wonderfully made; Your works are wonderful, I know that full well. My frame was not hidden from You when I was made in the secret place. When I was woven together in the depths of the earth, Your eyes saw my unformed body. All the days ordained for me were written in Your book before one of them came to be. (Psalms, 139:13-16)

Lift your eyes and look to the heavens: Who created all these? He Who brings out the starry host one by one, and calls them each by name. Because of His great power and mighty strength, not one of them is missing... The Lord is the everlasting God, the Creator of the ends of the earth. He will not grow tired or weary, and His understanding no one can fathom. (Isaiah, 40:26-28)

Others went out on the sea in ships; they were merchants on the mighty waters. **They saw the works of the Lord, His wonderful deeds in the deep.** (Psalms, 107:23-24)

This is what the **Lord says**—your Redeemer, **Who formed you in the womb:** I am the Lord, **Who has made all things, Who alone stretched out the heavens, Who spread out the earth by Myself...** (Isaiah, 44:24)

I will remember the deeds of the Lord; yes, I will remember Your miracles of long ago. **I will meditate on all Your works and consider all Your mighty deeds.** (Psalms, 77:11-12)

Many, O Lord my God, **are the wonders You have done.** The things You planned for us no one can recount to You; **were I to speak and tell of them, they would be too many to declare.** (Psalms, 40:5)

Great are the works of the Lord; they are pondered by all who delight in them. Glorious and majestic are His deeds... He has caused His wonders to be remembered; the Lord is gracious and compassionate. (Psalms, 111:2-4)

Let them give thanks to the Lord for His unfailing love and **His wonderful deeds for men,** for He satisfies the thirsty and fills the hungry with good things. (Psalms, 107:8-9)

You will have plenty to eat, until you are full, and **you will praise the name of the Lord your God, Who has worked wonders for you...** (Joel, 2:26)

... I will meditate on Your wonderful works. They will tell of the power of Your awesome works, and I will proclaim Your great deeds. (Psalms, 145:5-6)

For You are great and **do marvelous deeds;** You alone are God. (Psalms, 86:10)

... Teach me Your decrees. Let me understand the teaching of Your precepts; then **I will meditate on Your wonders.** (Psalms, 119:26-27)

Praise be to the Lord God... **Who alone does marvelous deeds.** (Psalms, 72:18)

... He Who made the earth, the Lord Who formed it and established it—the Lord is His name. (Jeremiah, 33:2)

He Who forms the mountains, creates the wind, and reveals His thoughts to man, He Who turns dawn to darkness, and treads the high places of the earth—the Lord God Almighty is His name. (Amos, 4:13)

He Who made the Pleiades and Orion, **Who turns blackness into dawn and darkens day into night, Who calls for the waters of the sea and pours them out over the face of the land**—the Lord is His name. (Amos, 5:8)

... You forget the Lord **your Maker, Who stretched out the heavens and laid the foundations of the earth... (**Isaiah, 51:13)

For this is what the Lord says -**He Who created the heavens,** He is God; **He Who fashioned and made the Earth, He founded it**; He did not create it to be empty, but formed it to be inhabited- He says: "I am the Lord, and there is no other." (Isaiah, 45:18)

 I form the light and create darkness, I bring prosperity and create disaster; I, the Lord, do all these things. (Isaiah, 45:7)

Did not He Who made me in the womb make them? Did not the same One form us both within our mothers? (Job, 31:15)

Ears that hear and eyes that see—the Lord has made them both. (Proverbs, 20:12)

... The Maker of heaven and earth, the sea, and everything in them... (Psalms, 146:6)

This is the account of the heavens and the earth when they were created. When **the Lord God made the earth and the heavens**—and no shrub of the field had yet appeared on the earth and no plant of the field had yet sprung up, for the Lord God had not sent rain on the earth and there was no man to work the ground, but streams came up from the earth and watered the whole surface of the ground—the **Lord God formed the Adam from the dust of the ground and breathed into his nostrils the breath of life, and the man became a living being.** (Genesis, 2:4-7)

He **[the Prophet Solomon (pbuh)] described plant life**, from the cedar of Lebanon to the hyssop that grows out of walls. He also **taught about animals and birds, reptiles and fish.** Men of all nations came to listen to Solomon's wisdom, sent by all the kings of the world, who had heard of his wisdom. (1 Kings, 4:33-34)

For, before the harvest, when the blossom is gone and **the flower becomes a ripening grape**... (Isaiah, 18:5)

Let us go early to the vineyards **to see if the vines have budded, if their blossoms have opened, and if the pomegranates are in bloom**... The mandrakes send out their fragrance, and at our doors are **all sorts of fruit**, both new and old... (Song of Solomon, 7:12-13)

WISDOM AND SOUND ADVICE FROM THE TORAH

I went down to **the grove of nut trees to look at the new growth in the valley, to see if the vines had budded or the pomegranates were in bloom.** (Song of Solomon, 6:11)

Then God said, "Let the land produce vegetation: **seed-bearing plants and trees on the land that bear fruit with seed in it, according to their various kinds.**" And it was so. (Genesis, 1:11)

... He shall **blossom as the lily**, and cast forth his roots as Lebanon. His branches shall spread, and **his beauty shall be as the olive-tree**, and his fragrance as Lebanon. They that dwell under his shadow shall again **make corn to grow, and shall blossom as the vine**... (Hoshea, 14:6-8)

Statements from the Torah Regarding the Transient Nature of This World

All our days pass away under Your wrath; we finish our years with a moan. **The length of our days is seventy years—or eighty, if we have the strength; yet their span is but trouble and sorrow, for they quickly pass, and we fly away.** (Psalms, 90:9-10)

... **Our days on earth are like a shadow...** (1 Chronicles, 29:15)

Neither their silver nor their gold will be able to save them... (Zephaniah, 1:18)

Man is like a breath; his days are like a fleeting shadow... (Psalms, 144:4)

The **youthful vigor that fills his bones will lie with him in the dust.** (Job, 20:11)

... For **death is the destiny of every man**; the living should take this to heart. (Ecclesiastes, 7:2)

By the sweat of your brow, you will eat your food **until you return to the ground**, since from it you were taken; **for dust you are and to dust you will return**. (Genesis, 3:19)

And said: "**Naked I came from my mother's womb, and naked I will depart.** The Lord gave and the Lord has taken away; may the name of the Lord be praised." (Job, 1:21)

He springs up like a flower and **withers away; like a fleeting shadow, he does not endure**. (Job, 14:2)

My heart grew hot within me, and as I meditated, the fire burned; then I spoke with my tongue: Show me, O Lord, **my** life's end and the number of my days; let me know how fleeting is my life. You have made my days a mere handbreadth; the span of my years is as nothing before You. Each man's life is but a breath. Man is a mere phantom as he goes to and fro: He bustles about, but only in vain; he heaps up wealth, not knowing who will get it. "But now, Lord, what do I look for? My hope is in You." (Psalms, 39:3-7)

For He knows how we are formed, He remembers that we are dust. **As for man, His days are like grass, He flourishes like a flower of the field; the wind blows over it and it is gone, and its place remembers it no more.** But from everlasting to everlasting the Lord's love is with those who fear Him... (Psalms, 103:14-18)

Hear this, all you peoples; listen, **all who live in this world, both low and high, rich and poor alike**... Those who trust in their wealth and boast of their great riches? No man can redeem the life of another or give to God a ransom for Him—the ransom for a life is costly, no payment is ever enough—that he should live on forever and not see decay. For all can see that wise men die; the foolish and the senseless alike perish and **leave their wealth to others. Their tombs will remain their houses forever, their dwellings for endless generations**, though they had named lands after themselves. **But man, despite his riches, does not endure;** he is like the beasts that perish... Do not be overawed when a man grows rich, when the splendor of his house increases; **for he will take nothing with him when he dies, his splendor will not descend with him.** Though while he lived he counted himself blessed—and men praise you when you prosper—he will join the generation of his fathers, who will never see the light of life. A man who has riches without understanding is like the beasts that perish. (Psalms, 49:1-2, 6-20)

They will perish, but You remain; they will all wear out like a garment. Like clothing You will change them and **they will be discarded.** But You remain the same, and your years will never end. (Psalms, 102:26-27)

With Me are riches and honor, enduring wealth and prosperity. (Proverbs, 8:18)

... **Riches do not endure forever,** and a crown is not secure for all generations. (Proverbs, 27:24)

Charm is deceptive, and beauty is fleeting; but a woman who fears the Lord is to be praised. (Proverbs, 31:30)

Whoever trusts in his riches will fall, but the righteous will thrive like a green leaf. (Proverbs, 11:28)

... The wealth they acquired is gone. (Jeremiah, 48:36)

In that day the Lord will snatch away their finery: the bangles and headbands and crescent necklaces, the earrings and bracelets and veils, the headdresses and ankle chains and sashes, the perfume bottles and charms, the signet rings and nose rings, the fine robes and the capes and cloaks, the purses and mirrors, and the linen garments and tiaras and shawls. **Instead of fragrance there will be a stench; instead of a sash, a rope; instead of well-dressed hair, baldness; instead of fine clothing, sackcloth; instead of beauty, branding.** (Isaiah, 3:18-24)

What will you do on the Day of Reckoning, when disaster comes from afar? To whom will you run for help? **Where will you leave your riches?** (Isaiah, 10:3)

Cast but a glance at riches, and they are gone, for they will surely sprout wings and fly off to the sky like an eagle. (Proverbs, 23:5)

Wealth is worthless in the day of wrath... (Proverbs, 11:4)

A man's riches may ransom his life... (Proverbs, 13:8)

He will not enjoy the streams, the rivers flowing with honey and cream. What he toiled for he must give back uneaten; he will not enjoy the profit from his trading... **He cannot save himself by his treasure.** (Job, 20:17-20)

My spirit is broken, my days are cut short, the grave awaits me. (Job, 17:1)

Then the Lord said, "My Spirit will not contend with man forever, **for he is mortal..."** (Genesis, 6:3)

At the end of your life you will groan, **when your flesh and body are spent.** (Proverbs, 5:11)

Stop trusting in man, who has but a breath in his nostrils. **Of what account is he?** (Isaiah, 2:22)

... During the few and meaningless days he passes through like a shadow? Who can tell him what will happen under the Sun after he is gone? (Ecclesiastes, 6:12)

No man has power over the wind to contain it; so **no one has power over the day of his death**... (Ecclesiastes, 8:8)

You sweep men away in the sleep of death; they are like the new grass of the morning- though in the morning it springs up new, by evening it is dry and withered. (Psalms, 90:5-6)

I undertook great projects: I built houses for myself and planted vineyards. I made gardens and parks and planted all kinds of fruit trees in them. I made reservoirs to water groves of flourishing trees… I also owned more herds and flocks than anyone… I amassed silver and gold for myself, and the treasure of kings and provinces… I became greater by far than anyone… I denied myself nothing my eyes desired; I refused my heart no pleasure… Yet **when I surveyed all that my hands had done and what I had toiled to achieve, everything was meaningless, a chasing after the wind**; nothing was gained under the Sun. (Ecclesiastes, 2:411)

… Wealth hoarded to the harm of its owner, or wealth lost through some misfortune… as he comes, so he departs. **He takes nothing from his labor that he can carry in his hand… As a man comes, so he departs…** (Ecclesiastes, 5:13-16)

… for **youth and vigor are meaningless**. (Ecclesiastes, 11:10)

Remember Him—before the silver cord is severed, or the golden bowl is broken; before the pitcher is shattered at the spring, or the wheel broken at the well, and **the dust returns to the ground it came from, and the spirit returns to God Who gave it.** "Meaningless! Meaningless!" says the Teacher. "Everything is meaningless!" (Ecclesiastes, 12:6-8)

THE ATTRIBUTES OF GOD ACCORDING TO THE TORAH

The Oneness of God

I am the Lord, and there is no other; apart from Me there is no God... so that from the rising of the Sun to the place of its setting men may know **there is none besides Me. I am the Lord, and there is no other.** (Isaiah, 45:5-6)

... I am God, and there is no other; I am God, and there is none like Me. (Isaiah, 46:9)

... so that all the peoples of the earth may know that **the Lord is God and that there is no other.** (1 Kings, 8:60)

Turn to Me and be saved, all you ends of the earth; **for I am God, and there is no other.** (Isaiah, 45:22)

This is what the Lord says... "Surely God is with you, and **there is no other; there is no other God."** (Isaiah, 45:14)

... The Lord our God, the **Lord is one.** (Deuteronomy, 6:4)

... **O Lord; no deeds can compare with Yours.** All the nations You have made will come and worship before You, O Lord; they will bring glory to

Your name. For You are great and do marvelous deeds; **You alone are God.** (Psalms, 86:8-10)

O Lord... You alone are God over all the kingdoms of the earth. You have made heaven and earth. (Isaiah, 37:16)

... All kingdoms on earth may know that **You alone, O Lord, are God**. (Isaiah, 37:20)

This is what the Lord says—your Redeemer, Who formed you in the womb: **I am the Lord,** Who has made all things, **Who alone stretched out the heavens, Who spread out the earth by Myself.** (Isaiah, 44:24)

Since ancient times no one has heard, no ear has perceived, no eye has seen **any God besides You,** who acts on behalf of those who wait for Him. (Isaiah, 64:4)

For this is what the Lord says—He Who created the heavens, He is God; He Who fashioned and made the earth, He founded it; He did not create it to be empty, but formed it to be inhabited— **He says: "I am the Lord, and there is no other."** (Isaiah, 45:18)

... Was it not I, the Lord? And **there is no god apart from Me,** a righteous God and a Savior; **there is none but Me**. (Isaiah, 45:21)

See now that I Myself am He! **There is no god besides Me.** I put to death and I bring to life, I have wounded and I will heal... (Deuteronomy, 32:39)

... You may know **there is no one like the Lord our God.** (Exodus, 8:10)

O Lord... **there is no god like You in heaven above or on earth below...** (1 Kings, 8:23; 2 Chronicles, 6:14)

Then Asa called to the Lord his God and said, **"Lord, there is no one like You** to help the powerless against the mighty..." (2 Chronicles, 14:11)

I, **even I, am the Lord, and apart from Me there is no savior.** (Isaiah, 43:11)

There is no one like You, O Lord, and there is no god but You, as we have heard with our own ears. (1 Chronicles, 17:20; 2 Samuel, 7:22)

There is no one holy like the Lord; there is no one besides You; there is no strength like our God. (1 Samuel, 2:2)

For You are great and do marvelous deeds; **You alone are God.** (Psalms, 86:10)

You alone are the Lord. You made the heavens, even the highest heavens, and all their starry host, the earth and all that is on it, the seas and all that is in them. You give life to everything, and the multitudes of heaven worship You. (Nehemiah, 9:6)

They will say of Me, **"In the Lord alone are righteousness and strength."**... (Isaiah, 45:24)

You were shown these things so that **you might know that the Lord is God; besides Him there is no other.** (Deuteronomy, 4:35)

... Is there any god besides Me? No, there is no other strong one; I know not one. (Isaiah, 44:8)

God's Being Eternal and Infinite

This is what the Lord says—**I am the first and I am the last; apart from Me there is no god.** (Isaiah, 44:6)

Who has done this and carried it through, calling forth the generations from the beginning? **I, the Lord—with the first of them and with the last—I am He.** (Isaiah, 41:4)

O Lord, **are You not from everlasting?** My God, my Holy One... (Habakkuk 1:12)

I know that everything God does will endure forever; nothing can be added to it and nothing taken from it. God does it so that men will revere Him. (Ecclesiastes, 3:14)

Before the mountains were born or You brought forth the earth and the world, **from everlasting to everlasting You are God.** (Psalms, 90:2)

Your throne, O God, **will last for ever and ever...** (Psalms, 45:6)

For this is what the high and lofty One says—**He Who lives forever,** Whose name is holy... (Isaiah, 57:15)

Daniel answered and said: "Praise be to the name of **God for ever and ever;** wisdom and power are His." (Daniel, 2:20)

He has made everything beautiful in its time. **He has also set eternity in the hearts of men;** yet they cannot fathom what God has done from beginning to end. (Ecclesiastes, 3:11)

... For **He is the living God and He endures forever**... **His dominion will never end.** (Daniel, 6:26)

WISDOM AND SOUND ADVICE FROM THE TORAH

Praise be to **the Lord... from everlasting to everlasting**... (1 Chronicles, 16:36)

But You, **O Lord, are exalted forever**. (Psalms, 92:8)

The grass withers and the flowers fall, but **the word of our God stands forever.** (Isaiah, 40:8)

God, the Creator of All Things

In the beginning **God created the heavens and the earth.** Now the earth was formless and empty, darkness was over the surface of the deep, and the Spirit of God was hovering over the waters. **And God said, "Let there be light," and there was light.** (Genesis, 1:1-3)

And God said, "Let there be an expanse between the waters to separate water from water." So **God made the expanse and separated the water under the expanse from the water above it.** And it was so. (Genesis, 1:6-7)

And God said, **"Let the water under the sky be gathered to one place, and let dry ground appear." And it was so**. (Genesis, 1:9)

Then God said, **"Let the land produce vegetation: seed-bearing plants and trees on the land that bear fruit with seed in it, according to their various kinds." And it was so.** The land produced vegetation: plants bearing seed according to their kinds and trees bearing fruit with seed in it according to their kinds... (Genesis, 1:11-12)

And God said, "Let there be lights in the expanse of the sky to separate the day from the night, and let them serve as signs to mark seasons and days and years, and let them be lights in the expanse of the sky to give light on the earth." And it was so. **God made two great lights—the greater light to govern the day and the lesser light to govern the night. He also made the stars.** (Genesis, 1:14-16)

... I have raised my hand to the Lord, God Most High, **Creator of heaven and earth,** and have taken an oath. (Genesis, 14:22)

And God said, "Let the water teem with living creatures, and let birds fly above the earth across the expanse of the sky." **So God created the great creatures of the sea and every living and moving thing with which the water teems...** (Genesis, 1:20-21)

And God said, "Let the land produce living creatures according to their kinds: livestock, creatures that move along the ground, and wild animals, each according to its kind." And it was so. **God made the wild animals according to their kinds, the livestock according to their kinds, and all the creatures that move along the ground according to their kinds...** (Genesis, 1:24-25)

Then God said, "Let us make man... and let them rule over the fish of the sea and the birds of the air, over the livestock, over all the earth, and over all the creatures that move along the ground." **So God created man... He created him; male and female He created them.** (Genesis, 1:26-27)

Who among the gods is like You, O Lord? Who is like You—majestic in holiness, awesome in glory, **working wonders?** (Exodus, 15:11)

Is He not... **your Creator, Who made you and formed you**? (Deuteronomy, 32:6)

Ears that hear and eyes that see—the Lord has made them both. (Proverbs, 20:12)

... He abandoned **the God Who made him...** (Deuteronomy, 32:15)

... You forgot the **God Who gave you birth.** (Deuteronomy, 32:18)

... **God Most High, Creator of heaven and earth.** (Genesis, 14:19)

For all the gods of the nations are idols, but **the Lord made the heavens.** (1 Chronicles, 16:26)

He is the Maker of the Bear and Orion, the Pleiades and the **constellations of the south.** (Job, 9:9)

Did not **He Who made me in the womb** make them? Did not the same one form us both within our mothers? (Job, 31:15)

He Who forms the hearts of all, Who considers everything they do. (Psalms, 33:15)

... **Who alone does marvelous deeds.** (Psalms, 72:18)

It was You Who set all the boundaries of the earth; You made both summer and winter. (Psalms, 74:17)

You are the God Who performs miracles; You display Your power... (Psalms, 77:14)

Come, let us bow down in worship, let us kneel before **the Lord our Maker.** (Psalms, 95:6)

For all the gods of the nations are idols, but **the Lord made the heavens.** (Psalms, 96:5)

Know that the Lord is God. **It is He Who made us,** and we are His; we are His people, the sheep of His pasture. (Psalms, 100:3)

May you be blessed by **the Lord, the Maker of heaven and earth.** (Psalms, 115:15)

My help comes from **the Lord the Maker of heaven and earth.** (Psalms, 121:2)

Our help is in the name of **the Lord, the Maker of heaven and earth.** (Psalms, 124:8)

The Maker of heaven and earth, the sea, and everything in them. (Psalms, 146:6)

As you do not know the path of the wind, or how the body is formed in a mother's womb, so you cannot understand the work of **God, the Maker of all things.** (Ecclesiastes, 11:5)

Do you not know? Have you not heard? The Lord is the everlasting God, **the Creator of the ends of the earth.** He will not grow tired or weary, and His understanding no one can fathom. (Isaiah, 40:28)

But now, this is what the Lord says—**He Who created you... He Who formed you...** (Isaiah, 43:1)

This is what the Lord says—**He Who made you, Who formed you in the womb,** and Who will help you... (Isaiah, 44:2)

This is what the Lord says—your Redeemer, **Who formed you in the womb: Who has made all things, Who alone stretched out the heavens, Who spread out the earth by Myself...** (Isaiah, 44:24)

I form the light and create darkness, I bring prosperity and create disaster; **I, the Lord, do all these things.** (Isaiah, 45:7)

... that you forget **the Lord your Maker, Who stretched out the heavens and laid the foundations of the earth**... (Isaiah, 51:13)

But **God made the earth** by His power; **He founded the world** by His wisdom and stretched out the heavens by His understanding. (Jeremiah, 10:12)

This is what the Lord says, **He Who made the earth, the Lord Who formed it and established it**—the Lord is His name. (Jeremiah, 33:2)

He Who forms the mountains, creates the wind, and reveals His thoughts to man, He Who turns dawn to darkness, and treads the high places of the earth—the Lord God Almighty is His name. (Amos, 4:13)

He Who made the Pleiades and Orion, Who turns blackness into dawn and darkens day into night, Who calls for the waters of the sea and pours them out over the face of the land—the Lord is His name. (Amos, 5:8)

… I worship **the Lord, the God of heaven, Who made the sea and the land.** (Jonah, 1:9)

You alone are the Lord. **You made the heavens, even the highest heavens, and all their starry host, the earth and all that is on it, the seas and all that is in them. You give life to everything**, and the multitudes of heaven worship You. (Nehemiah, 9:6)

God the All-Seeing, All-Hearing and Omniscient

You know when I sit and when I rise; You perceive my thoughts from afar. You discern my going out and my lying down; **You are familiar with all my ways.** Before a word is on my tongue **You know it completely, O Lord.** (Psalms, 139:2-4)

Does He Who implanted the ear not hear? Does He Who formed the eye not see? (Psalms, 94:9)

Do not keep talking so proudly or let your mouth speak such arrogance, **for the Lord is a God Who knows...** (1 Samuel, 2:3)

But You, O God, **do see trouble and grief; You consider it to take it in hand.** The victim commits himself to You; You are the helper of the fatherless. (Psalms, 10:14)

I obey Your precepts and Your statutes, **for all my ways are known to You.** (Psalms, 119:168)

In the morning, **O Lord, You hear my voice;** in the morning I lay my requests before You and wait in expectation. (Psalms, 5:3)

You hear, O Lord, the desire of the afflicted; You encourage them, and **You listen to their cry.** (Psalms, 10:17)

... since You know his heart [for You alone know the hearts of all men]. (1 Kings, 8:39)

All my longings lie open before You, O Lord; my sighing is not hidden from You. (Psalms, 38:9)

... It is You Who know my way. (Psalms, 142:3)

Yet You know me, O Lord; You see me and test my thoughts about You... (Jeremiah, 12:3)

... What passes my lips is open before You. (Jeremiah, 17:16)

... [They said,] **"God is with you in everything you do"**. (Genesis, 21:22)

And you, my son Solomon, acknowledge the God of your father, and serve Him with wholehearted devotion and with a willing mind, **for the Lord searches every heart and understands every motive behind the thoughts.** If you seek Him, He will be found by you; but if you forsake Him, He will reject you forever. (1 Chronicles, 28:9)

... Even though no one is with us, remember that God is a witness between you and me. (Genesis, 31:50)

He [God] changes times and seasons; He sets up kings and deposes them. He gives wisdom to the wise and knowledge to the discerning. **He reveals deep and hidden things; He knows what lies in darkness...** (Daniel, 2:21-22)

You know my folly, O God; **my guilt is not hidden from You**. (Psalms, 69:5)

My frame was not hidden from You when I was made in the secret place. When I was woven together in the depths of the earth. (Psalms, 139:15)

**You know when I sit and when I rise; You perceive my thoughts from afar... You are familiar with all my ways. Before a word is on my tongue You know it completely, O Lord... (Psalms, 139:2-5)

For **God will bring every deed into judgment, including every hidden thing**... (Ecclesiastes, 12:14)

God, the Only Power and Will

The Almighty is beyond our reach and exalted in power... (Job, 37:23)

The Lord sends poverty and wealth; He humbles and He exalts. (1 Samuel, 2:7)

Daniel answered and said: "Praise be to the name of God for ever and ever; **wisdom and power are His.** He changes times and seasons; He sets up kings and deposes them. He gives wisdom to the wise and knowledge to the discerning. He reveals deep and hidden things; He knows what lies in darkness, and light dwells with Him." (Daniel, 2:20-22)

... The Lord appeared to him and said, **"I am God Almighty; walk before Me and be blameless."** (Genesis, 17:1)

May God Almighty bless you and make you fruitful and increase your numbers until you become a community of peoples. (Genesis, 28:3)

And God said to him, "I am God Almighty..." (Genesis, 35:11)

And may **God Almighty** grant you mercy before the man... (Genesis, 43:14)

But if you will look to God and plead with the **Almighty.** (Job, 8:5)

In His hand is the life of every creature and the breath of all humanity. (Job, 12:10)

To God belong wisdom and **power;** counsel and understanding are His. (Job, 12:13)

But remember the **Lord your God, for it is He Who gives you the ability to produce wealth...** (Deuteronomy, 8:18)

What He tears down cannot be rebuilt; the man He imprisons cannot be released. If He holds back the waters, there is drought; if He lets them loose, they devastate the land. **To Him belong strength and victory...** He reveals the deep things of darkness and brings deep shadows into the light. He makes nations great, and destroys them; He enlarges nations, and disperses them. (Job, 12:14-16; 22-23)

O Sovereign Lord... For what God is there in heaven or on earth Who can do the deeds and mighty works You do? (Deuteronomy, 3:24)

Then Job... : "**I know that You can do all things; no plan of Yours can be thwarted**." (Job, 42:1-2)

No one is like You, O Lord; You are great, and **Your name is mighty in power.** (Jeremiah, 10:6)

He Who forms the mountains, creates the wind, and reveals His thoughts to man, He Who turns dawn to darkness... **the Lord God Almighty** is His name. (Amos, 4:13)

He Who made the Pleiades and Orion, Who turns blackness

into dawn and darkens day into night, Who calls for the waters of the sea and pours them out over the face of the land—the Lord is His name. (Amos, 5:8)

God's Bestowal of the Human Soul

But **it is the spirit in a man, the breath of the Almighty, that gives him understanding.** (Job, 32:8)

The Spirit of God has made me; the breath of the Almighty gives me life. (Job, 33:4)

Remember Him before… the dust returns to the ground it came from, and **the spirit returns to God Who gave it.** (Ecclesiastes, 12:7)

This is what God the Lord says—He Who created the heavens and stretched them out, Who spread out the earth and all that comes out of it, **Who gives breath to its people, and life** to those who walk on it. (Isaiah, 42:5)

This is what the Sovereign Lord says to these bones: **"I will make breath enter you, and you will come to life."** (Ezekiel, 37:5)

I will attach tendons to you and make flesh come upon you and cover you with skin; **I will put breath in you, and you will come to life.** Then you will know that I am the Lord. (Ezekiel, 37:6)

But as for me, I am filled with power, **with the Spirit of the Lord.** (Micah, 3:8)

I will give you a new heart and put a new spirit in you; I will remove from you your heart of stone and give you a heart of flesh. And **I will put My Spirit in you** and move you to follow My decrees and be careful to keep My laws. (Ezekiel 36:26-27)

God, the Infinitely Just

So listen to me, you men of understanding. **Far be it from God to do evil, from the Almighty to do wrong.** (Job, 34:10)

It is unthinkable that God would do wrong, that the Almighty would pervert justice. (Job, 34:12)

The Almighty is beyond our reach and exalted in power; **in His justice and great righteousness, He does not oppress.** (Job, 37:23)

The Lord works righteousness and justice for all the oppressed. (Psalms, 103:6)

The Lord is exalted... **will fill... with justice and righteousness.** (Isaiah, 33:5)

Many seek an audience with a ruler, but it is from the **Lord that man gets justice.** (Proverbs, 29:26)

... His works are perfect, and all His ways are just. A faithful **God Who does no wrong, upright and just is He.** (Deuteronomy, 32:4)

... **The Lord is upright... and there is no wickedness in Him.** (Psalms, 92:15)

For I, the Lord, love justice; I hate robbery and iniquity... (Isaiah, 61:8)

But from everlasting to everlasting the Lord's love is with those who fear Him, and **His righteousness** with their children's children. [For those who abide by, are loyal to, God's commandments.]. (Psalms, 103:17-18)

Yet the Lord longs to be gracious to you; He rises to show you compassion. For **the Lord is a God of justice.** Blessed are all who wait for Him! (Isaiah, 30:18)

... His works are perfect, and **all His ways are just. A faithful God Who does no wrong, upright and just is He.** (Deuteronomy, 32:4)

I**n all that has happened to us, You have been just**; You have acted faithfully, while we did wrong. (Nehemiah, 9:33)

... Everlasting joy will be theirs. For **I, the Lord, love justice** ... (Isaiah, 61:7-8)

This is what the Lord says: "Let not the wise man boast of his wisdom or the strong man boast of his strength or the rich man boast of his riches, but let him who boasts boast about this: that he understands and knows Me, that **I am the Lord, Who exercises kindness, justice and righteousness on earth, for in these I delight**," declares the Lord. (Yeremiah, 9:23-24)

But, **O Lord Almighty, You Who judge righteously** and test the heart and mind... for to You I have committed my cause. (Jeremiah, 11:20)

But **the Lord Almighty will be exalted by His justice**... (Isaiah, 5:16)

Your righteousness is everlasting and Your law is true. (Psalms, 119:142)

I will sing of Your love and justice; to You, O Lord, I will sing praise. (Psalms, 101:1)

Say among the nations, "The Lord reigns." The world is firmly established, it cannot be moved; **He will judge the peoples with equity... He will judge the world in righteousness** and the peoples in His truth. (Psalms, 96:10-13)

In You, O Lord, I have taken refuge; let me never be put to shame; **deliver me in Your righteousness.** (Psalms, 31:1)

The Lord loves righteousness and justice; the earth is full of His unfailing love. (Psalms, 33:5)

O righteous God... bring to an end the violence of the wicked and make the righteous secure... **God is a righteous judge [judges with justice]...** (Psalms, 7:9-11)

... And there is no God apart from Me, **a righteous God** and a Savior; there is none but Me. (Isaiah, 45:21)

... **For the Lord our God is righteous in everything he does;** yet we have not obeyed Him. (Daniel, 9:14)

Who is wise? He will realize these things. Who is discerning? He will understand them. **The ways of the Lord are right**; the righteous walk in them, but the rebellious stumble in them. (Hosea, 14:9)

The Lord is righteous in all His ways and loving toward all He has made. (Psalms, 145:17)

I will praise You with an upright heart **as I learn Your righteous laws.** I will obey Your decrees... (Psalms, 119:7-8)

I know, O Lord, that **Your laws are righteous**... I have taken an oath and confirmed it, that **I will follow Your righteous laws.** (Psalms, 119:75-106)

Righteous are You, O Lord, and Your laws are right... Your righteousness is everlasting and Your law is true. (Psalms, 119:137-142)

Your righteousness is like the mighty mountains, Your justice like the great deep. O Lord, You preserve both man and beast. (Psalms, 36:6)

The works of His hands are faithful and just; all His precepts are trustworthy. They are steadfast for ever and ever, done in faithfulness and uprightness. (Psalms, 111:7-8)

The Lord is gracious and righteous; our God is full of compassion. (Psalms, 116:5)

God, the Loving, Compassionate and All-Forgiving

But **with You there is forgiveness...** (Psalms, 130:4)

Perhaps... when each of them will turn from his wicked way; then **I will forgive their wickedness and their sin.** (Jeremiah, 36:3)

The Lord our God is merciful and forgiving, even though we have rebelled against Him. (Daniel, 9:9)

You are forgiving and good, O Lord, abounding in love to all who call to You. (Psalms, 86:5)

Yet **He was merciful; He forgave their iniquities** and did not destroy them... (Psalms, 78:38)

... [They] refused to listen and failed to remember the miracles You performed among them. They became stiff-necked and in their rebellion appointed a leader in order to return to their slavery. But **You are a forgiving God, gracious and compassionate... and abounding in love.** Therefore You did not desert them. (Nehemiah, 9:17)

The Lord... abounding in love and forgiving sin and rebellion. Yet He does not leave the guilty unpunished... (Numbers, 14:18)

... Maintaining love to thousands, and forgiving wickedness, rebellion and sin. Yet He does not leave the guilty unpunished... (Exodus, 34:7)

Who forgives all your sins and heals all your diseases. (Psalms, 103:3)

... The Lord has compassion on those who fear Him. (Psalms, 103:13)

The Lord is compassionate and gracious... abounding in love... For as high as the heavens are above the earth, so great is His love for those who fear Him. (Psalms, 103:8, 11)

The Lord is gracious and compassionate... rich in love. The Lord is good to all; **He has compassion on all He has made.** (Psalms, 145:8-9)

Surely it is **You Who love the people...** (Deuteronomy, 33:3)

Love the Lord, all His saints! **The Lord preserves the faithful,** but the proud He pays back in full. (Psalms, 31:23)

You are my hiding place; You will protect me from trouble and surround me with songs of deliverance. (Psalms, 32:7)

The Lord will protect him and preserve his life; He will bless him in the land and not surrender him to the desire of his foes. (Psalms, 41:2)

Let those who love the Lord hate evil, for **He guards the lives of His faithful ones** and delivers them from the hand of the wicked. (Psalms, 97:10)

The Lord is gracious and righteous; our God is full of compassion. The Lord protects the simple hearted; when I was in great need, He saved me. (Psalms, 116:5-6)

WISDOM AND SOUND ADVICE FROM THE TORAH

The Lord will keep you from all harm—He will watch over your life. (Psalms, 121:7)

Though I walk in the midst of trouble, You preserve my life... You save me. (Psalms, 138:7)

The Lord watches over all who love Him, but all the wicked He will destroy. (Psalms, 145:20)

The Lord watches over the alien and sustains the fatherless and the widow, but He frustrates the ways of the wicked. (Psalms, 146:9)

... for **He guards the course of the just and protects the way of His faithful ones.** (Proverbs, 2:8)

The Lord is good, a refuge in times of trouble. He cares for those who trust in Him. (Nahum, 1:7)

He who conceals his sins does not prosper, but **whoever confesses and renounces them finds mercy.** (Proverbs, 28:13)

He Who has compassion on them will guide them and lead them beside springs of water. (Isaiah, 49:10)

Shout for joy, O heavens; rejoice, O earth; burst into song, O mountains! **For the Lord comforts His people and will have compassion on His afflicted ones.** (Isaiah, 49:13)

Let the wicked forsake his way and the evil man his thoughts. Let him turn to the Lord, and **He will have mercy on him,** and to our God, for **He will freely pardon.** (Isaiah, 55:7)

For men are not cast off by the Lord forever. Though He brings grief, **He will show compassion, so great is His unfailing love.** (Lamentations, 3:31-32)

Because of the Lord's great love we are not consumed, for His compassions never fail. (Lamentations, 3:22)

The Lord loves righteousness and justice; **the earth is full of His unfailing love.** (Psalms, 33:5)

Give thanks to the Lord, for **He is good; His love endures forever.** (1 Chronicles, 16:34)

But **You, O Lord, are a compassionate and gracious God... abounding in love and faithfulness.** (Psalms, 86:15)

... "I am merciful," declares the Lord... (Jeremiah, 3:12)

The Lord is righteous in all His ways and loving toward all **He has made.** The Lord is near to all who call on Him, to all who call on Him in truth. (Psalms, 145: 17-18)

Turn to me and have mercy on me, as You always do to those who love Your name. Your compassion is great, O Lord; preserve my life according to Your laws. (Psalms, 119:132, 156)

He has caused His wonders to be remembered; the **Lord is gracious and compassionate.** (Psalms, 111:4)

For surely, O Lord, You bless the righteous; **You surround them with Your favor as with a shield.** (Psalms, 5:12)

... Lord your God loves you. (Deuteronomy, 23:5)

For great is His love toward us, and the faithfulness of the Lord endures forever. Praise the Lord. (Psalms, 117:2)

... **He [God] is gracious and compassionate... and abounding in love...** (Joel, 2: 13)

God's Being Omnipresent

Have I not commanded you? Be strong and courageous. Do not be terrified; do not be discouraged, for the Lord your **God will be with you wherever you go.** (Joshua, 1:9)

... to God, Who has been with me wherever I have gone. (Genesis, 35:3)

... **"Be strong... for I am with you," declares the Lord Almighty.** (Haggai, 2:4)

Joseph's master took him and put him in prison, the place where the king's prisoners were confined. But **while Joseph was there in the prison, the Lord was with him...** (Genesis, 39:20-21)

... because **the Lord was with Joseph** and gave him success in whatever he did. (Genesis, 39:23)

... O Lord... **You hem me in—behind and before**... (Psalms, 139:4-5)

[He] said to Abraham, **"God is with you in everything you do."** (Genesis, 21:22)

And the Lord was with him; he was successful in whatever he undertook... (2 Kings, 18:7)

And David became more and more powerful, because **the Lord Almighty was with him.** (1 Chronicles, 11:9)

The Lord was with Samuel as he grew up... (1 Samuel, 3:19)

How precious to me are Your thoughts, O God! How vast is the sum of them! Were I to count them, they would outnumber the grains of sand. **When I awake, I am still with You.** (Psalms 139: 17-18)

... for his God had given him rest on every side. (2 Chronicles, 20:30)

... They sought God eagerly, and he was found by them. **So the Lord gave them rest on every side.** (2 Chronicles, 15:15)

In everything he did he had great success, because **the Lord was with him.** (1 Samuel, 18:14)

God, the Provider of Sustenance

Then God said, "I give you every seed-bearing plant on the face of the whole earth and every tree that has fruit with seed in it. **They will be yours for food."** (Genesis, 1:29)

And to all the beasts of the earth and all the birds of the air and all the creatures that move on the ground... **I give every green plant for food.** (Genesis, 1:30)

Everything that lives and moves will be food for you. Just as I gave you the green plants, I now give you everything. (Genesis, 9:3)

He defends the cause of the fatherless and the widow, and loves the alien, **giving him food and clothing.** (Deuteronomy, 10:18)

... [God] **Who gives food to every creature.** His love endures forever. Give thanks to the God of Heaven. His love endures forever. (Psalms, 136:25-26)

He covers the sky with clouds; **He supplies the earth with rain and makes grass grow on the hills. He provides food for the cattle and for the young ravens when they call.** (Psalms, 147:8-9)

... **You gave them water for their thirst.** For forty years You sustained them in the desert; they lacked nothing... They took possession of houses filled with all kinds of good things, wells already dug, vineyards, olive groves and fruit trees in abundance. **They ate to the full and were well-nourished**; they reveled in Your great goodness. (Nehemiah, 9:20-21, 25)

He has caused His wonders to be remembered; the Lord is gracious and compassionate. **He provides food for those who fear Him...** (Psalms, 111:4-5)

God, the All-Encompassing Ruler

To the Lord your God belong the heavens, even the highest heavens, the earth and everything in it. (Deuteronomy, 10:14)

He is the Lord our God; His judgments are in all the earth. (1 Chronicles, 16:14; Psalms, 105:7)

If I go up to the heavens, You are there; if I make my bed in the depths, You are there. If I rise on the wings of the dawn, if I settle on the far side of the sea, even there Your hand will guide me... (Psalms, 139:8-10)

You hem me in—behind and before; You have laid Your hand upon me. (Psalms, 139:5)

Yours, O Lord, is the greatness and the power and the glory and the majesty and the splendor, for **everything in heaven and earth is yours.** Yours, O Lord, is the kingdom; **You are exalted as head over all.** Wealth and honor come from you;

You are the ruler of all things. In Your hands are strength and power to exalt and give strength to all. (1 Chronicles, 29:11-12)

He rescues and He saves; **He performs signs and wonders in the heavens and on the earth.** (Daniel, 6:27)

But **God made the earth by His power**; He founded the world by His wisdom and stretched out the heavens by His understanding. (Jeremiah, 10:12)

O Lord, our Lord, how majestic is Your name in all the earth! **You have set Your glory above the heavens.** (Psalms, 8:1)

I form the light and create darkness, I bring prosperity and create disaster; **I, the Lord, do all these things.** (Isaiah, 45:7)

The Lord your God is God in heaven above and on the earth below. (Joshua, 2:11)

Praise Him for His acts of power; praise Him for **His surpassing greatness.** (Psalms, 150:2)

His wisdom is profound, His power is vast. Who has resisted Him and come out unscathed. (Job, 9:4)

God's Being Free from All Imperfection

The eternal God is your refuge, and **underneath are the everlasting arms...** (Deuteronomy, 33:27)

Do you not know? Have you not heard? The Lord is the everlasting God, the Creator of the ends of the earth. **He will not grow tired or weary,** and His understanding no one can fathom. (Isaiah, 40:28)

BELIEF IN THE HEREAFTER ACCORDING TO THE TORAH

Resurrection

Multitudes who sleep in the dust of the earth will awake: some to everlasting life, others to shame and everlasting contempt. (Daniel, 12:2)

"**And you will know that I am the Lord, when I open your graves and bring you up from them. I will put My Spirit in you and you will live**"... declares the Lord. (Ezekiel, 37:13-14)

But your dead will live; their bodies will rise. You who dwell in the dust, wake up and shout for joy... **The earth will give birth to her dead.** (Isaiah, 26:19)

O Lord, **You brought me up from the grave; You spared me** from going down into the pit [hell]. (Psalms, 30:3)

As for you, go your way **till the end. You will rest, and then at the end of the days you will rise to receive your allotted inheritance.** (Daniel, 12:13)

The Lord brings death and makes alive; **He brings down to the grave and raises up.** (1 Samuel, 2:6)

The Last Day

Multitudes, multitudes in the valley of decision! **For the day of the Lord is** near in the valley of decision. **The Sun and Moon will be darkened, and the stars no longer shine**... **The earth and the sky will tremble.** (Joel, 3:14-16)

I will show wonders in the heavens and on the earth, blood and fire and billows of smoke. The Sun will be turned to darkness and the Moon to blood before the coming of the great and dreadful day of the Lord. (Joel, 2:30-31)

Before them the earth shakes, the sky trembles, the Sun and Moon are darkened, and the stars no longer shine... The day of the Lord is great; it is dreadful. Who can endure it? (Joel, 2:10-11)

Their slain will be thrown out... **All the stars of the heavens will be dissolved and the sky rolled up like a scroll; all the starry host will fall like withered leaves from the vine, like shriveled figs from the fig tree.** (Isaiah, 34:3-4)

The great day of the Lord is near—near and coming quickly. **Listen! The cry on the day of the Lord will be bitter, the shouting of the warrior there.** That day will be a day of wrath, a day of distress and anguish, a day of trouble and ruin, a day of darkness and gloom, a day of clouds and blackness, a day of trumpet and battle cry against the fortified cities and against the corner towers. **I will bring distress on the**

people and they will walk like blind men, because they have sinned against the Lord... **Neither their silver nor their gold will be able to save them on the day of the Lord's wrath...** (Zephaniah, 1:14-18)

Alas for that day! **For the day of the Lord is near; it will come like destruction** from the Almighty. (Joel, 1:15)

... Let all who live in the land tremble, for **the day of the Lord is coming. It is close** at hand. (Joel, 2:1)

... For the day of the Lord is near; it will come like destruction from the Almighty. Because of this, all hands will go limp, every man's heart will melt. Terror will seize them, pain and anguish will grip them; they will writhe like a woman in labor. They will look aghast at each other, their faces aflame. See, the day of the Lord is coming—a cruel day, with wrath and fierce anger—to make the land desolate and destroy the sinners within it. **The stars of heaven and their constellations will not show their light. The rising Sun will be darkened and the Moon will not give its light.** I will punish the world for its evil, the wicked for their sins. I will put an end to the arrogance of the haughty and will humble the pride of the ruthless. (Isaiah, 13:6-11)

"Surely the day is coming; it will burn like a furnace. All the arrogant and every evildoer will be stubble, and that day that is coming will set them on fire," says the Lord Almighty. "Not a root or a branch will be left to them." (Malachi, 4:1)

Men will flee to caves in the rocks and to holes in the ground from dread of the Lord and the splendor of His majesty, **when He rises to shake the earth.** (Isaiah, 2:19)

... That day will be darkness, not light. It will be as though a man fled from a lion only to meet a bear, as though he entered his house and rested his hand on the wall only to have a snake bite him. Will not the **day of the Lord** be darkness, not light—**pitch-dark, without a ray of brightness?** (Amos, 5:18-20)

Every valley shall be raised up, every mountain and hill made low; **the rough ground shall become level, the rugged places a plain.** And the glory of the Lord will be revealed, and all humanity together will see it. For the mouth of the Lord has spoken." (Isaiah, 40:4-5)

He lifts up a banner for the distant nations, He whistles for those at the ends of the earth. Here they come, swiftly and speedily... If one looks at the land, he will see darkness and distress; even the **light will be darkened by the clouds.** (Isaiah, 5:26, 30)

The Day of Judgment

Multitudes, **multitudes in the valley of decision!** For the day of the Lord is near **in the valley of decision.** (Joel, 3:14)

"O profane [those who do not obey the laws of God}... whose day has come, whose **time of punishment has reached its climax..."** this is what the Sovereign Lord says: ... It will not be as it was: The lowly will be exalted and the exalted will be brought low. (Ezekiel, 21:25-26)

The day of the Lord is near for all nations. **As you have done, it will be done to you; your deeds will return upon your own head.** (Obadiah, 1:15)

Not so the wicked! They are like chaff that the wind blows away. Therefore **the wicked will not stand in the judgment, nor sinners in the assembly of the righteous.** For the Lord watches over the way of the righteous, but the way of the wicked will perish. (Psalms, 1:4-6)

The Lord is known by His justice; the wicked are ensnared by the work of their hands. **The wicked return to the underworld [hell],** all the nations that forget God. (Psalms, 9:16-17)

Tell the righteous it will be well with them, **for they will enjoy the fruit of their deeds.** Woe to the wicked! Disaster is upon them! They will be paid back for what their hands have done. (Isaiah, 3:10-11)

... whose day has come, **whose time of punishment has reached** its climax. (Ezekiel, 21:29)

The day of your watchmen has come, the day God visits you. Now is the time of their confusion. (Micah 7:4)

The great day of the Lord is near, it is near and coming very quickly. Listen! The cry on the day of the Lord will be bitter, the shouting of the warrior there. That day will be a day of wrath, **a day of distress and anguish, a day of trouble and ruin, a day of darkness and gloom**, a day of clouds and blackness... **and they will walk like blind men**... Even their silver and their gold will not be able to keep them safe in the day of the Lord's wrath.

Hell

(The references to the underworld [sheol, hell] in the Torah are used in the sense of hell)

... Trembling grips the godless: **"Who of us can dwell with the consuming fire? Who of us can dwell with everlasting burning?"** (Isaiah, 33:14)

... **Before I go to the place of no return, to the land of gloom and deep shadow, to the land of deepest night, of deep shadow and disorder, where even the light is like darkness.** (Job, 10:21-22)

... Some to everlasting life [paradise], **others to shame and everlasting contempt.** (Daniel, 12:3)

As heat and drought snatch away the melted snow, so **the grave [hell] snatches away those who have sinned.** (Job, 24:19)

As a cloud vanishes and is gone, so **he who goes down to the grave [hell] does not return.** (Job, 7:9)

Death and destruction are never satisfied... (Proverbs, 27:20)

For great is Your love toward me; **You have delivered me from the depths of the grave [hell].** (Psalms, 86:13)

I will set My face against them... **The fire will yet consume them.** (Ezekiel, 15:7)

For a fire has been kindled by My wrath, one that burns to the realm of death [hell] below... (Deuteronomy, 32:22)

Therefore the grave [hell] enlarges its appetite and opens its mouth without limit... So man will be brought low and mankind humbled, the eyes of the arrogant humbled. (Isaiah, 5:14-15)

... Let them go down alive to the grave [hell], for evil finds lodging among them. (Psalms, 55:15)

So they... went down alive into the grave [hell], with everything they owned... (Numbers, 16:33)

There are three things that never are satisfied, and the fourth **never say, "Enough!": the grave [hell]...** (Proverbs, 30:15-16)

This is the fate of those who trust in themselves, and of their followers, who approve their sayings. Like sheep they are destined for the grave... **Their forms will decay in the grave [hell], far from their princely mansions. But God will redeem my life from the grave [hell];** He will surely take me to Himself. (Psalms, 49:13-15)

But you are **brought down to the grave, to the depths of the pit [hell].** Those who see you stare at you, they ponder your fate: "Is this the man who shook the earth and made kingdoms tremble, the man who made the world a desert, who overthrew its cities and would not let his captives go home?" (Isaiah, 14:15-17)

Woe to those who draw sin along with cords of deceit, and wickedness as with cart ropes... Woe to those who call evil good and good evil, who put darkness for light and light for darkness, who put bitter for sweet and sweet for bitter. Woe to those who are wise in their own eyes and clever in their own sight. Woe to those who are heroes at drinking wine and champions at mixing drinks, who acquit the guilty for a bribe, but deny justice to the innocent. Therefore, **as tongues of fire lick up straw and as dry grass sinks down in the flames, so their roots will decay and their flowers blow away like dust**; for they have rejected the law of the Lord Almighty... (Isaiah, 5:18-24)

... O Lord, for I have cried out to You; but let the wicked be put to shame and **lie silent in the underworld [hell]**. (Psalms, 31:17)

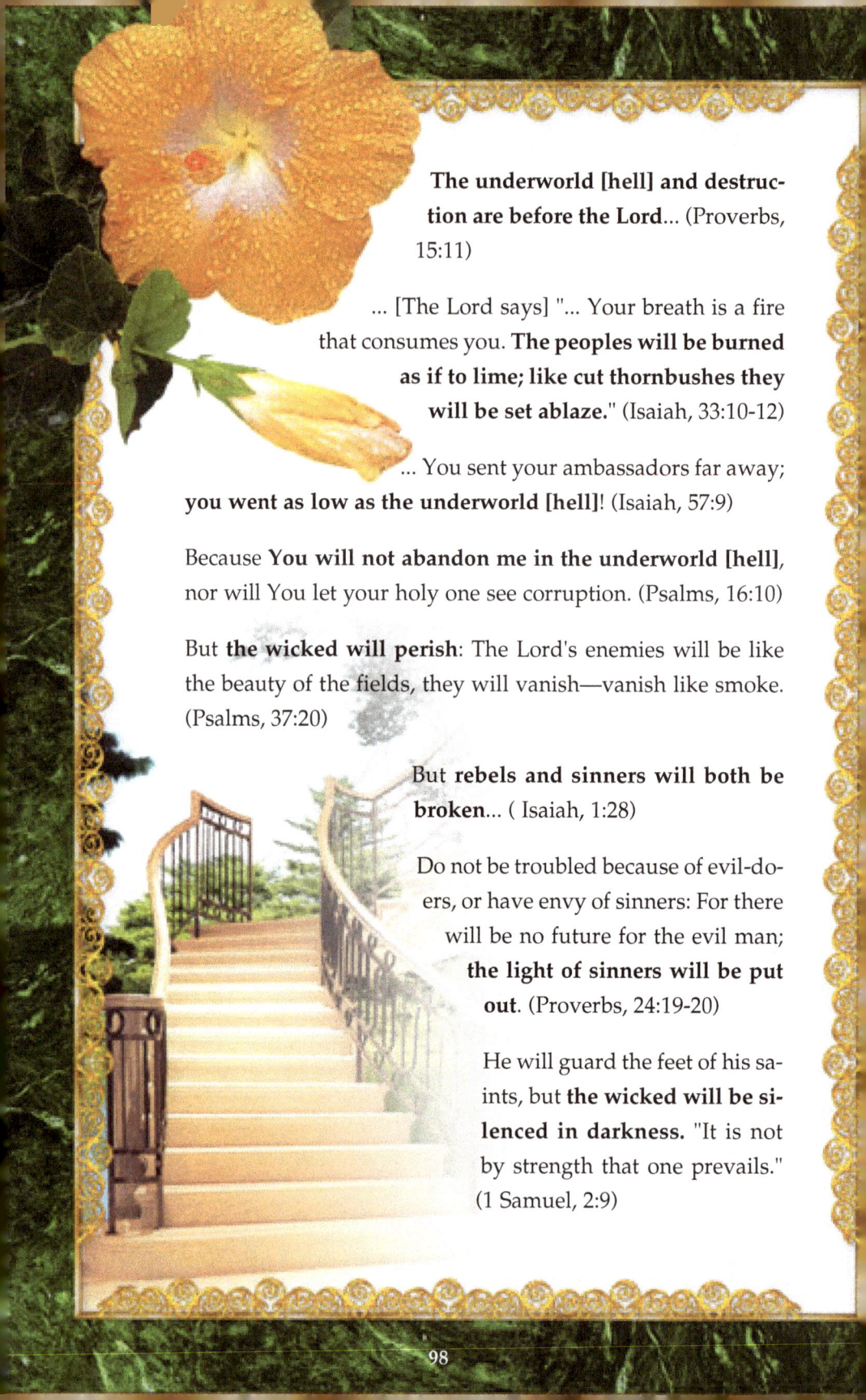

The underworld [hell] and destruction are before the Lord... (Proverbs, 15:11)

... [The Lord says] "... Your breath is a fire that consumes you. **The peoples will be burned as if to lime; like cut thornbushes they will be set ablaze.**" (Isaiah, 33:10-12)

... You sent your ambassadors far away; **you went as low as the underworld [hell]**! (Isaiah, 57:9)

Because **You will not abandon me in the underworld [hell]**, nor will You let your holy one see corruption. (Psalms, 16:10)

But **the wicked will perish**: The Lord's enemies will be like the beauty of the fields, they will vanish—vanish like smoke. (Psalms, 37:20)

But **rebels and sinners will both be broken**... (Isaiah, 1:28)

Do not be troubled because of evil-doers, or have envy of sinners: For there will be no future for the evil man; **the light of sinners will be put out**. (Proverbs, 24:19-20)

He will guard the feet of his saints, but **the wicked will be silenced in darkness.** "It is not by strength that one prevails." (1 Samuel, 2:9)

But the wicked are like the tossing sea, which cannot rest, whose waves cast up mire and mud. **"There is no peace," says my God, "for the wicked."** (Isaiah, 57:20-21)

He will repay them for their sins and destroy them **for their wickedness; the Lord our God will destroy them**. (Psalms, 94:23)

Paradise

(The references to the everlasting life and land of the living in the Torah are used in the sense of paradise.)

... **Some to everlasting life,** others to shame and everlasting contempt. Those who are wise **will shine like the brightness of the heavens,** and those who lead many to righteousness, like the stars for ever and ever. (Daniel, 12:2-3)

The path of life [paradise] leads upward for the wise to keep him from going down to the grave [hell]. (Proverbs, 15:24)

I am still confident of this: I will see the **goodness of the Lord in the land of the living [paradise].** (Psalms, 27:13)

That I may walk before the Lord **in the land of the living [paradise].** (Psalms, 116:9)

... Then man goes to his eternal home [paradise]... and the dust returns to the ground it came from, and **the spirit returns to God Who gave it.** (Ecclesiastes, 12:5, 7)

He who walks righteously and speaks what is right, who rejects gain from extortion and keeps his hand from accepting bribes, who stops his ears against plots of murder and shuts his eyes against contemplating evil—**this is the man who will dwell on the heights, whose refuge will be the mountain fortress. His bread will be supplied, and water will not fail him.** (Isaiah, 33:15-16)

Wicked men are overthrown and are no more, but **the house of the righteous stands firm...** (Proverbs, 12:7)

... O God... lead me in the **way everlasting.** (Psalms, 139:23-24)

In that day they will say, "Surely this is our God; we trusted in Him, and **He saved us.** This is the Lord, we trusted in Him; let us rejoice and be glad in **His salvation."** (Isaiah, 25:9)

The fruit of the righteous is a tree of life... (Proverbs, 11:30)

The Prophet Adam (pbuh) and the Garden of Eden

Now the Lord God had **planted a garden in the east, in Eden;** and there He put the man [Adam] He had formed. (Genesis, 2:8)

... This is what the Sovereign Lord says: "You were the model of perfection, full of wisdom and perfect in beauty. **You were in Eden, the Garden of God;** every precious stone adorned you: ruby, topaz and emerald, chrysolite, onyx and jasper, sapphire, turquoise and beryl. Your settings and mountings were made of gold; **on the day you were created they were prepared."** (Ezekiel, 28:12)

So the Lord God banished him [Adam] **from the Garden of Eden** to work the ground from which he had been taken. (Genesis, 3:23)

THE OBLIGATIONS OF FAITH ACCORDING TO THE TORAH

Faith in God Without Idolatry

But I am the Lord your God... **You shall acknowledge no God but Me,** no Savior except Me. (Hosea, 13:4)

O Lord... **there is no God like You in heaven above or on earth below.** (1 Kings, 8:23)

I am the Lord, and there is no other; apart from Me there is no God... so that from the rising of the Sun to the place of its setting men may know **there is none besides Me. I am the Lord, and there is no other.** (Isaiah, 45:5-6)

I am the Lord your God... **You shall have no other gods before Me.** You shall not make for yourself an idol in the form of anything in heaven above or on the earth beneath or in the waters below. You shall not bow down to them or worship them... (Exodus, 20:2-5)

This is what the Lord says... the Lord Almighty: **I am the first and I am the last; apart from Me there is no God.** (Isaiah, 44:6)

All who make idols are nothing, and the things they treasure are worthless. Those who would speak up for them are blind; they are ignorant, to their own shame. Who shapes a god and casts an idol, which can profit him nothing? He and his kind will be put to shame; craftsmen are nothing but men. Let them all come together and take their stand; they will be brought down to terror and infamy. (Isaiah, 44:9-11)

... Ignorant are those who carry about idols of wood... **There is no God apart from Me,** a righteous God and a Savior; **there is none but Me.** "Turn to Me and be saved, all you ends of the earth; for I am God, and there is no other." (Isaiah, 45:20-22)

And you shall know... that **I am the Lord your God, and that there is no other**... (Joel, 2:27)

Fear the Lord your God, **serve Him only** and take your oaths in His name. **Do not follow other gods, the gods of the peoples around you.** (Deuteronomy, 6:13-14)

... Before Me no God was formed, nor will there be one after Me. **I, even I, am the Lord, and apart from Me there is no savior.** I have revealed and saved and proclaimed—I, and not some foreign god among you... I am God. Yes, and from ancient days I am He. When I act, who can reverse it? (Isaiah, 43:10-13)

Of what value is an idol, since a man has carved it? Or an image that teaches lies? For he who makes it trusts in his own Creation; he makes idols that cannot speak. Woe to him who says to wood, "Come to life!" or to lifeless stone, "Wake up!" Can it give guidance?

It is covered with gold and silver; there is no breath in it. (Habakkuk, 2:18-19)

See, they are all false! Their deeds amount to nothing; their images are but wind and confusion. (Isaiah, 41:29)

Many, O Lord my God, are the wonders You have done. The things You planned for us **no one can recount to You;** were I to speak and tell of them, they would be too many to declare. (Psalms, 40:5)

For who in the skies above can compare with the Lord?... O Lord God Almighty, who is like You?... The heavens are Yours, and Yours also the earth; You founded the world and all that is in it. (Psalms, 89:6, 8, 11)

But those who trust in idols, who say to images, "You are our gods," will be turned back in utter shame. (Isaiah, 42:17)

But if you turn away and forsake the decrees and commands I have given you and go off to serve other gods and worship them, then I will uproot... from My land, which I have given them... (2 Chronicles, 7:19-20)

Do not bow down before their gods or worship them or follow their practices. You must demolish them and break their sacred stones to pieces. **Worship the Lord your God**... (Exodus, 23:24-25)

If you violate the covenant of the Lord your God, which He commanded you, and go and serve other gods and bow down to them, the Lord's anger will burn against you, and you will quickly perish from the good land He has given you. (Joshua, 23:16)

Whoever sacrifices to any god other than the Lord must be destroyed. (Exodus, 22:20)

... You have forsaken Me and served other gods [God is beyon this]. (Judges, 10:13)

Gratitude to God

Moreover, when God gives any man wealth and possessions, and enables him to enjoy them, to accept his lot and be happy in his work—**this is a gift of God.** (Ecclesiastes, 5:19)

Sing to the Lord, you saints of His; **praise His holy name**... that my heart may sing to You and not be silent. O Lord my God, **I will give You thanks forever**. (Psalms, 30:4, 12)

I will praise You forever for what You have done... (Psalms, 52:9)

We give thanks to You, O God, we give thanks, for Your Name is near, men tell of Your wonderful deeds. (Psalms, 75:1)

Then we Your people... **will praise You forever;** from generation to generation we will recount Your praise. (Psalms, 79:13)

And said: "Naked I came from my mother's womb, and naked I will depart. The Lord gave and the Lord has taken away; **may the name of the Lord be praised.**" (Job, 1:21)

... There were... **songs of praise and thanksgiving to God**. (Nehemiah, 12:46)

Enter His gates with thanksgiving and His courts with praise; give thanks to Him and praise His name. For the Lord is good and His love endures forever; His faithfulness continues through all generations. (Psalms, 100:4-5)

I will praise You, O Lord, with all my heart; I will tell of all Your wonders. I will be glad and rejoice in You; I will sing praise to Your name, O Most High. (Psalms, 9:1-2)

Wealth and honor come from You; You are the ruler of all things. In Your hands are strength and power to exalt and give strength to all. Now, our God, **we give You thanks,** and praise Your glorious name. (1 Chronicles, 29:12-13)

Praise the Lord. Give thanks to the Lord, for He is good; His love endures forever. (Psalms, 106:1)

Praise the Lord. I will extol the Lord with all my heart in the council of the upright and in the assembly. (Psalms, 111:1)

Give thanks to the Lord, for He is good; His love endures forever... **Let them give thanks to the Lord** for His unfailing love and His wonderful deeds for men, for He satisfies the thirsty and fills the hungry with good things. (Psalms, 107:1, 7-9)

I will praise You, O Lord, with all my heart... I will sing Your praise... **will praise Your name for Your love and Your faithfulness...** When I called, You answered me; You made me bold and stouthearted. **May all the kings of the earth praise You, O Lord...** (Psalms, 138:1-4)

All You have made will praise You, O Lord; Your saints will extol You. (Psalms, 145:10)

I thank and praise You, O God of my fathers: **You have given me wisdom and power,** You have made known to me what we asked of You... (Daniel, 2:23)

I will praise You with an upright heart as I learn Your righteous laws. I will obey Your decrees; do not utterly forsake me. (Psalms, 119:7-8)

Give thanks to the Lord, for He is good; His love endures forever... Open for me the gates of righteousness; I will enter and give thanks to the Lord. This is the gate of the Lord through which the righteous may enter. **I will give You thanks,** for You answered me; You have become my salvation. You are my God, and **I will give You thanks;** You are my God, **and I will exalt You. Give thanks to the Lord,** for He is good; His love endures forever. (Psalms, 118:1, 19-21, 28-29)

I will praise You, O Lord my God, with all my heart; I will glorify Your name forever. For great is Your love toward me; You have delivered me from the depths of the grave. (Psalms, 86:12-13)

... **Give thanks to the Lord,** for His love endures forever. (2 Chronicles, 20:21)

WISDOM AND SOUND ADVICE FROM TORAH

Give thanks to the Lord, call on His name; make known among the nations what He has done. Sing to Him, sing praise to Him; tell of all His wonderful acts. Glory in His holy name; let the hearts of those who seek the Lord rejoice. (1 Chronicles, 16:8-10)

... They were also to stand **every morning to thank and praise the Lord. They were to do the same in the evening.** (1 Chronicles, 23:30)

It is good to **praise the Lord** and make music to Your name, O Most High, to proclaim Your love in the morning and Your faithfulness at night, to the music of the ten-stringed lyre and the melody of the harp. (Psalms, 92:1-3)

Rejoice in the Lord, you who are righteous, and **praise His holy name.** (Psalms, 97:12)

Give thanks to the Lord, call on His name; make known among the nations what He has done. Sing to Him, sing praise to Him; tell of all His wonderful acts. (Psalms, 105:1-2)

Give thanks to the Lord, for He is good. His love endures forever. (Psalms, 136:1)

... "**I will praise You,** O Lord. Surely God is my salvation; I will trust and not be afraid. The Lord, the Lord, is my strength and my song; He has become my salvation." In that day you will say: "**Give thanks to the Lord,** call on His name; make known among the nations what He has done, and proclaim that His name is exalted." (Isaiah, 12:1-4)

May the peoples praise You, O God; may all the peoples praise You. May the nations be glad and sing for joy, for You rule the peoples justly and guide the nations of the earth. (Psalms, 67:3-4)

Praise the Lord. Praise, O servants of the Lord, praise the name of the Lord. (Psalms, 113:1)

Submission to God

The Lord is my strength and my shield; my heart trusts in Him, and I am helped. (Psalms, 28:7)

Those who trust in the Lord... which cannot be shaken but endures forever. (Psalms, 125:1)

He said: **"The Lord is my strength, my fortress and my deliverer; my God... in Whom I take refuge, my shield and the horn of my salvation.** He is my stronghold, my refuge and my savior—from violent men You save me." (2 Samuel, 22:2-3)

Fear of man will prove to be a snare, but **whoever trusts in the Lord is kept safe.** (Proverbs, 29:25)

Surely **God is my help; the Lord is the One Who sustains me.** (Psalms, 54:4)

The Lord is my light and my salvation—whom shall I fear? The Lord is the stronghold of my life—of whom shall I be afraid? When evil men advance against me to devour my flesh, when my enemies and my foes attack me, they will stumble and fall. Though an army besiege me, my heart will not fear; though war break out against me, even then will I be confident. (Psalms, 27:1-3)

Trust in the Lord... Delight yourself in the Lord and He will give you the desires of your heart. **Commit your way to the Lord; trust in Him and He will do this.** (Psalms, 37:3-5)

Wait for the Lord and keep His way... When the wicked are cut off, you will see it. **The salvation of the righteous comes from the Lord; He is their stronghold in time of trouble. The Lord helps them and delivers them;** He delivers them from the wicked and saves them, **because they take refuge in Him.** (Psalms, 37:34, 39-40)

Whoever gives heed to instruction prospers, **and blessed is he who trusts in the Lord.** (Proverbs, 16:20)

A greedy man stirs up dissension, but **he who trusts in the Lord will prosper.** (Proverbs, 28:25)

Surely God is my salvation; **I will trust and not be afraid.** The Lord, **the Lord, is my strength** and my song; He has become my salvation. (Isaiah, 12:2)

You will keep in perfect peace him whose mind is steadfast, because he trusts in You. **Trust in the Lord forever, for the Lord, the Lord, is the eternal strength.** (Isaiah, 26:3-4)

This is what the Sovereign Lord... says: "In repentance and rest is your salvation, in quietness and **trust is your strength,** but you would have none of it." (Isaiah, 30:15)

... Let him who walks in the dark, who has no light, trust in the name of the Lord and rely on his God. (Isaiah, 50:10)

But blessed is the man who trusts in the Lord, whose confidence is in Him. He will be like a tree planted by the water that sends out its roots by the stream. It does not fear when heat comes; its leaves are always green. It has no worries in a year of drought and never fails to bear fruit. (Jeremiah, 17:7-8)

Have I not commanded you? Be strong and courageous. Do not be terrified; do not be discouraged, **for the Lord your God will be with you wherever you go.** (Joshua, 1:9)

... "**Surely God is with you,** and there is no other; there is no other god." (Isaiah, 45:14)

I am still confident of this: I will see the goodness of the Lord in the land of the living. **Wait for the Lord; be strong and take heart and wait for the Lord.** (Psalms, 27:13-14)

I love You, **O Lord, my strength. The Lord is my strength, my fortress and my deliverer; my God is my strength, in Whom I take refuge. He is my shield and the horn of my salvation, my stronghold.** I call to the Lord, Who is worthy of praise, and I am saved from my enemies. (Psalms, 18:1-3)

In my distress I called to the Lord; I cried to my God for help... He... drew me out of deep waters. He rescued me from my powerful enemy, from my foes, who were too strong for me. They confronted me in the day of my disaster, but **the Lord was my support. He brought me out into a spacious place; He rescued me** because He delighted in me. (Psalms, 18:6, 16-19)

You, O Lord, keep my lamp burning; my God turns my darkness into light. (Psalms, 18:28)

... He is a shield for all who take refuge in Him. For who is God besides the Lord? And who is the strength except our God? It is God Who arms me with strength and makes my way perfect. You give me Your shield of victory... You broaden the path beneath me, so that my ankles do not turn. (Psalms, 18:30-32, 35-36)

WISDOM AND SOUND ADVICE FROM THE TORAH

... Exalted be God my Savior! **Who saves me** from my enemies... from violent men **You rescued me**. (Psalms, 18:46, 48)

In You, O Lord, I have taken refuge; let me never be put to shame; deliver me in Your righteousness... Be my strength of refuge, a strong fortress to save me. Since You are my strength and my fortress, for the sake of Your name lead and guide me. Free me from the trap that is set for me, for **You are my refuge. Into Your hands I commit my spirit;** redeem me, O Lord the God of truth. I hate those who cling to worthless idols; I trust in the Lord. (Psalms, 31:1-6)

My soul finds rest in God alone; my salvation comes from Him. **He alone is my strength and my salvation; He is my fortress, I will never be shaken.** Find rest, O my soul, in God alone; my hope comes from Him. **He alone is my strength and my salvation; He is my fortress, I will not be shaken.** My salvation and my honor depend on God; **He is my... refuge. Trust in Him at all times,** O people; pour out your hearts to Him, for **God is our refuge.** (Psalms, 62:1-2, 5-8)

But I call to God, and **the Lord saves me... Cast your cares on the Lord and He will sustain you;** He will never let the righteous fall. But You, O God, will bring down the wicked into the pit of corruption... But as for me, **I trust in You.** (Psalms, 55:16, 22-23)

He trusted in the Lord, the God... He held fast to the Lord and did not cease to follow Him; he kept the commands the Lord had given Moses. And **the Lord was with him; he was successful in whatever he undertook...** (2 Kings, 18:5-7)

But **I trust in You, O Lord;** I say, "You are my God." **My times are in Your hands; deliver me** from my enemies and from those who pursue me. Let Your face shine on Your servant; save me in Your unfailing love. **In the shelter of Your presence** You hide them from the intrigues of men; **in Your dwelling You keep them safe** from accusing tongues... Love the Lord, all His saints! **The Lord preserves the faithful...** Be strong and take heart, all you who hope in the Lord. (Psalms, 31:14-16, 20-24)

You are my hiding place; You will protect me from trouble and surround me with songs of deliverance. (Psalms, 32:7)

Many are the woes of the wicked, **but the Lord's unfailing love surrounds the man who trusts in Him.** Rejoice in the Lord and be glad, you righteous; sing, all you who are upright in heart! (Psalms, 32:10-11)

... And put their trust in the Lord. **Blessed is the man who makes the Lord his trust,** who does not look to the proud, to those who turn aside to false gods. (Psalms, 40:3-4)

Be pleased, O Lord, to save me; O Lord, come quickly to help me... **You are my help and my deliverer;** O my God... (Psalms, 40:13, 17)

... The Lord delivers him in times of trouble. The Lord will protect him and preserve his life... The Lord will sustain him on his sickbed and restore him from his bed of illness. (Psalms, 41:1-3)

I do not trust in my bow, my sword does not bring me victory; but **You give us victory over our enemies...** (Psalms, 44:6-7)

Such is the destiny of all who forget God; so perishes the hope of the godless. What he trusts in is fragile; what he relies on is a spider's web. He leans on his web, but it gives way; he clings to it, but it does not hold. (Job, 8:13-15)

The Lord is a refuge for the oppressed, a stronghold in times of trouble. Those who know Your name will trust in You, for You, Lord, have never forsaken those who seek You. (Psalms, 9:9-10)

I have set the Lord always before me. Because He is at my right hand, I will not be shaken. Therefore my heart is glad and my tongue rejoices; **my body also will rest secure... You have made known to me the path of life;** You will fill me with joy in Your presence, with eternal pleasures at Your right hand. (Psalms, 16:8-11)

Some trust in chariots and some in horses, but **we trust in the name of the Lord our God.** They are brought to their knees and fall, but we rise up and stand firm. (Psalms, 20:7-8)

For the king **trusts in the Lord;** through the unfailing love of the Most High he will not be shaken. (Psalms, 21:7)

Even though I walk through the valley of the shadow of death, **I will fear no evil, for You are with me;** Your rod and Your staff, they comfort me... Surely goodness and love will follow me all the days of my life, and I will dwell in the house of the Lord forever. (Psalms, 23:4-6)

To You, O Lord, I lift up my soul; **in You I trust,** O my God... No one whose hope is in You will ever be put to shame, but they will be put to shame who are treacherous without excuse... **For You are God my Savior, and my hope is in You all day long.** (Psalms, 25:1-5)

... I have trusted in the Lord without wavering. (Psalms, 26:1)

I will lie down and sleep in peace, **for You alone, O Lord, make me dwell in safety.** (Psalms, 4:8)

... Have faith in the Lord your God and you will be upheld. Have faith in His Prophets and you will be successful. (2 Chronicles, 20:20)

Here now is the man who did not make God his stronghold... But I am like an olive tree flourishing in the house of God; **I trust in God's unfailing love for ever and ever.** (Psalms, 52:7-8)

When I am afraid, **I will trust in You. In God, Whose word I praise, in God I trust; I will not be afraid.** What can mortal man do to me?... I will know that God is for me. (Psalms, 56:3-4-9)

In God, Whose word I praise, in the Lord, Whose word I praise—in God I trust; I will not be afraid. What can man do to me?... For You have delivered me from death and my feet from tumbling, that I may walk before God in the light of life. (Psalms, 56:10-13)

And Asa called to the Lord his God and said, "Lord, there is no one like You to help the powerless against the mighty. **Help us, O Lord our God, for we rely on You,** and in Your name we have come against this vast army. O Lord, You are our God..." (2 Chronicles, 14:11)

Even though someone is pursuing you to take your life, the soul of my Lord shall be kept, as **in the bundle of the living by the Lord your God.** But the lives of your enemies He will hurl away as from the pocket of a sling. (1 Samuel, 25:29)

Have no fear of sudden disaster or of the ruin that overtakes the wicked, **for the Lord will be your confidence** and will keep your foot from being snared. (Proverbs, 3:25-26)

The Lord is with me; I will not be afraid. What can man do to me? **The Lord is with me; He is my helper... It is better to take refuge in the Lord than to trust in man...** I was pushed back and about to fall, but the Lord helped me. **The Lord is my strength** and my praise; He has become my salvation. (Psalms, 118:6-9, 13-14)

... Trust in the Lord—He is their help and shield. You who fear Him, **trust in the Lord—He is their help and shield.** (Psalms, 115:9, 11)

He will have no fear of bad news; his heart is steadfast, trusting in the Lord. His heart is secure, he will have no fear... (Psalms, 112:7-8)

For the Lord God is a Sun and shield; the Lord bestows favor and honor; no good thing does He withhold from those whose walk is blameless. O Lord Almighty, **blessed is the man who trusts in You.** (Psalms, 84:11-12)

Then they would put their trust in God and would not forget His deeds but would keep His commands. They would not be like their forefathers—a stubborn and rebellious generation, whose hearts were not loyal to God, whose spirits were not faithful to Him. (Psalms, 78:7-8)

In You, O Lord, I have taken refuge... Be my strength of refuge, to which I can always go... **You are my strength and my fortress.** Deliver me, O my God, from the hand of the wicked, from the grasp of evil and cruel men. For You have been my hope, O Sovereign Lord, **my confidence since my youth. From birth I have relied on You;** You brought me forth from my mother's womb. I will ever praise You. I have become like a portent to many, but You are my strong refuge. (Psalms, 71:1-7)

Have no fear of sudden disaster or of the ruin that overtakes the wicked, **for the Lord will be your confidence...** (Proverbs, 3:25-26)

Have I not commanded you? Be strong and courageous. Do not be terrified; do not be discouraged, for the Lord your God will be with you wherever you go. (Joshua, 1:9)

Be strong and courageous. Do not be afraid or terrified because of them, for the Lord your God goes with you; **He will never leave you nor forsake you.** (Deuteronomy, 31:6)

The Lord Himself goes before you and **will be with you;** He

will never leave you nor forsake you. **Do not be afraid; do not be discouraged.** (Deuteronomy, 31:8)

Be strong and courageous. Do not be afraid or discouraged because... there is a greater Power [God] with us than with him. (2 Chronicles, 32:7)

He Who dwells in the shelter of the Most High will rest in the shadow of the Almighty. I will say of the Lord, **"He is my refuge and my fortress, my God, in Whom I trust."** Surely He will save you from the fowler's snare and from the deadly pestilence. He will cover you with His feathers, and under His wings you will find refuge; His faithfulness will be your shield and rampart. You will not fear the terror of night, nor the arrow that flies by day, nor the pestilence that stalks in the darkness, nor the plague that destroys at midday... **If you make the Most High your dwelling—even the Lord, Who is my refuge—then no harm will befall you, no disaster will come near your tent.** For He will command His angels concerning you to guard you in all your ways; they will lift you up in their hands, so that you will not strike your foot against a stone. You will tread upon the lion and the cobra; you will trample the great lion and the serpent. **"Because he loves Me," says the Lord, "I will rescue him; I will protect him, for he acknowledges My name. He will call upon Me, and I will answer him; I will be with him in trouble,** I will deliver him and honor him. With long life will I satisfy him and show him My salvation." (Psalms, 91:1-7, 9-16)

Then **they cried out to the Lord in their trouble, and He delivered them from their distress.** (Psalms, 107:6)

In my anguish I cried to the Lord, and He answered me [and]... set me free [from all of them]. (Psalms, 118:5)

The righteous cry out... the Lord... delivers them from all their troubles. (Psalms, 34:17)

God is our refuge and strength... (Psalms, 46:1)

Commit your works to the Lord, and your purposes will be made certain. The Lord has made everything for its own ends. (Proverbs, 16:3-4)

Obedience to God's Commandments

So be careful to do what the Lord your God has commanded you; do not turn aside to the right or to the left. Walk in all the way that the Lord your God has commanded **you, so that you may live and prosper and prolong your days in the land that you will possess.** (Deuteronomy, 5:32-33)

Oh, that their hearts would be inclined to fear Me and **keep all My commands always,** so that it might go well with them and their children forever! (Deuteronomy, 5:29)

Be sure to keep the commands of the Lord your God and the stipulations and decrees He has given you. Do what is right and good in the Lord's sight, so that it may go well with you and you may go in and take over the good land that the Lord promised on oath to your forefathers. (Deuteronomy, 6:17-18)

WISDOM AND SOUND ADVICE FROM THE TORAH

The Lord commanded us to obey all these decrees and to fear the Lord our God, so that we might always prosper and be kept alive, as is the case today. And **if we are careful to obey all this law** before the Lord our God, as He has commanded us, that will be our righteousness. (Deuteronomy, 6:24-25)

Remember how the Lord your God... **test you** in order to know what was in your heart, **whether or not you would keep His commands.** (Deuteronomy, 8:2)

You must obey My laws and be careful to follow My decrees. I am the Lord your God. **Keep My decrees and laws,** for the man who obeys them will live by them. I am the Lord. (Leviticus, 18:4-5)

... Repent! **Turn away from all your offenses;** then sin will not be your downfall. **Rid yourselves of all the offenses** you have committed, and get a new heart and a new spirit. (Ezekiel, 18:30-31)

... Your people whom You brought out of Egypt have become corrupt. **They have turned away quickly from what I commanded them** and have made a cast idol for themselves. And the Lord said to me... **They are a stiff-necked people indeed!**... I may destroy them and blot out their name from under heaven. (Deuteronomy, 9:12-14)

... **But you rebelled against the command of the Lord your God.** You did not trust Him or **obey Him.** You have been rebellious against the Lord ever since I have known you. (Deuteronomy, 9:23-24)

Circumcise your hearts, therefore, and **do not be stiff-necked**

any longer. For the Lord your God is... the great God, mighty and awesome... (Deuteronomy, 10:16-17)

... Lord your God, Who brought you out of Egypt and redeemed you from the land of slavery; **he [wicked one] has tried to turn you from the way the Lord your God commanded you to** follow. You must purge the evil from among you. (Deuteronomy, 13:5)

... He is to... **learn to revere the Lord his God and follow carefully all the words of this law** and these decrees and not consider himself better than his brothers and **turn from the law...** (Deuteronomy, 17:19-20)

The Lord your God commands you this day to follow these decrees and laws; carefully observe them with all your heart and with all your soul. You have declared this day that the Lord is your God and that you will walk in His ways, that you will keep His decrees, commands and laws, and **that you will obey Him...** that you are to keep all His commands. (Deuteronomy, 26:16-18)

Cursed is the man who does not uphold the words of this law by carrying them out. Then all the people shall say, "Amen!" (Deuteronomy, 27:26)

"You acted foolishly," Samuel said. "You have not kept the command the Lord your God gave you... (1 Samuel, 13:13)

... To obey is better than sacrifice, and to heed is better than the fat of rams... Because you have rejected the word of the Lord, He has rejected you as king. (1 Samuel, 15:22-23)

A man who remains stiff-necked after many rebukes will suddenly be destroyed—without remedy. (Proverbs, 29:1)

... For you are a stiff-necked people... you have been rebellious against the Lord. (Deuteronomy, 9:6-7)

They refused to listen and failed to remember the miracles You performed among them. They became stiff-necked and in their rebellion appointed a leader in order to return to their slavery. But You are a forgiving God, gracious and compassionate...and abounding in love. Therefore You did not desert them... (Nehemiah, 9:17)

However, **if you do not obey the Lord your God and do not carefully follow all His commands and decrees I am giving you today, all these curses will come upon you and overtake you:** You will be cursed in the city and cursed in the country. Your basket and your kneading trough will be cursed. The fruit of your womb will be cursed, and the crops of your land, and the calves of your herds and the lambs of your flocks. You will be cursed when you come in and cursed when you go out. The Lord will send on you curses, confusion and rebuke in everything you put your hand to, until you are destroyed and come to sudden ruin **because of the evil you have done in forsaking Him.** The Lord will plague you with diseases until He has destroyed you from the land you are entering to possess. (Deuteronomy, 28:15-21)

If you do not carefully follow all the words of this law, which are written in this book, and do not revere this glorious and awesome name—the Lord your God—the Lord will send fearful plagues on you and your descendants, harsh and pro-

longed disasters, and severe and lingering illnesses. He will bring upon you all the diseases of Egypt that you dreaded, and they will cling to you. The Lord will also bring on you every kind of sickness and disaster not recorded in this Book of the Law, until you are destroyed. (Deuteronomy, 28:58-61)

I know how rebellious and stiff-necked you are. If you have been rebellious against the Lord while I am still alive and with you, how much more will you rebel after I die! (Deuteronomy, 31:27)

"Woe to the obstinate children," declares the Lord... heaping sin upon sin. (Isaiah, 30:1)

... Those who oppose You will be as nothing and perish. (Isaiah, 41:11)

They are all hardened rebels... They are bronze and iron; they all act corruptly. (Jeremiah, 6:28)

Yet they did not listen or pay attention; they were stiff-necked and would not listen or respond to discipline. (Jeremiah, 17:23)

This is what the Lord Almighty... says: "Listen! I am going to bring on this city and the villages around it every disaster I pronounced against them, because they were stiff-necked and would not listen to My words." (Jeremiah, 19:15)

... They and their fathers have been in revolt against Me to this very day. The people to whom I am sending you are obstinate and stubborn. Say to them, "This is what the Sovereign Lord says." And whether they listen or fail to listen—for they are a rebellious house—they will know that a Prophet has been among them. And you, son of man, do not be afraid of them or their words. Do not be afraid, though briers and thorns are all around you and you live among scorpions. Do not be afraid of what they say or terrified by them, though they are a rebellious house. You must speak My words to them, whether they listen or fail to listen, for they are rebellious. (Ezekiel, 2:3-7)

... "Do not be afraid of them or terrified by them, though they are a rebellious house." And He said to me, "Son of man, listen carefully and take to heart all the words I speak to you. Go now to your countrymen in exile and speak to them. Say to them, 'This is what the Sovereign Lord says,' whether they listen or fail to listen." (Ezekiel, 3:9-11)

... **Those who oppose the Lord will be shattered.** He will thunder against them from heaven; the Lord will judge the ends of the earth. (1 Samuel, 2:10)

If you fear the Lord and serve and **obey Him and do not rebel against His commands,** and if both you and the king who reigns over you follow the Lord your God-good! But if you do not obey the Lord, and if you rebel against His commands,

His hand will be against you, as it was against your fathers. (1 Samuel, 12:14-15)

They... refused to live by His law. They forgot what He had done, the wonders He had shown them. But they... rebelled against the Most High; they did not keep His statutes. Like their fathers they were disloyal and faithless, as unreliable as a faulty bow. (Psalms, 78:10-11, 56-57)

For they had rebelled against the words of God and despised the counsel of the Most High... Some became fools through their rebellious ways and suffered affliction because of their iniquities. (Psalms, 107:11, 17)

You have laid down precepts that are to be fully obeyed. Oh, that my ways were steadfast in obeying Your decrees! Then I would not be put to shame when I consider all Your commands. I will praise You with an upright heart as I learn Your righteous laws. **I will obey Your decrees; do not utterly forsake me.** (Psalms, 119:4-8)

... I obey Your precepts. I have kept my feet from every evil path so that I might obey Your word. **I have not departed from Your laws, for You yourself have taught me.** How sweet are Your words to my taste, sweeter than honey to my mouth! **I gain understanding from Your precepts;** therefore I hate every wrong path. Your word is a lamp to my feet and a light for my path. **I have taken an oath and confirmed it, that I will follow Your righteous laws.** (Psalms, 119:100-106)

The Lord detests all the proud of heart. Be sure of this: They will not go unpunished. (Proverbs, 16:5)

... I said, **"Obey Me and do everything I command you...** But they did not listen or pay attention; instead, they followed the stubbornness of their evil hearts. So I brought on them all the curses of the covenant I had commanded them to follow but that they did not keep." (Jeremiah, 11:4, 8)

Because you have burned incense and have sinned against the Lord and have not obeyed Him or followed His law or His decrees or His stipulations, this disaster has come upon you, as you now see." (Jeremiah, 44:23)

And if you reject My decrees and abhor My laws and fail to carry out all My commands and so violate My covenant, then I will do this to you: I will bring upon you sudden terror, wasting diseases and fever that will destroy your sight and drain away your life. You will plant seed in vain, because your enemies will eat it. (Leviticus, 26:15-16)

"If you remain hostile toward Me and refuse to listen to Me, I will multiply your afflictions seven times over, as your sins deserve... If in spite of these things you do not accept My correction but continue to be hostile toward Me, I myself will be hostile toward you and will afflict you for your sins seven times over... If in spite of this you still do not listen to Me but continue to be hostile toward Me... I myself will punish you for your sins seven times over." (Leviticus, 26:21-28)

Because he has despised the Lord's word and broken His commands, that person must surely be cut off; his guilt remains on him. (Numbers, 15:31)

So I told you, but you would not listen. You rebelled against the Lord's command and in your arrogance you marched up into the hill country. (Deuteronomy, 1:43)

... She has rejected My laws and has not followed My decrees. Therefore this is what the Sovereign Lord says: "You have been more unruly than the nations around you and have not followed My decrees or kept My laws. You have not even conformed to the standards of the nations around you." Therefore this is what the Sovereign Lord says: "I Myself am against you... and I will inflict punishment on you in the sight of the nations." (Ezekiel, 5:6-8)

But they rebelled against Me and would not listen to Me; they did not get rid of the vile images they had set their eyes on, nor did they forsake the idols of Egypt. (Ezekiel, 20:8)

But the children rebelled against Me: They did not follow My decrees, they were not careful to keep My laws—although the man who obeys them will live by them... I will purge you of those who revolt and rebel against Me. Although I will bring them out of the land where they are living... (Ezekiel, 20:21, 38)

I dealt with them according to their uncleanness and their offenses... (Ezekiel, 39:24)

Because you did not obey the Lord... the Lord has done this to you today. (1 Samuel, 28:18)

But if you or your sons turn away from Me and do not observe the commands and decrees I have given you and go off to serve other gods and worship them, then I will cut off... the land I have given them... (1 Kings, 9:6-7)

... Be careful to follow all the commands of the Lord your God, that you may possess this good land and pass it on as an inheritance to your descendants forever. (1 Chronicles, 28:8)

... He [Zechariah] stood before the people and said, "This is what God says: "Why do you disobey the Lord's commands? You will not prosper. Because you have forsaken the Lord, He has forsaken you." (2 Chronicles, 24:20)

Whoever does not obey the law of your God... must surely be punished by death, banishment, confiscation of property, or imprisonment. (Ezra, 7:26)

... O our God, what can we say after this? For we have disregarded the commands You gave through Your servants the Prophets... (Ezra, 9:10-11)

We have acted very wickedly toward You. We have not obeyed the commands, decrees and laws You gave Your servant Moses. "Remember the instruction You gave Your servant Moses, saying, 'If you are unfaithful, I will scatter you among the nations, but **if you return to Me and obey My commands**, then even if your exiled people are at the farthest horizon, I will gather them from there and bring them to the place I have chosen as a dwelling for My Name'." (Nehemiah, 1:7-9)

You warned them to return to Your law, but they became arrogant and disobeyed Your commands. They sinned against Your ordinances, by which a man will live if he obeys them.

Stubbornly they turned their backs on You, became stiff-necked and refused to listen. (Nehemiah, 9:29)

... [They] bind themselves with a curse and **an oath to follow the Law of God given through Moses the servant of God and to obey carefully all the commands, regulations and decrees of the Lord our Lord.** (Nehemiah, 10:29)

... We have not obeyed the Lord our God or kept the laws He gave us through His servants the Prophets... has transgressed Your law and turned away, refusing to obey You. "Therefore the curses and sworn judgments written in the Law of Moses, the servant of God, have been poured out on us, because we have sinned against You. You have fulfilled the words spoken against us and against our rulers by bringing upon us great disaster... Just as it is written in the Law of Moses, all this disaster has come upon us, yet we have not sought the favor of the Lord our God by turning from our sins and giving attention to Your truth." (Daniel, 9:10-13)

This is what the Lord says: "... I will not turn back [My wrath]. Because they have rejected the law of the Lord and have not kept His decrees, because they have been led astray by false gods, the gods their ancestors followed." (Amos, 2:4)

Heeding the Conscience

I will maintain my righteousness and never let go of it; **my conscience will not reproach me as long as I live.** (Job, 27:6)

I will praise the Lord, Who counsels me; **even at night my heart instructs me.** (Psalms, 16:7)

A man tormented by the guilt of murder will be a fugitive till death... (Proverbs, 28:17)

... I have done this with **a clear conscience** and clean hands. (Genesis, 20:5)

... My bones have no soundness because of my sin. **My guilt has overwhelmed me like a burden too heavy to bear.** (Psalms, 38:3-4)

Timelessness and Belief in Destiny

For **a thousand years in Your sight are like a day that has just gone by, or like a watch in the night.** (Psalms, 90:4)

I thought in my heart, **"God** will bring to judgment both the righteous and the wicked, **for there will be a time for every activity, a time for every deed."** (Ecclesiastes, 3:17)

The lot is cast into the lap, but **its every decision is from the Lord.** (Proverbs, 16:33)

Before I formed you in the womb I knew you, before you were born I set you apart; I appointed you as a Prophet to the nations. (Jeremiah, 1:5)

I know that **everything God does will endure forever; nothing can be added to it and nothing taken from it.** God does it so that men should fear before Him. Whatever is has already been, and what will be has been before... (Ecclesiastes, 3:14-15)

Remember the former things, those of long ago; I am God, and there is no other; I am God, and there is none like Me. **I make** known the end from the beginning, from ancient times, what is still to come. (Isaiah, 46:9-10)

Your eyes saw my unformed body. **All the days ordained for me were written in Your book before one of them came to be.** (Psalms, 139:16)

There is a time for everything, and a season for every activity under heaven. (Ecclesiastes, 3:1)

[There is] a time to be born and a time to die, a time to plant and a time to uproot. (Ecclesiastes, 3:2)

... **[There is] a time to heal, a time to tear down and a time to build**... He has made everything beautiful in its time... (Ecclesiastes, 3:3, 11)

Man's days are determined; You have decreed the number of his months and have set limits he cannot exceed. (Job, 14:5)

Many are the plans in a man's heart, but it is the Lord's purpose that prevails. (Proverbs, 19:21)

Before a word is on my tongue, You know it completely, O Lord. (Psalms, 139:4)

... **All the days ordained for me were written in Your book before one of them came to be**. (Psalms, 139:16)

... **It [the time of the end] will still come at the appointed time.** (Daniel 11:35)

Moreover, **no man knows when his hour will come:** As fish are caught in a cruel net, or birds are taken in a snare, so men are trapped by evil times that fall unexpectedly upon them. (Ecclesiastes, 9:12)

Even from birth the wicked go astray; from the womb they are wayward and speak lies. (Psalms, 58:3)

Listen to me, you islands; hear this, you distant nations: **Before I was born the Lord called me; from my birth He has made mention of my name.** (Isaiah, 49:1)

The lot is cast into the lap, **but its every decision is from the Lord.** (Proverbs, 16:33)

Have you not heard? **Long ago I ordained it. In days of old I planned it; now I have brought it to pass**, that you have turned fortified cities into piles of stone... But I know where you stay and when you come and go... (Isaiah, 37:26,28)

... But you did **not look to the One Who made it, or have regard for the One Who planned it** long ago... "Till your dying day this sin will not be atoned for"... (Isaiah, 22:11, 14)

Let this be written for a future generation, that a people not yet created may praise the Lord. (Psalms, 102:18)

... All the curses written in this book will fall upon him, and the Lord will blot out his name from under heaven. (Deuteronomy, 29:20)

... I am going to bring disaster on this place and its people— **all the curses written in the book...** (2 Chronicles, 34:24)

"Have you not heard? **Long ago I ordained it. In days of old I planned it; now I have brought it to pass,** that you have turned fortified cities into piles of stone." (2 Kings, 19:25)

The Importance of Prayer

The Lord is near to all who call on Him, to all who call on Him in truth. He fulfills the desires of those who fear Him; He hears their cry and saves them. The Lord watches over all who love Him... (Psalms, 145:18-20)

... Let us go at once **to entreat the Lord and seek the Lord Almighty...** (Zechariah, 8:21)

Ask the Lord for rain in the springtime; it is the Lord Who makes the storm clouds. (Zechariah, 10:1)

"When my life was ebbing away... and my prayer rose to You." (Jonah, 2:7)

So **I turned to the Lord God and pleaded with Him in prayer and petition, in fasting,** and in sackcloth and ashes. **I prayed to the Lord my God and confessed:** "O Lord, the great and awesome God, Who keeps His covenant of love with all who love Him and obey His commands." (Daniel, 9:3-4)

... At night His song is with me—**a prayer to the God** of my life. (Psalms, 42:8)

He [Job (pbuh)] prays to God and finds favor with Him, he sees God's face and shouts for joy; he is restored by God... (Job, 33:26)

... **But I prayed, "Now strengthen my hands."** (Nehemiah, 6:9)

I cry aloud to the Lord; I lift up my voice to the Lord for mercy... I cry to You, O Lord; I say, "You are my refuge, my portion in the land of the living." (Psalms, 142:1, 5)

... If My people, who are called by My name, will humble themselves and **pray and seek My face** and turn from their wicked ways, then will I... forgive their sin and will heal their land. (2 Chronicles, 7:14)

But **we prayed to our God**... (Nehemiah, 4:9)

You alone are the Lord. You made the heavens, even the highest heavens, and all their starry host, the earth and all that is on it, the seas and all that is in them. You give life to everything, and the multitudes of heaven worship You. (Nehemiah, 9:6)

This is what the Lord says, He Who made the earth, the Lord Who formed it and established it—the Lord is His name: **"Call to Me and I will answer you** and tell you great and unsearchable things you do not know." (Jeremiah, 33:2-3)

I cry aloud to the Lord; I lift up my voice to the Lord... When my spirit grows faint within me, it is You Who know my way. In the path where I walk men have hidden a snare for me... **I cry to You, O Lord; I say, "You are my refuge, my portion in**

the land of the living." Listen to my cry, for I am in desperate need; rescue me from those who pursue me, for they are too strong for me. (Psalms, 142:1-6)

From inside the fish **Jonah prayed to the Lord his God**. He said: "In my distress **I called to the Lord, and He answered me... I called for help, and You listened to my cry.** You hurled me into the deep, into the very heart of the seas, and the currents swirled about me; all Your waves and breakers swept over me... But You brought my life up from the pit, O Lord my God. When my life was ebbing away, I remembered You, Lord, and **my prayer rose to You**, what I have vowed I will make good. Salvation comes from the Lord." (Jonah, 2:1-9)

O Lord, hear **my prayer,** listen to **my cry for mercy**; in Your faithfulness and righteousness come to my relief... I spread out my hands to You; my soul thirsts for You like a parched land. Answer me quickly, O Lord; my spirit fails. Do not hide Your face from me or I will be like those who go down to the pit. Let the morning bring me word of Your unfailing love, for I have put my trust in You. Show me the way I should go, for **to You I lift up my soul.** Rescue me from my enemies, O Lord, for I hide myself in You. Teach me to do Your will, for You are my God; may Your good Spirit lead me on level ground. For Your name's sake, O Lord, preserve my life; in Your righteousness, bring me out of trouble... (Psalms, 143:1, 6-12)

Then Hannah **prayed** and said: "My heart rejoices in the Lord; in the Lord my horn is lifted high... There is no one holy like the Lord; there is no one besides You; there is no strength like our God... For the Lord is a God Who knows, and by Him deeds are weighed... The Lord brings death and makes alive;

He brings down to the grave and raises up." The Lord sends poverty and wealth; He humbles and He exalts. He raises the poor from the dust and lifts the needy from the ash heap... "For the foundations of the earth are the Lord's... He will guard the feet of His saints, but the wicked will be silenced in darkness. It is not by strength that one prevails." (1 Samuel, 2:1-9)

Then Abraham **prayed to God,** and God healed... they could have children again. (Genesis, 20:17)

Then he **prayed,** "O Lord, God of my master Abraham, give me success today, and show kindness to my master Abraham." (Genesis, 24:12)

Moses then left Pharaoh and **prayed to the Lord.** (Exodus, 10:18, 8:30)

... But Hezekiah **prayed** for them, saying, "May the Lord... pardon everyone who sets his heart on seeking God—the Lord, the God of his fathers?" (2 Chronicles, 30:18-19)

... **Three times a day he [Daniel] got down on his knees and prayed,** giving thanks to his God, just as he had done before. Then these men went as a group and found Daniel **praying and asking** God for help. (Daniel, 6:10-11)

Then Solomon stood... spread out his hands toward heaven and said: "O Lord... there is no god like You in heaven above or on earth below—You Who keep Your covenant of love with Your servants who continue wholeheartedly in Your way. O Lord my God. **Hear the cry and the prayer that Your servant is praying in Your presence** this day... **You will hear the prayer Your servant prays** toward this place. Hear the supplication of Your servant and of Your people... **when they pray** toward this place. When a man wrongs his neighbor and is required to take an oath and he comes and swears the oath before Your altar in this house... judge between your servants, condemning the guilty and bringing down on his own head what he has done... when they turn back to You and confess Your name, **praying and making supplication to You** in this house, then... forgive the sin of Your people... and bring them back to the land You gave to their fathers. When the heavens are shut up and there is no rain because Your people have sinned against You, and **when they pray** toward this place and confess Your name and turn from their sin... then forgive the sin of Your servants... Teach them the right way to live, and send rain on the land You gave Your people for an inheritance. When famine or plague comes to the land, or blight or mildew, locusts or grasshoppers, or when an enemy besieges them in any of their cities, whatever disaster or disease may come, and **when a prayer** or plea is made by any of Your people...—each one aware of the afflictions of his own heart, and spreading out his hands toward this house—then... forgive... since You know his heart (for You alone know the hearts of all men), so that they will fear You all the time they live in the land You gave our fathers. As for the foreigner... has come from a distant land because of Your name—for men will hear of Your great name and Your mighty hand and Your outstretched arm—when he comes and **prays** toward this house... so that all the peoples of the earth may know Your name and fear You... and say, 'We have sinned, we have done wrong, we have acted wickedly'; and if they turn back to You with all their heart and soul in the land of their enemies who took them captive, and **pray** to You toward the land You gave their fathers, toward the city You have chosen and the house I have built for Your Name; then... hear **their prayer** and their plea, and uphold their cause. And forgive Your people, who have sinned against You; forgive all the offenses they have committed against You... may You listen to them whenever they cry out to You." **When Solomon had finished all these prayers and supplications to the Lord,** he rose from before the altar of the Lord, where he had been kneeling with his hands spread out toward heaven. (1 Kings, 8:22-54)

So I turned to the Lord God and **pleaded with Him in prayer and petition, in fasting. I prayed to the Lord my God** and confessed: "O Lord... we have sinned and done wrong. We have been wicked and have rebelled; we have turned away from Your commands and laws. We have not listened to Your servants the Prophets, who spoke in Your name to our kings, our princes and our fathers, and to all the people of the land.

"Lord, You are righteous, but this day we are covered with shame... in all the countries where You have scattered us because of our unfaithfulness to You. O Lord, we and our kings, our princes and our fathers are covered with shame because we have sinned against You. The Lord our God is merciful and forgiving, even though we have rebelled against Him; we have not obeyed the Lord our God or kept the laws He gave us through His servants the Prophets... Therefore the curses and sworn judgments written in the Law of Moses, the servant of God, have been poured out on us, because we have sinned against You. You have fulfilled the words spoken against us and against our rulers by bringing upon us great disaster... Just as it is written in the Law of Moses, all this disaster has come upon us, yet we have not sought the favor of the Lord our God by turning from our sins and giving attention to Your truth. Now, our God, **hear the prayers and petitions of Your servant**... We do not make requests of You because we are righteous, but because of Your great mercy. O Lord, forgive!... For Your sake, O my God, do not delay... (Daniel, 9:3-19)

... The Prophet Elijah stepped forward and **prayed:** "... I am Your servant and have done all these things at Your command. Answer me, O Lord, answer me... and that You are turning their hearts back again." (1 Kings, 18:36-37)

... I mourned and fasted and **prayed before the God of heaven. "O Lord, God of heaven, the great and awesome God... hear the prayer Your servant is praying** before You day and night... Give your servant success today." (Nehemiah, 1:4-7, 11)

Hezekiah received the letter... and spread it **prayed "O Lord**

Almighty... You alone are God over all the kingdoms of the earth. You have made heaven and earth." (Isaiah, 37:14-16)

And seek the peace of the city... and **pray to the Lord** for it... (Jeremiah, 29:7)

Therefore **pray** for the remnant that still survives. (2 Kings, 19:4)

... **[They] pray** for the well-being... (Ezra, 6:10)

And **Hezekiah prayed to the Lord**: "O Lord... You alone are God over all the kingdoms of the earth. You have made heaven and earth." (2 Kings, 19:15)

And **Elisha prayed** and said, "O Lord, open his eyes so he may see..." (2 Kings, 6:17)

Then he stretched himself out on the boy three times and **cried to the Lord,** "O Lord my God, let this boy's life return to him!" (1 Kings, 17:21)

Hear my voice when I call, O Lord... Do not reject me or forsake me, O God my Savior... Teach me your way, O Lord; lead me in a straight path... (Psalms, 27:7-11)

Belief in Angels

For He will command His angels concerning you to guard you in all your ways; they will lift you up in their hands, so that you will not strike your foot against a stone. You will tread upon the lion and the cobra; you will trample the great lion and the serpent. "Because he loves Me," says the Lord, "I will rescue him; I will protect him, for he acknowledges My name. He will call upon Me, and I will answer him; I will be with him in trouble, I will deliver him and honor him. With long life will I satisfy him and show him My salvation." (Psalms, 91:11-16)

... All at once an angel touched him and said, "Get up and eat." He looked around, and there by his head was a cake of bread baked over hot coals, and a jar of water. He ate and drank and then lay down again. **The angel of the Lord came back a second time** and touched him and said, "Get up and eat, for the journey is too much for you." So he got up and ate and drank. Strengthened by that food, he traveled forty days and forty nights until he reached Horeb, the mountain of God. (1 Kings, 19:5-8)

He replied, **"The Lord, before Whom I have walked, will send His angel with you** and make your journey a success." (Genesis, 24:40)

The Lord replied... "Now go, lead the people to the place I spoke of, and **My angel will go before you.** However, when the time comes for Me to punish, I will punish them for their sin." (Exodus, 32:33-34)

Jacob also went on his way, and the **angels of God** met him. (Genesis, 32:1)

But when we cried out to the Lord, He heard our cry and **sent an angel** and brought us out of Egypt. (Numbers, 20:16)

Then the **Lord spoke to the angel,** and he put his sword back into its sheath. (1 Chronicles, 21:27)

WISDOM AND SOUND ADVICE FROM TORAH

With the coming of dawn, **the angels urged Lot,** saying, "Hurry! Take... your two daughters who are here..." (Genesis, 19:15)

The two angels arrived at Sodom in the evening, and Lot was sitting in the gateway of the city. When he saw them, he got up to meet them... (Genesis, 19:1)

"See, **I am sending an angel ahead of you** to guard you along the way and to bring you to the place I have prepared. Pay attention to him and listen to what he says. Do not rebel against him; he will not forgive your rebellion, since My Name is in him. If you listen carefully to what he says and do all that I say, I will be an enemy to your enemies and will oppose those who oppose you. **My angel will go ahead of you...**" (Exodus, 23:20-23)

I will send an angel before you... to the land flowing with milk and honey. (Exodus, 33:2-3)

And the **Lord sent an angel,** who annihilated all the fighting men and the leaders and officers in the camp of the Assyrian king. So he withdrew to his own land in disgrace. (2 Chronicles, 32:21)

Praise the Lord, **you His angels,** you mighty ones who do His orders, who obey His word. Praise the Lord, all His heavenly hosts, you His servants who do His will. Praise the Lord, all His works everywhere in His dominion. Praise the Lord, O my soul. (Psalms, 103:20-22)

Praise Him, **all His angels,** praise Him, all His heavenly hosts. (Psalms, 148:2)

I asked, "What are these, my lord?" **The angel who was talking** with me answered, "I will show you what they are." Then the man standing among the myrtle trees explained, "They are the ones the Lord has sent to go throughout the earth." And they reported to the **angel of the Lord,** who was standing among the myrtle trees, "We have gone throughout the earth and found the whole world at rest and in peace." (Zechariah, 1:9-11)

Then the angel who talked with me answered me, "Don't you know what these are?"... And he answered, and spoke to me, saying: "This is the word of the Lord..." (Zechariah, 4:5-6)

When the angel of the Lord appeared to Gideon, he said, "The Lord is with you, mighty warrior." (Judges, 6:12)

The angel of the Lord appeared to her and said, "You are sterile and childless, but you are going to conceive and have a son... **The angel of God came again** to the woman while she was out in the field." (Judges, 13:3, 9)

MORAL VIRTUES RECOMMENDED IN THE TORAH

Humility: Avoiding Pride and Arrogance

He did evil in the eyes of the Lord, his God and **did not humble himself** before Jeremiah the Prophet, who spoke the word of the Lord. (2 Chronicles, 36:12)

A little while, and the wicked will be no more; though you look for them, they will not be found. But the **meek will inherit the land and enjoy great peace.** (Psalms, 37:10-11)

When pride comes, then comes disgrace, **but with humility comes wisdom.** (Proverbs, 11:2)

Pride goes before destruction, a haughty spirit before a fall. (Proverbs, 16:18)

Humility and the fear of the Lord bring wealth and honor and life. (Proverbs, 22:4)

... He [God] **looks upon the lowly,** but the proud He knows from afar. (Psalms, 138:6)

The fear of the Lord teaches a man wisdom, and **humility comes before honor.** (Proverbs, 15:33)

This is the one I esteem: he who is humble and contrite in spirit, and trembles at My word. (Isaiah, 66:2)

He [God] has showed you, O man, what is good. And what does the Lord require of you? To act justly and to love mercy and **to walk humbly with your God.** (Micah, 6:8)

By your great skill in trading you have increased your wealth, and **because of your wealth your heart has grown proud.** (Ezekiel, 28:5)

Your heart became proud on account of your beauty and you corrupted your wisdom because of your splendor. So I threw you to the earth; I made a spectacle of you before kings. (Ezekiel, 28:17)

But when **his heart became arrogant and hardened with pride,** he was deposed from his royal throne and stripped of his glory. (Daniel, 5:20)

When I fed them, they were satisfied; **when they were satisfied, they became proud; then they forgot Me.** (Hosea, 13:6)

The pride of your heart has deceived you, you who live in the clefts of the rocks and make your home on the heights, you who say to yourself, "Who can bring me down to the ground?" Though you soar like the eagle and make your nest among the stars, from there I will bring you down," declares the Lord. (Obadiah, 1:3-4)

This is what the Sovereign Lord says:... It will not be as it was: **The lowly will be exalted** and the exalted will be brought low. (Ezekiel, 21:26)

Seek the Lord, all you humble of the land, you who do what He commands. Seek righteousness, **seek humility**; perhaps you will be sheltered... (Zephaniah, 2:3)

... He crowns the humble with salvation. (Psalms, 149:4)

You save the humble but bring low those whose eyes are haughty. (Psalms, 18:27)

Hear and pay attention, **do not be arrogant,** for the Lord has spoken. (Jeremiah, 13:15)

He guides the humble in what is right and teaches them His way. (Psalms, 25:9)

He [Lord] mocks proud mockers but **gives grace to the humble.** (Proverbs, 3:34)

This is what the Lord... says: "How long will you refuse to humble yourself before Me?" (Exodus, 10:3)

Moses was a very humble man, more humble than anyone else on the face of the earth. (Numbers, 12:3)

You save the humble, but Your eyes are on the haughty to bring them low. (2 Samuel, 22:28)

He went around meekly... **he has humbled himself, I will not bring this disaster in his day...** (1 Kings, 21:27-29)

If... [they] humble themselves and pray and seek My face and turn from their wicked ways, then... I will forgive their sin and will heal their land. (2 Chronicles, 7:14)

When the Lord saw that they humbled themselves, this word of the Lord came... : "Since they have humbled themselves, I will not destroy them..." (2 Chronicles, 12:7)

But... (he) was proud and he did not respond to the kindness shown him... **Then (he) repented of the pride of his heart...** therefore the Lord's wrath did not come upon them. (2 Chronicles, 32:25-26)

... **He humbled himself greatly before God**... (2 Chronicles, 33:12)

I proclaimed a fast, so that **we might humble ourselves before our God** and ask Him for a safe journey for us and our children, with all our possessions. (Ezra, 8:21)

Yet when they were ill, I put on sackcloth and **humbled myself** with fasting. (Psalms, 35:13-14)

... **A contrite heart, O God, you will not despise.** (Psalms, 51:17)

Pride goes before destruction, a haughty spirit before a fall. Better to be lowly in spirit and among the oppressed than to share plunder with the proud. Whoever gives heed to instruction prospers, and blessed is he who trusts in the Lord. (Proverbs, 16:18-20)

Before his downfall a man's heart is proud, **but humility comes before honor.** (Proverbs, 18:12)

An angry man stirs up dissension, and a hot-tempered one commits many sins. A man's pride brings him low, **but a man of lowly spirit gains honor.** (Proverbs, 29:22-23)

For this is what the high and lofty One says, He Who lives forever, Whose name is holy: "I am with him who is **contrite and lowly in spirit,** to revive the spirit of the lowly." (Isaiah, 57:15)

"And **I hate a man's covering himself with violence as well as with his garment,"** says the Lord Almighty. So guard yourself in your spirit, and do not break faith. (Malachi, 2:16)

There are six things the Lord hates, seven **that are detestable to Him: haughty eyes,** a lying tongue, hands that shed innocent blood, a heart that devises wicked schemes, feet that are quick to rush into evil, a false witness who pours out lies and a man who stirs up dissension among brothers. (Proverbs, 6:16-19)

Because I will remove from this city those who rejoice in their pride. **Never again you will be haughty...** But **I will leave within you the meek and humble**, who trust in the name of the Lord. (Zephaniah, 3:11-12)

To fear the Lord is to hate evil; **I hate pride and arrogance,** evil behavior and perverse speech. (Proverbs, 8:13)

Pride only breeds quarrels, but wisdom is found in those who take advice. (Proverbs, 13:10)

They have no struggles; their bodies are healthy and strong. They are free from the burdens common to man; they are not plagued by human ills. **Therefore pride is their necklace;** they clothe themselves with violence. From their callous hearts comes iniquity; the evil conceits of their minds know no limits. **They scoff, and speak with malice; in their arrogance they threaten oppression.** Their mouths lay claim to Heaven, and their tongues take possession of the earth. (Psalms, 73:4-9)

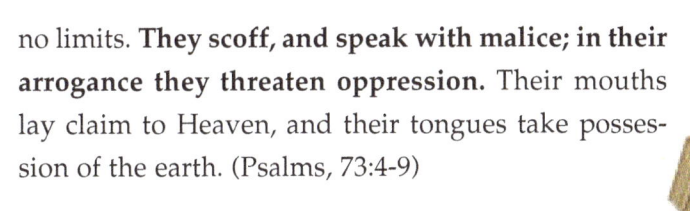

The Lord tears down the proud man's house... He who listens to a life-giving rebuke will be at home among the wise. (Proverbs, 15:25, 31)

Haughty eyes and a proud heart, the lamp of the wicked, are sin! (Proverbs, 21:4)

The end of a matter is better than its beginning, and **patience is better than pride.** (Ecclesiastes, 7:8)

The Lord Almighty has a day in store for all the **proud and lofty, for all that is exalted (and they will be humbled),** the Lord alone will be exalted in that day. (Isaiah, 2:12-13)

I will punish... for the willful pride of his heart and the haughty look in his eyes. (Isaiah, 10:12)

I will punish the world for its evil, the wicked for their sins. **I will put an end to the arrogance of the haughty and will humble the pride of the ruthless.** (Isaiah, 13:11)

But after... **became powerful, his pride led to his downfall.** He was unfaithful to the Lord his God. (2 Chronicles, 26:16)

But they, our forefathers, became **arrogant and stiff-necked, and did not obey Your commands.** They refused to listen and failed to remember the miracles You performed among them. They became stiff-necked and in their rebellion appointed a leader in order to return to their slavery. (Nehemiah, 9:16-17)

He may speak in their ears and terrify them with warnings, to turn man from wrongdoing and **keep him from pride, to preserve his soul from the pit [Hell],** his life from perishing by the sword. (Job, 33:16-18)

... Men cry out because of the arrogance of the wicked. (Job, 35:12)

He tells them what they have done that **they have sinned arrogantly.** He makes them listen to correction and commands them to repent of their evil. If they obey and serve Him, they will spend the rest of their days in prosperity and their years in contentment. But if they do not listen, they will perish by the sword and die without knowledge. (Job, 36:9-12)

In his arrogance **the wicked man hunts down the weak,** who are caught in the schemes he devises. **He boasts of the cravings of his heart... In his pride the wicked** does not seek

Him... His ways are always prosperous; **he is haughty and Your laws are far from him;** he sneers at all his enemies. (Psalms, 10:2-5)

Blessed is the man who makes the Lord his trust, **who does not look to the proud**, to those who turn aside to false gods. (Psalms, 40:4)

He rules forever by His power... the nations let not the rebellious rise up against Him. (Psalms, 66:7)

"**We have heard of his pride and arrogance and the haughtiness of his heart**. I know his insolence but it is futile," declares the Lord, "**and his boasts accomplish nothing**." (Jeremiah, 48:29-30)

I will put an end to the pride of the mighty... When terror comes, they will seek peace, but there will be none. (Ezekiel, 7:24-25)

"Now **this was the sin of your sister Sodom: She and her daughters were arrogant,** overfed and unconcerned; they did not help the poor and needy... You will bear the consequences of your lewdness and your detestable practices," declares the Lord. (Ezekiel, 16:49, 58)

In the pride of your heart you say, "I am a god; I sit on the throne of a god in the heart of the seas." [God is beyond this.] But you are a man and not a god... (Ezekiel, 28:2)

His arrogance testifies against him, but despite all this he does not return to the Lord his God or search for Him. (Hosea, 7:10)

WISDOM AND SOUND ADVICE FROM THE TORAH

You warned them to return to Your law, but they **became arrogant and disobeyed Your commands.** They sinned against Your ordinances, by which a man will live if he obeys them. **Stubbornly they turned their backs on You, became stiff-necked and refused to listen.** (Nehemiah, 9:29)

To the arrogant I say, **"Boast no more,"** and to the wicked, "Do not lift up your horns. **Do not lift your horns... do not speak with outstretched neck."** No one from the east or the west or from the desert can exalt a man. But it is God Who judges: He brings one down, He exalts another. (Psalms, 75:4-7)

Whoever slanders his neighbor in secret, him will I put to silence; **whoever has haughty eyes and a proud heart,** him will I not endure. (Psalms, 101:5)

My heart is not proud, O Lord, my eyes are not haughty... (Psalms, 131:1)

The proud and arrogant man—"Mocker" is his name; he behaves with overweening pride. (Proverbs, 21:24)

Do not keep talking so proudly or let your mouth speak such arrogance, for the Lord is a God Who knows, and by Him deeds are weighed. (1 Samuel, 2:3)

Overcoming Anger

Do not be quickly provoked in your spirit, for anger resides in the lap of fools. (Ecclesiastes, 7:9)

A patient man has great understanding, but a quick-tempered man displays folly. (Proverbs, 14:29)

A quick-tempered man does foolish things... (Proverbs, 14:17)

If a ruler's anger rises against you, do not leave your post; calmness can lay great errors to rest. (Ecclesiastes, 10:4)

A gift given in secret soothes anger. (Proverbs, 21:14)

Mockers stir up a city, but **wise men turn away anger.** If a wise man goes to court with a fool, the fool rages and scoffs, and there is no peace. (Proverbs, 29:8-9)

An angry man stirs up dissension and a hot-tempered one commits many sins. (Proverbs, 29:22)

... **Do not fret** when men succeed in their ways, when they carry out their wicked schemes. **Refrain from anger and turn from wrath; do not fret—it leads only to evil.** For evil men will be cut off, but those who hope in the Lord will inherit the land. (Psalms, 37:7-9)

For as churning the milk produces butter... so **stirring up anger produces strife.** (Proverbs, 30:33)

Do not make friends with a hot-tempered man, **do not associate with one easily angered,** or you may learn his ways and get yourself ensnared. (Proverbs, 22:24-25)

Anger is cruel and fury overwhelming... (Proverbs, 27:4)

A fool shows his annoyance at once, but a prudent man overlooks an insult. (Proverbs, 12:16)

Let me not enter their council, let me not join their assembly, **for they have killed men in their anger** and hamstrung oxen as they pleased. **Cursed be their anger, so fierce, and their fury, so cruel!** (Genesis, 49:6-7)

Do not fret because of evil men... (Psalms, 37:1)

Forgiveness

Hatred stirs up dissension, but **love covers over all wrongs.** (Proverbs, 10:12)

A man's wisdom gives him patience; **it is to his glory to overlook an offense.** (Proverbs, 19:11)

He who covers over an offense promotes love, but whoever repeats the matter separates close friends. (Proverbs, 17:9)

Do not say, "I'll do to him as he has done to me; I'll pay that man back for what he did." (Proverbs, 24:29)

Through love and faithfulness sin is atoned for; through the fear of the Lord a man avoids evil. (Proverbs, 16:6)

Do not seek revenge or bear a grudge against one of your people, but love your neighbor as yourself. (Leviticus, 19:18)

Compassion and Affection

He who despises his neighbor sins, but **blessed is he who is kind to the needy.** (Proverbs, 14:21)

He who oppresses the poor shows contempt for their Maker, but **whoever is kind to the needy honors God.** (Proverbs, 14:31)

If your enemy is hungry, give him food to eat; if he is thirsty, give him water to drink. In doing this, you will heap burning coals on his head, and the Lord will reward you. (Proverbs, 25:21-22)

If there is a poor man among your brothers in any of the towns of the land that the Lord your God is giving you, **do not be hardhearted or tightfisted toward your poor brother.** (Deuteronomy, 15:7)

Defend the cause of the weak and fatherless; maintain the rights of the poor and oppressed. Rescue the weak and needy; deliver them from the hand of the wicked. (Psalms, 82:3-4)

This is what the Lord Almighty says: "Administer true justice; show mercy and compassion to one another. **Do not oppress the widow or the fatherless, the alien or the poor.** In your hearts do not think evil of each other." (Zechariah, 7:9-10)

[A virtuous wife] opens her arms to the poor and extends her hands to the needy. (Proverbs, 31:20)

If **I have denied the desires of the poor or let the eyes of the widow grow weary, if I have kept my bread to myself, not sharing it with the fatherless**—but from my youth I reared

him as would a father, and from my birth I guided the widow—if I have seen anyone perishing for lack of clothing, or a needy man without a garment, and his heart did not bless me for warming him with the fleece from my sheep, if I have raised my hand against the fatherless,** knowing that I had influence in court, **then let my arm fall from the shoulder, let it be broken off at the joint.** For **I dreaded destruction from God,** and for fear of his splendor I could not do such things. (Job, 31:16-23)

Blessed is he who has regard for the weak; the Lord delivers him in times of trouble. (Psalms, 41:1)

A ruler who oppresses the poor is like a driving rain that leaves no crops. (Proverbs, 28:3)

He who gives to the poor will lack nothing, but he who closes his eyes to them receives many curses. (Proverbs, 28:27)

If a man shuts his ears to the cry of the poor, he too will cry out and not be answered. (Proverbs, 21:13)

A generous man will himself be blessed, for **he shares his food with the poor.** (Proverbs, 22:9)

Is it not **to share your food with the hungry** and **to provide the poor wanderer with shelter—when you see the naked, to clothe him, and not to turn away from your own flesh and blood?** Then your light will break forth like the dawn, and your healing will quickly appear; then your righteousness will go before you, and the glory of the Lord will be your rear guard. (Isaiah, 58:7-8)

... And if you spend yourselves in behalf of the hungry and

satisfy the needs of the oppressed, then your light will rise in the darkness, and your night will become like the noonday. The Lord will guide you always; He will satisfy your needs in a sun-scorched land and will strengthen your frame. You will be like a well-watered garden, like a spring whose waters never fail. (Isaiah, 58:10-11)

Do not deprive the alien or the fatherless of justice, or take the cloak of the widow as a pledge... When you are harvesting in your field and you overlook a sheaf, do not go back to get it. **Leave it for the alien, the fatherless and the widow,** so that the Lord your God may bless you in all the work of your hands. When you beat the olives from your trees, **do not go over the branches a second time. Leave what remains for the alien, the fatherless and the widow.** When you harvest the grapes in your vineyard, **do not go over the vines again. Leave what remains for the alien, the fatherless and the widow.** (Deuteronomy, 24:17-21)

... You shall give it to... the alien, the fatherless and the widow, so that they may eat in your towns and be satisfied. Then say to the Lord your God: "I have given it to... the alien, the fatherless and the widow, according to all You commanded. I have not turned aside from Your commands nor have I forgotten any of them. (Deuteronomy, 26:12-13)

Learn to do right! Seek justice, encourage the oppressed. **Defend the cause of the fatherless, plead the case of the widow.** (Isaiah, 1:17)

Cursed is the man who leads the blind astray on the road... Cursed is the man who withholds justice from the alien, the fatherless or the widow. Then all the people shall say, "Amen." (Deuteronomy, 27:18-19)

You have not strengthened the weak or healed the sick or bound up the injured. You have not brought back the strays or searched for the lost. You have ruled them harshly and brutally. (Ezekiel, 34:4)

If you really change your ways and your actions and deal with each other justly, if you **do not oppress the alien, the fatherless or the widow** and do not shed innocent blood in this place... then I will let you live in this place, in the land I gave your forefathers for ever and ever. (Jeremiah, 7:5-7)

Woe to those who make unjust laws... to deprive the poor of their rights and withhold justice from the oppressed of my people, making widows their prey and robbing the fatherless. (Isaiah, 10:1-2)

"Now this was the sin... She and her daughters were arrogant, overfed and unconcerned; they did not help the poor and needy." (Ezekiel, 16:49-50)

He made them also to be pitied of all those that carried them captive. (Psalms, 106:46)

And **may God Almighty grant you mercy** before the man... (Genesis, 43:14)

... [A man who] **gives his food to the hungry and provides clothing for the naked.** (Ezekiel, 18:7)

They are waxed fat, they shine: yea, they overpass in deeds of wickedness; they plead not the cause, the cause of the fatherless, that they may prosper; and the right of the needy do they not judge. (Jeremiah, 5:28)

The people of the land practice extortion and commit robbery; they oppress the poor and needy and mistreat the alien, denying them justice. (Ezekiel, 22:29)

He defends the cause of the fatherless and the widow, and loves the alien, giving him food and clothing. And you are to love those who are aliens. (Deuteronomy, 10:18-19)

Do not rule over them with rigor, but fear your God. (Leviticus, 25:43)

Ruling with Justice and Defending the Truth

This is what the Lord Almighty says: **"Administer true justice;** show mercy and compassion to one another." (Zechariah, 7:9)

He has showed you, O man, what is good. And **what does the Lord require of you? To act justly** and to love mercy and to walk humbly with your God. (Micah, 6:8)

For **I, the Lord, love justice;** I hate robbery and iniquity. In My faithfulness I will reward them and make an everlasting covenant with them. (Isaiah, 61:8)

The righteous care about justice for the poor, but the wicked have no such concern. (Proverbs, 29:7)

If a king judges the poor with fairness, his throne will always be secure. (Proverbs, 29:14)

For I have chosen him, so that he will direct his children and his household after him to keep the way of the Lord **by doing what is right and just,** so that the Lord will bring about for

Abraham what He has promised him. (Genesis, 18:19)

He whose walk is blameless and **who does what is righteous, who speaks the truth from his heart** and has no slander on his tongue, who does his neighbor no wrong and casts no slur on his fellowman. (Psalms, 15:2-3)

The Lord loves righteousness and justice; the earth is full of His unfailing love. (Psalms, 33:5)

The mouth of the righteous man utters wisdom, and **his tongue speaks what is just.** The law of his God is in his heart; his feet do not slip. (Psalms, 37:30-31)

He [the king] will judge your people with righteousness, and your poor with justice. The mountains shall bring peace to the people, and the hills, **in righteousness. He will judge the poor of the people,** He will save the children of the needy... (Psalms, 72:2-4)

Blessed are they who maintain justice, who constantly do what is right. (Psalms, 106:3)

Good will come to him who is generous and lends freely, who **conducts his affairs with justice. Surely he will never be shaken; a righteous man will be remembered forever.** (Psalms, 112:5-6)

He guards the course of the just and protects the way of His faithful ones. Then you will understand what is right and just and fair—every good path. (Proverbs, 2:8-9)

Evil men do not understand justice, but those who seek the Lord understand it fully. (Proverbs, 28:5)

The plans of the righteous are just, but the advice of the wicked is deceitful. (Proverbs, 12:5)

The lips of a king speak as an oracle, and **his mouth should not betray justice...** Kings detest wrongdoing, for **a throne is established through righteousness.** Kings take pleasure in honest lips; they value a man who speaks the truth. (Proverbs, 16:10-13)

A wicked man accepts a bribe in secret to pervert the course of justice. (Proverbs, 17:23)

To do what is right and just is more acceptable to the Lord than sacrifice. (Proverbs, 21:3)

The righteous one takes note of the house of the wicked and brings the wicked to ruin. (Proverbs, 21:12)

By justice a king gives a country stability... If a king judges the poor with fairness, his throne will always be secure. (Proverbs, 29:4, 14)

Many seek an audience with a ruler, but **it is from the Lord that man gets justice.** The righteous detest the dishonest; the wicked detest the upright. (Proverbs, 29:26-27)

Speak up and judge fairly; defend the rights of the poor and needy. (Proverbs, 31:9)

Learn to do right! Seek justice, encourage the oppressed. Defend the cause of the fatherless plead the case of the widow. (Isaiah, 1:17)

This is what the Lord says: **"Maintain justice and do what is right... "** (Isaiah, 56:1)

If you really change your ways and your actions and **deal with each other justly**... (Jeremiah, 7:5)

"... but let him who boasts boast about this: that he understands and knows Me, that I am **the Lord, Who exercises kindness, justice and righteousness on earth,** for in these I delight," declares the Lord. (Jeremiah, 9:24)

... What the Lord says: **"Execute justice** in the morning, and deliver him who is robbed out of the hand of the oppressor..." (Jeremiah, 21:12)

This is what the Lord says: **Do what is just and right.** Rescue from the hand of his oppressor the one who has been robbed. **Do no wrong** or violence to the alien, the fatherless or the widow, and do not shed innocent blood in this place. (Jeremiah, 22:3)

Do not pervert justice; do not show partiality to the poor or favoritism to the great, but **judge your neighbor fairly.** (Leviticus, 19:15)

... **Judge fairly... do not show partiality in judging, hear both small and great alike.** Do not be afraid of any man... (Deuteronomy, 1:16-17)

... A king who will reign wisely and **do what is just and right** in the land. (Jeremiah, 23:5)

But if a wicked man turns away from the wickedness he has committed and **does what is just and right, he will save his life.** (Ezekiel, 18:27)

And if a wicked man turns away from his wickedness and **does what is just and right,** he will live by doing so. (Ezekiel, 33:19)

This is what the Sovereign Lord says: "You have gone far enough... Give up your violence and oppression and **do what is just and right."** (Ezekiel, 45:9)

But you must return to your God; **maintain** love and **justice**... (Hosea, 12:6)

... **Maintain justice in the courts...** (Amos, 5:15)

But let **justice roll on like a river, righteousness like a never-failing stream.** (Amos, 5:24)

These are the things you are to do: "**Speak the truth to each other, and render true and sound judgment in your courts;** do not plot evil against your neighbor, and do not love to swear falsely. I hate all this," declares the Lord. (Zechariah, 8:16-17)

"**Do not spread false reports. Do not help a wicked man by being a malicious witness. Do not follow the crowd in doing** wrong. **When you give testimony in a lawsuit, do not pervert justice by siding with the crowd... Do not deny justice to your poor people in their lawsuits. Have nothing to do with a false charge** and do not put an innocent or honest person to death, for I will not acquit the guilty. Do not accept a bribe, for a bribe blinds those who see and twists the words of the righteous." (Exodus, 23:1-8)

... [If a man] **judges fairly** between man and man... (Ezekiel, 18:8)

... **Should you not know justice?...** But as for me, I am filled with power, with the Spirit of the Lord, and **with justice and might.** Hear this, you leaders... who despise justice and distort all that is right. (Micah, 3:1, 8-9)

No one calls for justice; no one pleads his case with integrity. They rely on empty arguments and speak lies; they conceive trouble and give birth to evil. (Isaiah, 59:4)

The way of peace they do not know; there is no justice in their paths. They have turned them into crooked roads; no one who walks in them will know peace. So justice is far from us, and righteousness does not reach us. We look for light, but all is darkness; for brightness, but we walk in deep shadows... **We look for justice,** but find none; for deliverance, but it is far away. (Isaiah, 59:8-9, 11)

Appoint judges and officials for each of your tribes in every town the Lord your God is giving you, and they shall **judge the people fairly. Do not pervert justice or show partiality.** Do not accept a bribe, for a bribe blinds the eyes of the wise and twists the words of the righteous. (Deuteronomy, 16:18-19)

... God... has made you king, **to maintain justice and righteousness.** (1 Kings, 10:9)

... David reigned... and **he executed justice and righteousness unto all his people**. (1 Chronicles, 18:14)

Since it was customary for the king **to consult experts in matters of law and justice,** he spoke with the wise men who understood the times. (Esther, 1:13)

I put on righteousness as my clothing; **justice was my robe and my turban.** I was eyes to the blind and feet to the lame. I was a father to the needy; I took up the case of the stranger. (Job, 29:14-16)

It is not only the old who are wise, not only the aged who **understand what is right.** (Job, 32:9)

... **You have asked for discernment in administering justice,** I will do what you have asked... (1 Kings, 3:11-12)

But **with righteousness he will judge the needy, with justice he will give decisions for the poor of the earth.** He will strike the earth with the rod of his mouth; with the breath of his lips he will slay the wicked. **Righteousness will be his belt** and faithfulness the sash around his waist. (Isaiah, 11:4-5)

In love a throne will be established; in faithfulness a man will sit on it... **one who in judging seeks justice and speeds the cause of righteousness.** (Isaiah, 16: 5)

See, a king will reign in righteousness and **rulers will rule with justice... Justice will dwell in the desert and righteousness live in the fertile field.** The fruit of righteousness will be peace; the effect of righteousness will be quietness and confidence forever. (Isaiah, 32:1, 16-17)

Here is My servant, whom I uphold, My chosen one in whom I delight; I will put My Spirit on him and **he will bring justice to the nations.** He will not shout or cry out, or raise his voice in the streets. A bruised reed he will not break, and a smoldering wick he will not snuff out. **In faithfulness he will bring forth justice; he will not falter or be discouraged till he establishes justice on earth.** In his law the islands will put their hope. (Isaiah, 42:1-5)

Woe to those who make unjust laws, to those who issue oppressive decrees, to deprive the poor of their rights and **withhold justice from the oppressed of My people,** making widows their prey and robbing the fatherless. (Isaiah, 10:1-2)

Go up and down the streets... look around and consider... If you can find but one person **who deals honestly and seeks the truth,** I will forgive this city. (Jeremiah, 5:1)

Do you rulers indeed speak justly? Do you judge uprightly among men? No, in your heart you devise injustice, and your hands mete out violence on the earth. (Psalms, 58:1-2)

So God said to him, "Since you have asked for this and not for long life or wealth for yourself, nor have asked for the death of your enemies but for **discernment in administering justice,** I will do what you have asked. I will give you a wise and discerning heart, so that there will never have been anyone like you, nor will there ever be"... They held the king in awe, because they saw that he [Solomon] **had wisdom from God to administer justice.** (1 Kings, 3:11-12, 28)

Judgment will again be founded on righteousness, and all the upright in heart will follow it. (Psalms, 94:15)

The king is mighty, **he loves justice—you have established equity... You have done what is just and right.** (Psalms, 99:4)

For acquiring a disciplined and prudent life, **doing what is right and just and fair;** for giving prudence to the simple, knowledge and discretion to the young. (Proverbs, 1:3-4)

It is not good to be partial to the wicked or to deprive the innocent of justice. (Proverbs, 18:5)

A corrupt witness mocks at justice, and the mouth of the wicked gulps down evil. (Proverbs, 19:28)

"**Do not use dishonest standards when measuring length, weight or quantity. Use honest scales and honest weights, an honest ephah and an honest hin...** Keep all My decrees and all My laws and follow them. I am the Lord." (Leviticus, 19:35-37)

Helping Others

If you see the donkey of someone who hates you fallen down under its load, do not leave it there; **be sure you help him with it.** (Exodus, 23:5)

If one of your countrymen becomes poor and is unable to support himself among you, **help him** as you would an alien or a temporary resident, so he can continue to live among you. (Leviticus, 25:35)

Do the same if you find your brother's donkey or his cloak or anything he loses. Do not ignore it. If you see your brother's donkey or his ox fallen on the road, **do not ignore it. Help him** get it to its feet. (Deuteronomy, 22:3-4)

But **let your hand be open to give him the use of whatever he is in need of**... You do not show ill will toward your needy brother and give him nothing. He may then appeal to the Lord against you, and you will be found guilty of sin. Give generously to him and **do so without a grudging heart;** then because of this the Lord your God will bless you in all your work and in everything you put your hand to. There will always be poor people in the land. Therefore **I command you to be openhanded** toward your brothers and toward the poor and needy in your land. (Deuteronomy, 15:8-11)

Because **I rescued the poor who cried for help, and the fatherless who had none to assist him.** The man who was dying blessed me; I made the widow's heart sing. I put on righteousness as my clothing; justice was my robe and my turban. **I was**

eyes to the blind and feet to the lame. I was a father to the needy; I took up the case of the stranger. (Job, 29:12-16)

For He has not despised or disdained the suffering of the afflicted one; He has not hidden his face from him but **has listened to his cry for help.** (Psalms, 22:24)

Each helps the other and says to his brother, "Be strong!" (Isaiah, 41:6)

Is it not to **share your food with the hungry and to provide the poor wanderer with shelter—when you see the naked, to clothe him,** and not to turn away from your own flesh and blood? Then your light will break forth like the dawn, and your healing will quickly appear... (Isaiah, 58:7-8)

Now this was the sin of your sister Sodom: She and her daughters were arrogant, overfed and unconcerned; they did not help the poor and needy. (Ezekiel, 16:49)

Day after day men came to help David... (1 Chronicles, 12:22)

Doing Good and Turning from Evil

Turn from evil and do good; seek peace and pursue it. (Psalms, 34:14)

Do not oppress the widow or the fatherless, the alien or the poor. **In your hearts do not think evil of each other.** (Zechariah, 7:10)

Seek good, not evil, that you may live. Then the Lord God Almighty will be with you, just as you say He is. (Amos, 5:14)

Turn from evil and do good; then you will dwell in the land forever. (Psalms, 37:27)

Do not be wise in your own eyes; fear the Lord and **shun evil.** This will bring health to your body and nourishment to your bones. (Proverbs, 3:7-8)

He who seeks good finds goodwill, but evil comes to him who searches for it. The fruit of the righteous is a tree of life, and he who wins souls is wise. (Proverbs, 11:27, 30)

Do not those who plot evil go astray? But **those who plan what is good** find love and faithfulness. (Proverbs, 14:22)

Hate evil, love good... (Amos, 5:15)

A wise man fears the Lord and **shuns evil,** but a fool is hot-headed and reckless. (Proverbs, 14:16)

An oracle is within my heart concerning the sinfulness of the wicked: There is no fear of God before his eyes. For in his own eyes he flatters himself too much to detect or hate his sin. The words of his mouth are wicked and deceitful; he has ceased to be wise and to do good. Even on his bed he plots evil; he commits himself to a sinful course and does not reject what is wrong. (Psalms, 36:1-4)

Trust in the Lord and **do good;** dwell in the land and enjoy safe pasture. (Psalms, 37:3)

Let not my heart be drawn to what is evil, to take part in wicked deeds with men who are evildoers... Let a righteous man strike me—it is a kindness; let him rebuke me—it is oil on my head. My head will not refuse it. Yet my prayer is ever against the deeds of evildoers. (Psalms, 141:4-5)

He who is kind to the poor lends to the Lord, and **He will reward him for what he has done.** (Proverbs, 19:17)

Tell the righteous it will be well with them, **for they will enjoy the fruit of their deeds.** Woe to the wicked! Disaster is upon them! They will be paid back for what their hands have done. (Isaiah, 3:10-11)

Therefore, O King, be pleased to accept my advice: Renounce your sins by doing what is right, and **your wickedness by being kind to the oppressed.** It may be that then your prosperity will continue. (Daniel, 4:27)

... Your sins have deprived you of good. Among My people are wicked men... Like cages full of birds, their houses are full of deceit; they have become rich and powerful and have grown fat and sleek. Their evil deeds have no limit; they do not plead the case of the fatherless to win it, they do not defend the rights of the poor. (Jeremiah, 5:25-28)

Truthfulness and Honesty

Follow justice and justice alone, so that you may live and possess the land the Lord your God is giving you. (Deuteronomy, 16:20)

He holds victory in store for the upright, He is a shield to those whose walk is blameless. (Proverbs, 2:7)

For surely, O Lord, **You bless the righteous; You surround them with Your favor as with a shield.** (Psalms, 5:12)

The man of integrity walks securely, but he who takes crooked paths will be found out. (Proverbs, 10:9)

Folly delights a man who lacks judgment, but **a man of understanding keeps a straight course.** (Proverbs, 15:21)

The highway of the upright avoids evil; he who guards his way guards his life. (Proverbs, 16:17)

The way of the Lord is a refuge for the righteous, but it is the ruin of those who do evil. **The righteous will never be uprooted,** but the wicked will not remain in the land. (Proverbs, 10:29-30)

The integrity of the upright guides them, but the unfaithful are destroyed by their duplicity. Wealth is worthless in the day of wrath, but **righteousness delivers from death.** (Proverbs, 11:3-4)

The righteousness of the blameless makes a straight way for them, but the wicked are brought down by their own wickedness. (Proverbs, 11:5)

The righteousness of the upright delivers them, but the unfaithful are trapped by evil desires. (Proverbs, 11:6)

Righteousness guards the man of integrity, but wickedness overthrows the sinner. (Proverbs, 13:6)

The righteous man is rescued from trouble, and it comes on the wicked instead. (Proverbs, 11:8)

The Lord detests men of perverse heart but **He delights in those whose ways are blameless.** (Proverbs, 11:20)

But **with righteousness he will judge** the needy, with justice he will give decisions for the poor of the earth... (Isaiah, 11:4)

The path of the righteous is level... (Isaiah, 26:7)

Let the Lord judge the peoples. Judge me, O Lord, **according to my righteousness, according to my integrity,** O Most High. (Psalms, 7:8)

Fools mock at making amends for sin, but **goodwill is found among the upright.** (Proverbs, 14:9)

Thus you will **walk in the ways of good men and keep to the paths of the righteous. For the upright will live in the land, and the blameless will remain in it;** but the wicked will be cut off from the land, and the unfaithful will be torn from it. (Proverbs, 2:20-22)

I will be careful **to lead a blameless life...** (Psalms, 101:2)

The righteous man leads a blameless life; blessed are his children after him. (Proverbs, 20:7)

Those who walk uprightly enter into peace... (Isaiah, 57:2)

... Not one upright man remains... Both hands are skilled in doing evil; the ruler demands gifts, the judge accepts bribes, the powerful dictate what they desire—they all conspire together. The best of them is like a brier, the most upright worse than a thorn hedge. The day of your watchmen has come, the day God visits you. Now is the time of their confusion. (Micah, 7:2-4)

For the Lord God is a sun and shield; the Lord bestows favor and honor; **no good thing does He withhold from those whose walk is blameless.** (Psalms, 84:11)

... He who is walking in the right way will be My servant. (Psalms, 101:6)

Even in darkness light dawns for the upright, for the gracious and compassionate **and righteous man**. (Psalms, 112:4)

Surely the righteous will praise Your name and the upright will live before /ou. (Psalms, 140:13)

Better a poor man **whose walk is blameless than a fool whose lips are perverse.** (Proverbs, 19:1)

Better a poor man whose walk is blameless than a rich man whose ways are perverse. (Proverbs, 28:6)

But select capable men from all the people—men who fear God, **trustworthy men who hate dishonest gain**—and appoint them as officials over thousands, hundreds, fifties and tens. (Exodus, 18:21)

... Even in a land of uprightness they [the wicked] go on doing evil and regard not the majesty of the Lord. (Isaiah, 26:10)

O Lord, for **I have led a blameless life;** I have trusted in the Lord without wavering. (Psalms, 26:1)

In whose hands are wicked schemes, whose right hands are full of bribes. But **I lead a blameless life;** redeem me and be merciful to me. (Psalms, 26:10-11)

They did not require an accounting from those to whom they gave the money to pay the workers, **because they acted with complete honesty.** (2 Kings, 12:15)

... Because he was faithful to You and **righteous and upright in heart...** (1 Kings, 3:6)

... As surely as the Lord lives, **you have been reliable...** (1 Samuel, 29:6)

Bloodthirsty men hate a man of integrity and seek to kill the upright... (Proverbs, 29:10)

The righteous detest the dishonest; the wicked detest the upright. (Proverbs, 29:27)

Patience

Be still before the Lord and **wait patiently for Him**; do not fret when men succeed in their ways, when they carry out their wicked schemes. (Psalms, 37:7)

I waited patiently for the Lord; He turned to me and heard my cry. (Psalms, 40:1)

A hot-tempered man stirs up dissension, but **a patient man calms a quarrel.** (Proverbs, 15:18)

Better a patient man than a warrior, a man who controls his temper than one who takes a city. (Proverbs, 16:32)

A man's wisdom gives him patience; it is to his glory to overlook an offense. (Proverbs, 19:11)

The end of a matter is better than its beginning, and **patience is better than pride.** (Ecclesiastes, 7:8)

A man's spirit sustains him in sickness, but a crushed spirit who can bear? (Proverbs, 18:14)

Loyalty

Let love and **faithfulness never leave you; bind them around your neck, write them on the tablet of your heart.** Then you will win favor and a good name in the sight of God and man. (Proverbs, 3:3-4)

They would not be like their forefathers—a stubborn and rebellious generation, whose hearts were not loyal to God, whose spirits were not faithful to Him. (Psalms, 78:8)

Love and faithfulness keep a king safe; through love his throne is made secure. (Proverbs, 20:28)

Love and faithfulness meet together; righteousness and peace kiss each other. Faithfulness springs forth from the earth, and righteousness looks down from Heaven. (Psalms, 85:10-11)

... For they were faithful in consecrating themselves. (2 Chronicles, 31:18)

For He guards the course of the just and **protects the way of His faithful ones.** (Proverbs, 2:8)

All the ways of the Lord are loving and faithful for those who keep the demands of His covenant. (Psalms, 25:10)

To the faithful you show yourself faithful... (Psalms, 18:25)

My eyes will be on the faithful in the land... (Psalms, 101:6)

Righteousness will be his belt and **faithfulness the sash around his waist.** (Isaiah, 11:5)

Trust in the Lord and do good; dwell in the land and **enjoy faithfulness**. (Psalms, 37:3)

I have chosen **the way of faithfulness**... (Psalms, 119:30)

In love a throne will be established; **in faithfulness a man will sit on it...** one who in judging seeks justice... (Isaiah, 16:5)

... In faithfulness he will bring forth justice; he will not falter or be discouraged till he establishes justice on earth... (Isaiah, 42:3-4)

Help, Lord, for the godly are no more; the faithful have vanished from among men. Everyone lies to his neighbor; their flattering lips speak with deception. (Psalms, 12:1-2)

Because You will not abandon me to the underworld [Hell], nor will you let **Your faithful one** see decay. (Psalms, 16:10)

Love the Lord, all His saints! **The Lord preserves the faithful**, but the proud He pays back in full. (Psalms, 31:23)

For the Lord loves the just and **will not forsake His faithful ones. They will be protected forever,** but the offspring of the wicked will be cut off. (Psalms, 37:28)

Their hearts were not loyal to Him; they were not faithful to His covenant. (Psalms, 78:37)

Let those who love the Lord hate evil, for **He guards the lives of His faithful ones...** (Psalms, 97:10)

May your priests be clothed with righteousness; **may Your saints sing for joy...** I will clothe her priests with salvation, **and her saints will ever sing for joy.** (Psalms, 132:9, 16)

Many a man claims to have unfailing love, but a **faithful man** who can find? (Proverbs, 20:6)

"Son of man, if a country **sins against Me by being unfaithful** and I stretch out My hand against it to cut off its food supply and send famine upon it and kill its men and their animals... (Ezekiel, 14:13)

"I will make the land desolate because **they have been unfaithful**," declares the Sovereign Lord. (Ezekiel, 15:8)

... The Lord said: "I will ... execute judgment upon him there because **he was unfaithful to Me**." (Ezekiel, 17:19-20)

"But if a righteous man turns from his righteousness and commits sin and does the same detestable things the wicked man does, will he live? None of the righteous things he has done will be remembered. **Because of the unfaithfulness he is guilty** and because of the sins he has committed, he will die. (Ezekiel, 18:24)

"Lord, You are righteous... in all the countries where You have scattered us **because of our unfaithfulness to You**. (Daniel, 9:7)

... **There is no faithfulness**, no love, no acknowledgment of God in the land. There is only cursing, lying and murder, stealing and adultery; they break all bounds, and bloodshed follows bloodshed. (Hosea, 4:1-2)

See, he is puffed up; his desires are not upright—but **the righteous will live by his faith.** (Habakkuk, 2:4)

He has showed you, O man, what is good. And what does the Lord require of you? To act justly and to love mercy and **to walk humbly with your God.** (Micah, 6:8)

Avoiding Despotism

Wicked man suffers torment, the ruthless through all the years stored up for him. (Job, 15:20)

But God drags away the mighty by His power; though they become established, **they have no assurance of life.** (Job, 24:22)

The trouble he causes recoils on himself; his violence comes down on his own head. (Psalms, 7:16)

The Lord examines the righteous, **but the wicked and those who love violence His soul hates.** (Psalms, 11:5)

Do not trust in extortion or take pride in stolen goods; though your riches increase, do not set your heart on them. (Psalms, 62:10)

From the fruit of his lips a man enjoys good things, but the unfaithful have a craving for violence. (Proverbs, 13:2)

A violent man entices his neighbor and leads him down a path that is not good. (Proverbs, 16:29)

The violence of the wicked will drag them away, for they refuse to do what is right. (Proverbs, 21:7)

... Their deeds are evil deeds, and acts of violence are in their hands. Their feet rush into sin; they are swift to shed innocent blood. Their thoughts are evil thoughts; ruin and destruction mark their ways. The way of peace they do not know; there is no justice in their paths. They have turned them into crooked roads; **no one who walks in them will know peace.** (Isaiah, 59:6-8)

He who walks righteously and speaks what is right, **who rejects gain from extortion** and keeps his hand from accepting bribes, who stops his ears against plots of murder and shuts his eyes against contemplating evil- this is the man who will dwell on the heights... His bread will be supplied, and water will not fail him. (Isaiah, 33:15-16)

This is what the Sovereign Lord says: "You have gone far enough... **Give up your violence and oppression** and do what is just and right..." declares the Sovereign Lord. (Ezekiel, 45:9)

But let man and beast be covered with sackcloth. Let everyone call urgently on God. **Let them give up their evil ways and their violence.** (Jonah, 3:8)

Nations will see and be ashamed, deprived of all their power. They will lay their hands on their mouths and their ears will become deaf. (Micah, 7:16)

... "And **I hate a man's covering himself with violence** as well as with his garment," says the Lord Almighty. So guard yourself in your spirit, and do not break faith. (Malachi, 2:16)

"They do not know how to do right," declares the Lord, "who hoard plunder and loot in their fortresses." (Amos, 3:10)

The Importance of Peace and Friendship

When you march up to attack a city, make its people an offer of peace. (Deuteronomy, 20:10)

How good and pleasant it is **when brothers live together in unity!** (Psalms, 133:1)

For he [Solomon] ruled over all the kingdoms... and had peace on all sides. (1 Kings, 4:24)

There is deceit in the hearts of those who plot evil, but **joy for those who promote peace.** (Proverbs, 12:20)

WISDOM AND SOUND ADVICE FROM THE TORAH

Turn from evil and do good; **seek peace and pursue it.** (Psalms, 34:14)

... Did not one God create us? Why do we profane the covenant of our fathers by breaking faith with one another? (Malachi, 2:10)

And our elders and all those living in our country said to us, "Take provisions for your journey; go and meet them **and say to them, '... make a treaty with us'.**" (Joshua, 9:11)

Then Joshua **made a treaty of peace with them to** let them live, and the leaders of the assembly ratified it by oath. (Joshua, 9:15)

Then the whole assembly **sent an offer of peace...** (Judges, 21:13)

The Lord gave Solomon wisdom, just as He had promised him. **There were peaceful relations between Hiram and Solomon, and the two of them made a treaty.** (1 Kings, 5:12)

... For he thought, **"will there not be peace and security in my lifetime?"** (2 Kings, 20:19)

... **And the kingdom was at peace before Him.** (2 Chronicles, 14:5)

And the kingdom... was at peace, for his God had given him rest on every side. (2 Chronicles, 20:30)

Consider the blameless, observe the upright; **there is a future for the man of peace.** (Psalms, 37:37)

I am a man of peace; but when I speak, they are for war. (Psalms, 120:7)

All the lands are at rest and at peace; they break into singing. (Isaiah, 14:7)

Instead of bronze I will bring you gold, and silver in place of iron. Instead of wood I will bring you bronze, and iron in place of stones. **I will make peace your governor and righteousness your ruler.** (Isaiah, 60:17)

... And **the battle bow will be broken. He [your King] will proclaim peace to the nations...** (Zechariah, 9:10)

"These men are friendly toward us," they said. "Let them live in our land and trade in it; the land has plenty of room for them... " (Genesis, 34:21)

Then David and Jonathan **made a covenant,** because he loved him as himself. (1 Samuel, 18:3)

... and has no slander on his tongue, **who does his neighbor no wrong** and casts no slur on his fellowman. (Psalms, 15:3)

I am a friend to all who fear You, to all who follow Your precepts. (Psalms, 119:63)

A friend loves at all times, and a brother is born for adversity. (Proverbs, 17:17)

... But fear your God, **so that your brother may continue to live among you.** (Leviticus, 25:36)

"If one of your brother becomes poor among you and sells himself to you, do not make him work as a slave." (Leviticus, 25:39)

And I charged your judges at that time: Hear the disputes between your brothers and judge fairly... (Deuteronomy, 1:16)

This is how it is to be done: Every creditor shall cancel the loan he has made to his believer brother **He shall not require payment from believer brother**... (Deuteronomy, 15:2)

There will always be poor people in the land. Therefore I command you to **be openhanded toward your brothers and toward the poor and needy in your land.** (Deuteronomy, 15:11)

Do not abhor... for he is your brother. (Deuteronomy, 23:7)

Her ways are pleasant ways, **and all her paths are peace.** (Proverbs, 3:17)

The fruit of righteousness will be peace; the effect of righteousness will be quietness and confidence... will live in peaceful dwelling places, in secure homes, in undisturbed places of rest. (Isaiah, 32:17-18)

"... **Render true and sound judgment in your courts; do not plot evil against your neighbor...** I hate all this," declares the Lord. Again the word of the Lord Almighty came to me. This is what the Lord Almighty says: "... Therefore **love truth and peace."** (Zechariah, 8:16-18)

... **The whole world at rest and in peace.** (Zechariah, 1:11)

... "May those who love you be secure. **May there be peace within your walls and security within your citadels."** For the sake of my brothers and friends, I will say, "Peace be within you." (Psalms, 122:6-8)

The Importance of Reason and Wisdom

The fear of the Lord is the beginning of wisdom, and knowledge of the Holy One is understanding. (Proverbs, 9:10)

... **Better to get wisdom than gold, to choose understanding rather than silver!** (Proverbs, 16:16)

The fear of the Lord teaches a man wisdom, and humility comes before honor. (Proverbs, 15:33)

Coral and jasper are not worthy of mention; **the price of wisdom is beyond rubies.** (Job, 28:18)

And He said to man, **"The fear of the Lord—that is wisdom, and to shun evil is understanding."** (Job, 28:28)

But it is the **spirit in a man, the breath of the Almighty that gives him understanding.** It is not only the old who are wise, not only the aged who understand what is right. (Job, 32:8-9)

A wise man has great power, and a man of knowledge increases strength. (Proverbs, 24:5)

Blessed is the man who finds wisdom, the man who gains understanding. (Proverbs, 3:13)

[Wisdom] is a tree of life to those who embrace her; those who lay hold of her will be blessed. (Proverbs, 3:18)

Would **a wise man** answer with empty notions or fill his belly with the hot east wind? Would he argue with useless words, with speeches that have no value? (Job, 15:2-3)

A rebuke impresses **a man of discernment** more than a hundred lashes a fool. (Proverbs, 17:10)

The tongue of the wise commends knowledge, but the mouth of the fool gushes folly. (Proverbs, 15:2)

The lips of the wise spread knowledge; not so the hearts of fools. (Proverbs, 15:7)

Folly delights a man who lacks judgment, but **a man of understanding keeps a straight course.** (Proverbs, 15:21)

Who is like the wise man? Who knows the explanation of things? **Wisdom brightens a man's face and changes its hard appearance.** (Ecclesiastes, 8:1)

The wise man has eyes in his head, while the fool walks in the darkness. (Ecclesiastes, 2:14)

A wise person's heart leads the right way. The heart of a fool leads the wrong way. (Ecclesiastes, 10:2)

WISDOM AND SOUND ADVICE FROM THE TORAH

Words from a wise man's mouth are gracious, but a fool is consumed by his own lips. (Ecclesiastes, 10:12)

When a country is rebellious, it has many rulers, but **a man of understanding and knowledge maintains order.** (Proverbs, 28:2)

He who trusts in himself is a fool, but **he who walks in wisdom is kept safe.** (Proverbs, 28:26)

A man of knowledge uses words with restraint, and a man of understanding is even-tempered. Even a fool is thought wise if he keeps silent, and discerning if he holds his tongue. (Proverbs, 17:27-28)

The words of a man's mouth are deep waters, but **the fountain of wisdom is a bubbling brook.** (Proverbs, 18:4)

The heart of the discerning acquires knowledge; the ears of the wise seek it out. (Proverbs, 18:15)

He who listens to a life-giving rebuke will be at home among the wise. (Proverbs, 15:31)

King Solomon was greater in riches and wisdom than all the other kings of the earth. (1 Kings, 10:23)

The law of the Lord is perfect, reviving the soul. **The statutes of the Lord are trustworthy, making wise the simple.** (Psalms, 19:7)

The mouth of the righteous man utters wisdom, and his tongue speaks what is just. (Psalms, 37:30)

And He [God] would **disclose to you the secrets of wisdom,** for true wisdom has two sides. (Job, 11:6)

For wisdom is more precious than rubies, and nothing you desire can compare with her. "I, wisdom, dwell together with prudence; I possess knowledge and discretion." (Proverbs, 8:11-12)

Get wisdom, get understanding; do not forget my words or swerve from them. **Do not forsake wisdom, and she will protect you;** love her, and she will watch over you... **therefore get wisdom. Though it cost all you have, get understanding. Esteem her, and she will exalt you; embrace her, and she will honor you.** (Proverbs, 4:5-8)

My son, if you accept my words and store up my commands within you, **turning your ear to wisdom and applying your heart to understanding, and if you call out for insight and cry aloud for understanding. And if you look for it as for silver and search for it as for hidden treasure, then you will understand the fear of the Lord and find the knowledge of God.** (Proverbs, 2:1-5)

For the Lord gives wisdom, and from His mouth come knowledge and understanding. (Proverbs, 2:6)

For wisdom will enter your heart, and knowledge will be pleasant to your soul. Discretion will protect you, and **understanding will guard you.** Wisdom will save you from the ways of wicked men, from men whose words are perverse, who leave the straight paths to walk in dark ways. (Proverbs, 2:10-13)

When pride comes, then comes disgrace, but **with humility comes wisdom.** (Proverbs, 11:2)

Wisdom is found on the lips of the discerning, but a rod is for the back of him who lacks judgment. (Proverbs, 10:13)

A fool finds pleasure in evil conduct, but a man of understanding delights in wisdom. (Proverbs, 10:23)

Reckless words pierce like a sword, but **the tongue of the wise brings healing.** (Proverbs, 12:18)

A wise son heeds his father's instruction, but a mocker does not listen to rebuke. (Proverbs, 13:1)

Pride only breeds quarrels, but **wisdom is found in those who take advice.** (Proverbs, 13:10)

A patient man has great understanding, but a quick-tempered man displays folly. (Proverbs, 14:29)

Like tying a stone in a sling is the giving of honor to a fool. (Proverbs, 26:8)

The teaching of the wise is a fountain of life, turning a man from the snares of death. **Good understanding wins favor,** but the way of the unfaithful is hard. Every prudent man acts out of knowledge, but a fool exposes his folly. (Proverbs, 13:14-16)

The fear of the Lord is the beginning of knowledge, but fools despise wisdom and discipline. (Proverbs, 1:7)

"And now let Pharaoh look for a **discerning and wise man** and put him in charge of the land of Egypt"... Then Pharaoh said to Joseph, "Since God has made all this known to you, **there is no one so discerning and wise as you.** You shall be in charge of my palace, and all my people are to submit to your orders. I hereby put you in charge of the whole land of Egypt." (Genesis, 41:33, 39-41)

Your commands make me wiser than my enemies, for they are ever with me. **I have more insight than all my teachers, for I meditate on Your statutes. I have more understanding than the elders, for I obey Your precepts.** I have kept my feet from every evil path so that I might obey Your word. I have not departed from Your laws, for You Yourself have taught me. How sweet are Your words to my taste, sweeter than honey to my mouth! **I gain understanding from Your precepts;** therefore I hate every wrong path. (Psalms 119:98-104)

Choose some **wise, understanding and respected men from each of your tribes,** and I will set them over you."... So **I took the leading men** of your tribes, **wise and respected men,** and appointed them to have authority over you—as commanders of thousands, of hundreds, of fifties and of tens and as tribal officials. (Deuteronomy, 1:13, 15)

Observe them carefully, for this will show your **wisdom and understanding** to the nations, who will hear about all these decrees and say, "Surely this great nation is a **wise and understanding people."** (Deuteronomy, 4:6)

Is this the way you repay the Lord, O foolish and unwise people? Is He not... your Creator, Who made you and formed you? (Deuteronomy, 32:6)

The Lord was pleased that Solomon had asked for this. So God said to him, "Since you have asked for this and not for long life or wealth for yourself, nor have asked for the death of your enemies but for **discernment in administering justice,** I will do what you have asked. I will give you a **wise and discerning heart,** so that there will never have been anyone like you, nor will there ever be." (1 Kings, 3:10-12)

... They saw that **he [Solomon] had wisdom from God** to administer justice. (1 Kings, 3:28)

God gave Solomon wisdom and very great insight, and a breadth of understanding as measureless as the sand on the seashore. Solomon's wisdom was greater than the wisdom of all the men of the east, and greater than all the wisdom of Egypt. He was wiser than any other man... **Men of all nations came to listen to Solomon's wisdom,** sent by all the kings of the world, who had heard of his wisdom. (1 Kings, 4:29-34)

... He [David] said to the Lord, "I have sinned greatly in what I have done. Now, O Lord, I beg You, take away the guilt of Your servant. **I have done a very foolish thing."** (2 Samuel, 24:10)

And Hiram added: "Praise be to the Lord... Who made heaven and earth! He has given King David **a wise son, endowed** with intelligence and discernment"... "I am sending you... a man of great skill." (2 Chronicles, 2:12-13)

"**To God belong wisdom and power;** counsel and understanding are His. (Job, 12:13)

"Hear my words, **you wise men; listen to me, you men of learning.** For the ear tests words as the tongue tastes food. Let us discern for ourselves what is right; let us learn together what is good." (Job, 34:2-4)

Therefore, **you kings, be wise; be warned,** you rulers of the earth. Serve the Lord with fear and rejoice with trembling. (Psalms, 2:10-11)

The fool says in his heart, "there is no God" [God is beyond this]. They are corrupt, their deeds are vile; there is no one who does good... there are any who understand, any who seek God. All have turned aside, they have together become corrupt; there is no one who does good not even one. (Psalms, 14:1-3)

I was senseless and ignorant; I was a brute beast before You. Yet I am always with You... You guide me with Your counsel, and afterward You will take me into glory. (Psalms, 73:22-24)

How great are Your works, O Lord, how profound Your thoughts! The senseless man does not know, fools do not understand. (Psalms, 92:5-6)

Take heed, you senseless ones among the people; you fools, when will you become wise? Does He Who implanted the ear not hear? Does He Who formed the eye not see? (Psalms, 94:8-9)

The unfolding of Your words gives light; it gives understanding to the simple. (Psalms, 119:130)

Your statutes are forever right; **give me understanding that I may live.** (Psalms, 119:144)

May my cry come before You, O Lord; **give me understanding** according to Your word. (Psalms, 119:169)

Do not be wise in your own eyes; fear the Lord and shun evil. (Proverbs, 3:7)

I guide you in the way of wisdom and lead you along straight paths. (Proverbs, 4:11)

My son, **pay attention to my wisdom, listen well to my words of insight,** that you may maintain discretion and your lips may preserve knowledge. (Proverbs, 5:1-2)

... **Rebuke a wise man and he will love you. Instruct a wise man and he will be wiser still;** teach a righteous man and he will add to his learning. (Proverbs, 9:8-9)

If you are wise, your wisdom will reward you; if you are a mocker, you alone will suffer." (Proverbs, 9:12)

The woman folly is loud; she is undisciplined and without knowledge. (Proverbs, 9:13)

Wise men store up knowledge, but the mouth of a fool invites ruin. (Proverbs, 10:14)

The fruit of the righteous is a tree of life, and **he who wins souls is wise.** (Proverbs, 11:30)

He who walks with the wise grows wise, but a companion of fools suffers harm. (Proverbs, 13:20)

The mocker seeks wisdom and finds none, but **knowledge comes easily to the discerning.** (Proverbs, 14:6)

Stay away from a foolish man, for you will not find knowledge on his lips. (Proverbs, 14:7)

The wisdom of the prudent is to give thought to their ways, but the folly of fools is deception. (Proverbs, 14:8)

A wise man fears the Lord and shuns evil, but a fool is hotheaded and reckless. (Proverbs, 14:16)

The simple inherit folly, but the **prudent are crowned with knowledge.** (Proverbs, 14:18)

The wealth of the wise is their crown, but the folly of fools yields folly. (Proverbs, 14:24)

A wise king winnows out the wicked; he drives the threshing wheel over them. (Proverbs, 20:26)

Wisdom reposes in the heart of the discerning and even among fools she lets herself be known. (Proverbs, 14:33)

He who ignores discipline despises himself, **but whoever heeds correction gains understanding.** (Proverbs, 15:32)

The wise in heart are called discerning, and pleasant words promote instruction. (Proverbs, 16:21)

Discerning man keeps wisdom in view, but a fool's eyes wander to the ends of the earth. A foolish son brings grief to his father and bitterness to the one who bore him. (Proverbs, 17:24-25)

When a mocker is punished, the simple gain wisdom; **when a wise man is instructed, he gets knowledge.** (Proverbs, 21:11)

Pay attention and listen to the sayings of the wise; apply your heart to what I teach. (Proverbs, 22:17)

Do not speak to a fool, for he will scorn the wisdom of your words. (Proverbs, 23:9)

Listen, my son, and **be wise**, and keep your heart on the right path. (Proverbs, 23:19)

Buy the truth and do not sell it; **get wisdom, discipline and understanding.** (Proverbs, 23:23)

... **If you find it [wisdom], there is a future hope for you,** and your hope will not be cut off. (Proverbs, 24:14)

These also are **sayings of the wise**: To show partiality in judging is not good. (Proverbs, 24:23)

Do not answer a fool according to his folly, or you will be like him yourself. (Proverbs, 26:4)

Be wise, my son, and bring joy to my heart; then I can answer anyone who treats me with contempt. **The prudent see danger and take refuge,** but the simple keep going and suffer for it. (Proverbs, 27:11-12)

Mockers stir up a city, but **wise men turn away anger.** If a wise man goes to court with a fool, the fool rages and scoffs, and there is no peace. (Proverbs 29:8-9)

Now there lived in that city a man poor but wise, and **he saved the city by his wisdom**... So I said, "**Wisdom is better than strength**."... The quiet words of the wise are more to be heeded than the shouts of a ruler of fools. **Wisdom is better than weapons**... (Ecclesiastes, 9:15-18)

Wisdom makes one wise man more powerful than ten rulers in a city. (Ecclesiastes, 7:19)

Then the king ordered Ashpenaz, chief of his court officials, to bring in some of the believers from the royal family and the nobility- young men without any physical defect, handsome, **showing aptitude for every kind of learning, well informed, quick to understand,** and qualified to serve in the king's palace. (Daniel, 1:3-4)

I thank and praise You, O God... You have given me wisdom and power. (Daniel, 2:23)

I have heard that... **you have insight, intelligence and outstanding wisdom.** (Daniel, 5:14)

And to fear Your name is wisdom... (Micah, 6:9)

Answer a fool according to his folly, or he will be wise in his own eyes. (Proverbs, 26:5)

Like cutting off one's feet is the sending of a message by the hand of a fool. (Proverbs, 26:6)

Like a lame man's legs that hang limp is a proverb in the mouth of a fool. (Proverbs, 26:7)

Generosity and Avoiding Parsimony

One man gives freely, yet gains even more; another withholds unduly, but comes to poverty. **A generous man will prosper;** he who refreshes others will himself be refreshed. (Proverbs, 11:24-25)

The wicked borrow and do not repay, but **the righteous give generously.** (Psalms, 37:21)

... Do not be hardhearted or tightfisted toward your poor brother. Rather be openhanded... (Deuteronomy, 15:7-8)

A greedy man stirs up dissension, but he who trusts in the Lord will prosper. (Proverbs, 28:25)

They are always generous and lend freely; their children will be blessed. (Psalms, 37:26)

Good will come to him who is generous and lends freely, who conducts his affairs with justice. Surely he will never be shaken... (Psalms, 112:5-6)

Whoever loves money never has money enough; whoever loves wealth is never satisfied with his income. This too is meaningless. As goods increase, so do those who consume them. And what benefit are they to the owner except to feast his eyes on them? The sleep of a laborer is sweet, whether he eats little or much, but **the abundance of a rich man permits him no sleep.** (Ecclesiastes, 5:10-12)

A generous man will himself be blessed, for he shares his food with the poor. (Proverbs, 22:9)

... **Do not be hardhearted or tightfisted toward your poor brother... Give generously to him and do so without a grudging heart**; then because of this the Lord your God will bless you in all your work and in everything you put your hand to... Therefore **I command you to be openhanded** toward your brothers and toward the poor and needy in your land. (Deuteronomy, 15:7, 10-11)

Surely he will have no respite from his craving; he cannot save himself by his treasure. Nothing is left for him to devour; his prosperity will not endure. **In the midst of his plenty, distress will overtake him; the full force of misery will come upon him.** When he has filled his belly, God will rain down His blows upon him. (Job, 20:20-23)

Do not eat the food of a stingy man, do not crave his delicacies; for he is the kind of man who is always thinking about the cost. "Eat and drink," he says to you, but his heart is not with you. (Proverbs, 23:6-7)

A stingy man is eager to get rich and is unaware that poverty awaits him. (Proverbs, 28:22)

He who gives to the poor will lack nothing, but he who closes his eyes to them receives many curses. (Proverbs, 28:27)

You shall not... give him your food for profit. (Leviticus, 25:37)

A faithful man will be richly blessed, but one eager to get rich will not go unpunished. (Proverbs, 28:20)

The district officers, each in his month, supplied provisions for King Solomon and all who came to the king's table. **They saw to it that nothing was lacking.** (1 Kings, 4:27)

Trusting in God, not in Material Power

Bestowing wealth on those who love Me and making their treasuries full. (Proverbs, 8:21)

Those who trust in their wealth and boast of their great riches. (Psalms, 49:6)

The wealth of the rich is their fortified city; they imagine it an impassable wall. (Proverbs, 18:11)

Here now is the man who did not make God his stronghold but trusted in his great wealth and grew strong by destroying others! (Psalms, 52:7)

What will you do on the day of reckoning, when disaster comes from afar? To whom will you run for help? Where will you leave your riches? (Isaiah, 10:3)

The days of the blameless are known to the Lord, and their inheritance will endure forever. In times of disaster they will not wither; **in days of famine they will enjoy plenty. But the wicked will perish:** The Lord's enemies will be like the beauty of the fields, they will vanish—vanish like smoke. (Psalms, 37:18-20)

Wealth is worthless in the day of wrath, but righteousness delivers from death... When a wicked man dies, his hope perishes; **all he expected from his power comes to nothing.** (Proverbs, 11:4, 7)

By your great skill in trading you have increased your wealth, and **because of your wealth your heart has grown proud.** (Ezekiel, 28:5)

One man pretends to be rich, yet has nothing; another pretends to be poor, yet has great wealth. **A man's riches may ransom his life,** but a poor man hears no threat. (Proverbs, 13:7-8)

Do not wear yourself out to get rich; have the wisdom to show restraint. **Cast but a glance at riches, and they are gone,** for they will surely sprout wings and fly off to the sky like an eagle. (Proverbs, 23:4-5)

... wealth hoarded to the harm of its owner, or wealth lost... (Ecclesiastes, 5:13-14)

Would your wealth or even all your mighty efforts sustain you so you would not be in distress? (Job, 36:19)

Though he heaps up silver like dust and clothes like piles of clay, what he lays up the righteous will wear, and the innocent will divide his silver. The house he builds is like a moth's cocoon, like a hut made by a watchman. **He lies down wealthy, but will do so no more; when he opens his eyes, all is gone.** (Job, 27:16-19)

Avoiding Unfair Earnings

... **Woe to him who piles up stolen goods and makes himself wealthy by extortion!**... (Habakkuk, 2:6)

Be careful that no one entices you by riches; do not let a large bribe turn you aside. (Job, 36:18)

Like a partridge that hatches eggs it did not lay is the man who gains riches by unjust means. **When his life is half gone, they will desert him,** and in the end he will prove to be a fool. (Jeremiah, 17:11)

Dishonest money dwindles away, but he who gathers money little by little makes it grow. (Proverbs, 13:11)

Who lends his money without usury and does not accept a bribe against the innocent. He who does these things will never be shaken. (Psalms, 15:5)

Better the little that the righteous have than the wealth of many wicked. (Psalms, 37:16)

"Woe to him who builds his palace by unrighteousness... making his countrymen work for nothing, not paying them for their labor." (Jeremiah, 22:13)

He **who oppresses the poor to increase his wealth** and he who gives gifts to the rich—both **come to poverty**. (Proverbs, 22:16)

... O wicked house, your ill-gotten treasures and the short ephah, which is accursed? Shall I acquit a man with dishonest scales, with a bag of false weights? Her rich men are violent; her people are liars... (Micah, 6:10-12)

If a man denounces his friends for reward, the eyes of his children will fail. (Job, 17:5)

Extortion turns a wise man into a fool, and a bribe corrupts the heart. (Ecclesiastes, 7:7)

A kind man benefits himself, but a cruel man brings trouble **on himself. The wicked man earns deceptive wages,** but he who sows righteousness reaps a sure reward. (Proverbs, 11:17)

He does not oppress anyone, but returns what he took in pledge for a loan. He does not commit robbery but gives his food to the hungry and provides clothing for the naked. **He does not lend at usury or take any increase.** He withholds his hand from doing wrong and judges fairly between man and man. (Ezekiel, 18:7-8)

Woe to him who builds his realm by unjust gain... (Habakkuk, 2:9)

... But they do not put them into practice. With their mouths they express devotion, but their hearts are greedy for unjust gain. (Ezekiel, 33:31)

"... You take usury and increase and make unjust gain from your neighbors by extortion. And you have forgotten Me", declares the Sovereign Lord. (Ezekiel, 22:12)

A leader who is a great oppressor lacks understanding. But he who hates unjust gain will prolong his days. (Proverbs, 28:16)

He whose walk is blameless is kept safe, but **he whose ways are perverse will suddenly fall.** (Proverbs, 28:18)

Better a poor man whose walk is blameless than a rich man whose ways are perverse. (Proverbs, 28:6)

Such is the end of all who go after ill-gotten gain; it takes away the lives of those who get it. (Proverbs, 1:19)

... O Lord... **Turn my heart toward Your statutes and not toward selfish gain.** (Psalms, 119:33, 36)

But his sons did not walk in his ways. **They turned aside after dishonest gain and accepted bribes** and perverted justice. (1 Samuel, 8:3)

... They **sell the righteous for silver, and the needy for a pair of sandals.** (Amos, 2:6)

But select capable men from all the people—men who fear God, **trustworthy men who hate dishonest gain**—and appoint them as officials over thousands, hundreds, fifties and tens. (Exodus, 18:21)

Industry and Avoiding Sloth

All hard work brings a profit, but mere talk leads only to poverty. (Proverbs, 14:23)

The way of the sluggard is blocked with thorns, but the path of the upright is a highway. (Proverbs, 15:19)

Diligent hands will rule, but laziness ends in slave labor. (Proverbs, 12:24)

The sluggard craves and gets nothing, but **the desires of the diligent are fully satisfied.** (Proverbs, 13:4)

The sluggard's craving will be the death of him, because his hands refuse to work. (Proverbs, 21:25)

A lazy man does not roast his prey, but the **precious possession of a man is diligence.** (Proverbs, 12:27)

Lazy hands make a man poor, but **diligent hands bring wealth.** (Proverbs, 10:4)

Go to the ant, you sluggard; consider its ways and be wise! (Proverbs, 6:6)

Laziness brings on deep sleep, and the shiftless man goes hungry. (Proverbs, 19:15)

A sluggard does not plow in season; so at harvest time he looks but finds nothing. (Proverbs, 20:4)

He who works his land will have abundant food, but the one who chases fantasies will have his fill of poverty. (Proverbs, 28:19)

If a man is lazy, the rafters sag; if his hands are idle, the house leaks. (Ecclesiastes, 10:18)

As vinegar to the teeth and smoke to the eyes, so is a sluggard to those who send him. (Proverbs, 10:26)

She watches over the affairs of her household and **does not eat the bread of idleness.** (Proverbs, 31:27)

... was a man of standing, and when Solomon saw how well the young man did his work, he put him in charge of the whole labor force... (1 Kings, 11:28)

The men in charge of the work were diligent, and the repairs progressed under them... (2 Chronicles, 24:13)

The plans of the diligent lead to profit as surely as haste leads to poverty. (Proverbs, 21:5)

Avoiding Mockery

But they mocked God's messengers, despised His words and scoffed at his Prophets... (2 Chronicles, 36:16)

Drive out the mocker, and out goes strife; quarrels and insults are ended. (Proverbs, 22:10)

Mockers stir up a city, but wise men turn away anger. (Proverbs, 29:8)

You should not look down on your brother in the day of his misfortune, nor rejoice... in the day of their destruction, nor boast so much in the day of their trouble. (Obadiah, 1:12)

The mocker seeks wisdom and finds none, but knowledge comes easily to the discerning. (Proverbs, 14:6)

... Scorned by men and despised by the people. All who see me mock me; they hurl insults, shaking their heads: "He trusts in the Lord; let the Lord rescue him. Let Him deliver him, since He delights in him." Yet You brought me out of the womb; You made me trust in You even at my mother's breast. From birth I was cast upon You; from my mother's womb You have been my God. (Psalms, 22:6-10)

Penalties are prepared for mockers, and beatings for the backs of fools. (Proverbs, 19:29)

"How long will you simple ones love your simple ways? How long will mockers delight in mockery and fools hate knowledge? (Proverbs, 1:22)

Like the ungodly they maliciously mocked; they gnashed

their teeth at me... Rescue my life from their ravages... (Psalms, 35:16-17)

He [the Lord] mocks proud mockers but gives grace to the humble. (Proverbs, 3:34)

A mocker resents correction; he will not consult the wise. (Proverbs, 15:12)

He who mocks the poor shows contempt for their Maker... (Proverbs, 17:5)

When a mocker is punished, the simple gain wisdom; when a wise man is instructed, he gets knowledge. (Proverbs, 21:11)

The proud and arrogant man—"Mocker" is his name; he behaves with overweening pride. (Proverbs, 21:24)

Now stop your mocking, or your chains will become heavier; the Lord, the Lord Almighty, has told me of the destruction decreed against the whole land. (Isaiah, 28:22)

The ruthless will vanish, **the mockers will disappear,** and all who have an eye for evil will be cut down. (Isaiah, 29:20)

This is what they will get in return for their pride... and mocking... The Lord will be awesome to them... (Zephaniah, 2:10-11)

To his sin he adds rebellion; scornfully he claps his hands among us and multiplies his words against God. (Job, 34:37)

Avoiding Despair and Finding Peace Through Faith in God

"... Do not grieve, for the joy of the Lord is your strength." (Nehemiah, 8:10)

A heart at peace gives life to the body, but envy rots the bones. (Proverbs, 14:30)

Resentment kills a fool, and envy slays the simple. (Job, 5:2)

A happy heart makes the face cheerful, but heartache crushes the spirit. (Proverbs, 15:13)

... "In repentance and rest is your salvation, in quietness and trust is your strength, but you would have none of it." (Isaiah, 30:15)

The fruit of righteousness will be peace; **the effect of righteousness will be quietness and confidence forever.** (Isaiah, 32:17)

You have made known to me the path of life; You will **fill me with joy in Your presence, with eternal pleasures...** (Psalms, 16:11)

My soul finds rest in God alone; my salvation comes from Him. (Psalms, 62:1)

Find rest, O my soul, **in God alone; my hope comes from Him.** (Psalms, 62:5)

I said to the Lord, "You are my Lord; **apart from You I have no good thing."** (Psalms, 16:2)

He brought me out into a spacious place; He rescued me because He delighted in me. (2 Samuel, 22:20; Psalms, 18:19)

When I felt secure, I said, "I will never be shaken." (Psalms, 30:6)

But the meek will inherit the land and enjoy great peace. (Psalms, 37:11)

If you falter in times of trouble, how small is your strength! (Proverbs, 24:10)

Do not fret because of evil men or be envious of those who do wrong... Be still before the Lord and wait patiently for Him; **do not fret** when men succeed in their ways, when they carry out their wicked schemes... Refrain from anger and turn from wrath; **do not fret—it leads only to evil.** (Psalms, 37:1, 7-8)

Do not fret because of evil men or be envious of the wicked, for the evil man has no future hope, and the lamp of the wicked will be snuffed out. (Proverbs, 24:19-20)

The righteous man is rescued from trouble and it comes on the wicked instead. (Proverbs, 11:8)

When you are in distress and all these things have happened to you, then in later days you will return to the Lord your God and obey Him. (Deuteronomy, 4:30)

... **A righteous man escapes trouble.** (Proverbs, 12:13)

... **They went home, joyful and glad in heart for all the good** things the Lord had done... (1 Kings, 8:66)

How happy Your men must be! How happy Your officials, who continually stand before You and hear Your wisdom! (1 Kings, 10:8; 2 Chronicles, 9:7)

... Blessed are the people whose God is the Lord. (Psalms, 144:15)

... God keeps him occupied with gladness of heart. (Ecclesiastes, 5:20)

My servants will sing out of the joy of their hearts, but you will cry out from anguish of heart and wail in brokenness of spirit. (Isaiah, 65:14)

But blessed is the man who trusts in the Lord, whose confidence is in Him. (Jeremiah, 17:7)

But may all who seek You rejoice and be glad in You; may those who love Your salvation always say, "The Lord be exalted!" (Psalms, 40:16)

... **Their hearts will rejoice in the Lord.** (Zechariah, 10:7)

Be at rest once more, O my soul, for the Lord has been good to you. (Psalms, 116:7)

I run in the path of Your commands, for **You have set my heart free.** (Psalms, 119:32)

... **May those who love You be secure.** (Psalms, 122:6)

But **whoever listens to Me will live in safety and be at ease, without fear of harm."** (Proverbs, 1:33)

... **I was filled with delight day after day, rejoicing always in His presence.** (Proverbs, 8:30)

Spiritual Cleanliness

Blessed are they whose ways are blameless, who walk according to the law of the Lord. (Psalms, 119:1)

Wash away all my iniquity and cleanse me from my sin. (Psalms, 51:2)

... **Wash the evil from your heart and be saved.** How long will you harbor wicked thoughts? (Jeremiah, 4:14)

So Jacob said to his household and to all who were with him, "Get rid of the foreign gods you have with you, and **purify yourselves and change your clothes.**" (Genesis, 35:2)

They will no longer defile themselves with their idols and vile images or with any of their offenses, for I will save them from all their sinful backsliding, and I will cleanse them... (Ezekiel, 37:23)

Many **will be purified, made spotless and refined,** but the wicked will continue to be wicked. None of the wicked will understand, but those who are wise will understand. (Daniel, 12:10)

He who has clean hands and a pure heart, who does not lift up his soul to an idol or swear by what is false. He will receive blessing from the Lord and vindication from God his Savior. Such is the generation of those who seek Him... (Psalms, 24:4-6)

Nevertheless, the righteous will hold to their ways, and **those with clean hands will grow stronger.** (Job, 17:9)

... **The words of the pure are pleasing to Him [the Lord].** (Proverbs, 15:26)

My shield is God Most High, **Who saves the upright in heart.** (Psalms, 7:10)

Create in me a pure heart, O God, and renew a steadfast spirit within me. (Psalms, 51:10)

... **Because of the uncleanness and rebellion... whatever their sins have been.** He is to do the same for the Tent of Meeting, which is among them in the midst of their uncleanness. (Leviticus, 16:16)

... and **make them ceremonially clean.** (Numbers, 8:6)

When they... consecrated themselves, they went in **to purify the house of the Lord,** as the king had ordered, following the word of the Lord. (2 Chronicles, 29:15)

For You, O God, tested us; **You refined us like silver.** (Psalms, 66:10)

The crucible is for refining silver and the smelter for gold, but **the one who purifies hearts... is the Lord.** (Proverbs, 17:3)

Those **who are pure in their own eyes and yet are not cleansed of their filth.** (Proverbs, 30:12)

I will sprinkle clean water on you, and you will be clean; **I will cleanse you from all your impurities and from all your idols.** (Ezekiel, 36:25)

This is what the Sovereign Lord says: **On the day I cleanse you from all your sins,** I will resettle your towns, and the ruins will be rebuilt. (Ezekiel, 36:33)

Some of the wise will stumble, so that **they may be refined, purified and made spotless** until the time of the end, for it will still come at the appointed time. (Daniel, 11:35)

... A fountain will be opened... **to cleanse them from sin and impurity.** (Zechariah, 13:1)

The Lord has dealt with me according to my righteousness; **according to the cleanness of my hands He has rewarded me.** (2 Samuel, 22:21)

If you are pure and upright, even now He will... restore you to your rightful place. (Job, 8:6)

Rejoice in the Lord and be glad, you righteous; sing, **all you who are upright in heart!** (Psalms, 32:11)

Continue your love to those who know You, **Your righteousness to the upright in heart.** (Psalms, 36:10)

Let the righteous rejoice in the Lord and take refuge in Him;

let all the upright in heart praise Him! (Psalms, 64:10)

Surely God **is good... to those who are pure in heart.** (Psalms, 73:1)

Judgment will again be founded on righteousness, and **all the upright in heart** will follow it. (Psalms, 94:15)

Let those who love the Lord hate evil, for He guards the lives of His faithful ones and delivers them from the hand of the wicked. Light is **shed** upon the righteous and joy **on the upright in heart.** (Psalms, 97:10-11)

... O Lord, I will sing praise. **I will be careful to lead a blameless life**—when will You come to me? **I will walk** in my house **with blameless heart.** I will set before my eyes no vile thing... (Psalms, 101:1-3)

Blessed are they whose ways are blameless, who walk according to the law of the Lord. (Psalms, 119:1)

I will praise You with an upright heart as I learn Your righteous laws. (Psalms, 119:7)

Do good, O Lord, to those who are good, **to those who are upright in heart.** (Psalms, 125:4)

He who loves a pure heart and whose speech is gracious will have the king for his friend. (Proverbs, 22:11)

The Servants Promised Happiness by God

But blessed is the man who trusts in the Lord, whose confidence is in Him. (Jeremiah, 17:7)

Blessed are they who keep His statutes and seek Him with all their heart. (Psalms, 119:2)

Blessed are all who fear the Lord, who walk in His ways. (Psalms, 128:1)

Blessed is the man who makes the Lord his trust, who does not look to the proud, to those who turn aside to lies. (Psalms, 40:4)

Blessed are those whose strength is in You... (Psalms, 84:5)

Blessed are they whose ways are blameless, who walk according to the law of the Lord. (Psalms, 119:1)

Blessed is the man who does not walk in the counsel of the wicked or stand in the way of sinners or sit in the seat of mockers. (Psalms, 1:1)

Blessed is the man... whose spirit is no deceit. (Psalms, 32:2)

O Lord Almighty, **blessed is the man who trusts in You.** (Psalms, 84:12)

... Blessed is the man who fears the Lord, who finds great delight in His commands. (Psalms, 112:1)

Good will come to him who is generous and lends freely, who conducts his affairs with justice. (Psalms, 112:5)

Blessed are they who **maintain justice, who constantly do what is right.** (Psalms, 106:3)

Blessed is the man who finds wisdom, the man who gains understanding. (Proverbs, 3:13)

Blessed is the man whom God corrects... (Job, 5:17)

... [Wisdom] is a tree of life to those who embrace her; **those who lay hold of her will be blessed.** (Proverbs, 3:18)

Whoever gives heed to instruction prospers, and **blessed is he who trusts in the Lord.** (Proverbs, 16:20)

... The Lord is good; blessed is the man who takes refuge in Him. (Psalms, 34:8)

How happy Your officials, who continually stand before You and hear Your wisdom! (1 Kings, 10:8; 2 Chronicles, 9:7)

... Blessed are all who take refuge in Him. (Psalms, 2:12)

Blessed is he whose transgressions are forgiven, whose sins are covered. (Psalms, 32:1)

Blessed is he who has regard for the weak; the Lord delivers him in times of trouble. (Psalms, 41:1)

... Blessed are the people whose God is the Lord. (Psalms, 144:15)

... Blessed are those who keep My ways. (Proverbs, 8:32)

... Blessed is he who is kind to the needy. (Proverbs, 14:21)

Maintain justice and do what is right...Blessed is the man who does this, the man who holds it fast... (Isaiah, 56:1-2)

How blessed are the people who know the joyful sound! O Lord, **they walk in the light of Your countenance.** (Psalms, 89:15)

THE IMPORTANCE OF REMEMBERING GOD AND SAYING GOOD WORDS ACCORDING TO THE TORAH

Speaking of God

... In all your ways **acknowledge Him [Lord],** and He will make your paths straight. (Proverbs, 3:6)

Do not let this Book of the Law depart from your mouth; meditate on it day and night, so that you may be careful to do everything written in it. Then you will be prosperous and successful. (Joshua, 1:8)

Fix these words of Mine in your hearts and minds... Teach them to your children, **talking about them when you sit at home and when you walk along the road, when you lie down and when you get up.** (Deuteronomy, 11:18-19)

My mouth is filled with Your praise, declaring Your splendor all day long. (Psalms, 71:8)

In the night **I remember Your name,** O Lord, and I will keep Your law. (Psalms, 119:55)

I will extol the Lord at all times; **His praise will always be on my lips.** My soul will boast in the Lord... **Glorify the Lord with me;** let us exalt His name together. (Psalms, 34:1-3)

... The law of the Lord is to be on your lips. For the Lord brought you out of Egypt with His mighty hand. (Exodus, 13:9)

No, **the word** is very near you; it **is in your mouth** and in your heart so you may obey it. (Deuteronomy, 30:14)

In that day you will say: "Give thanks to the Lord, call on His name; **make known among the nations what He has done, and proclaim that His name is exalted.** Sing to the Lord, for He has done glorious things; **let this be known to all the world.** (Isaiah, 12:4-5)

Ascribe to the Lord, O families of nations, **ascribe to the Lord glory and strength.** (1 Chronicles, 16:28)

... O God, the God Who saves me, and **my tongue will sing of Your righteousness. O Lord, open my lips, and my mouth will declare Your praise.** (Psalms, 51:14-15)

The Spirit of the Lord spoke through me; **His word was on my tongue.** (2 Samuel, 23:2)

But I will sing of Your strength, in the morning I will **sing of Your love;** for You are my fortress, my refuge in times of trouble. O my strength, **I sing praise to You; You,** O God, are my fortress, my loving God. (Psalms, 59:16-17)

I cried out to Him with my mouth; **His praise was on my tongue.** (Psalms, 66:17)

My lips will shout for joy when I sing praise to You—I, whom You have redeemed. **My tongue will tell of Your righteous acts all day long...** (Psalms, 71:23-24)

... May they always say, "The Lord be exalted, Who delights in the well-being of His servant." **My tongue will speak of Your righteousness and of Your praises all day long.** (Psalms, 35:27-28)

... For it is pleasing when you keep them [My Words] in your heart **and have all of them ready on your lips.** (Proverbs, 22:18)

Because Your love is better than life, **my lips will glorify You.** I will praise You as long as I live, and in Your name I will lift up my hands... with singing lips **my mouth will praise You**. (Psalms, 63:3-5)

With my lips I recount all the laws that come from Your mouth. I rejoice in following Your statutes as one rejoices in great riches... **May my lips overflow with praise,** for You teach me Your decrees. **May my tongue sing of Your word,** for all Your commands are righteous. (Psalms, 119:13-14, 171-172)

... You shall read this law.... Assemble the people—men, women and children, and the aliens living in your towns—so they can listen and learn to fear the Lord your God and follow carefully all the words of this law. Their children, who do not know this law, must hear it and learn to fear the Lord your God... (Deuteronomy, 31:11-13)

... [We] will praise You forever; **from generation to generation we will recount Your praise.** (Psalms, 79:13)

"... My Spirit, Who is on you, and **My words that I have put in your mouth will not depart from your mouth, or from the mouths of your children, or from the mouths of their descendants from this time on and fore**ver," says the Lord. (Isaiah, 59:21)

These commandments that I give you today are to be upon your hearts. Impress them on your children. **Talk about them when you sit at home and when you walk along the road, when you lie down and when you get up**. (Deuteronomy, 6:6-7)

Speaking the Truth

The mouth of the righteous man utters wisdom, and his tongue speaks what is just. The law of his God is in his heart; his feet do not slip. (Psalms, 37:30-31)

Whoever of you loves life and desires to see many good days, **keep your tongue from evil and your lips from speaking lies.** (Psalms, 34:12-13)

These are the things you are to do: **"Speak the truth to each other...** and do not love to swear falsely..." declares the Lord. (Zechariah, 8:16-17)

A truthful witness gives honest testimony, but a false witness tells lies... **Truthful lips endure forever, but a lying tongue lasts only a moment.** There is deceit in the hearts of those who plot evil, but joy for those who promote peace. No harm befalls the righteous, but the wicked have their fill of trouble. **The Lord dislikes lying lips, but He delights in men who are truthful.** (Proverbs, 12:17-22)

The mouth of the righteous is a fountain of life, but violence overwhelms the mouth of the wicked. (Proverbs, 10:11)

The mouth of the righteous brings forth wisdom, but a perverse tongue will be cut out. **The lips of the righteous know what is fitting,** but the mouth of the wicked only what is perverse. (Proverbs, 10:31-32)

The righteous hate what is false, but the wicked bring shame and disgrace. (Proverbs, 13:5)

I said, "I will watch my ways and **keep my tongue from sin;** I will put a muzzle on my mouth as long as the wicked are in my presence." (Psalms, 39:1)

True instruction was in his mouth and nothing false was found on his lips. He walked with me in peace and uprightness, and turned many from sin. (Malachi, 2:6)

... I open my lips to speak what is right. My mouth speaks what is true, for my lips detest wickedness. **All the words of my mouth are just;** none of them is crooked or perverse. To the discerning all of them are right; they are faultless to those who have knowledge. (Proverbs, 8:6-9)

A scoundrel and villain, who goes about with a corrupt mouth. (Proverbs, 6:12)

A truthful witness does not deceive, but a false witness pours out lies. (Proverbs, 14:5)

... They take delight in lies. **With their mouths they bless, but in their hearts they curse.** (Psalms, 62:4)

... A malicious man **disguises himself with his lips, but in his heart he harbors deceit.** (Proverbs, 26:23-24)

As long as I have life within me, the breath of God in my nostrils, **my lips will not speak wickedness, and my tongue will utter no deceit.** (Job, 27:3-4)

Why do you boast of evil, you mighty man? Why do you boast all day long, you who are a disgrace in the eyes of God? Your tongue plots destruction; it is like a sharpened razor, you who practice deceit. **You love evil rather than good, falsehood rather than speaking the truth.** You love every harmful word, O you deceitful tongue! Surely God will bring you down to everlasting ruin: ... He will uproot you from the land of the living. (Psalms, 52:1-5)

Let their lying lips be silenced, for **with pride and contempt they speak arrogantly against the righteous.** (Psalms, 31:18)

The **words of his mouth are wicked and deceitful;** he has ceased to be wise and to do good. (Psalms, 36:3)

Like a club or a sword or a sharp arrow is the man who gives false testimony against his neighbor... As a north wind brings rain, so a sly tongue brings angry looks. (Proverbs, 25:18, 23)

A lying tongue hates those it hurts...(Proverbs, 26:28)

Save me, O Lord, from lying lips and from deceitful tongues. (Psalms, 120:2)

... Your lips have spoken lies, and your tongue mutters wicked things. No one calls for justice; no one pleads his case with integrity. **They rely on empty arguments and speak lies; they conceive trouble and give birth to evil.** (Isaiah, 59:3-4)

WISDOM AND SOUND ADVICE FROM THE TORAH

Friend deceives friend, and no one speaks the truth. They have taught their tongues to lie; they weary themselves with sinning... **Their tongue is a deadly arrow; it speaks with deceit.** With his mouth each speaks cordially to his neighbor, but in his heart he sets a trap for him. (Jeremiah, 9:5, 8)

You use your mouth for evil and harness your tongue to deceit. (Psalms, 50:19)

Whose mouths are full of lies, whose right hands are deceitful. (Psalms, 144:8)

He **who conceals his hatred has lying lips,** and whoever spreads slander is a fool. (Proverbs, 10:18)

The tongue of the righteous is choice silver, but the heart of the wicked is of little value. **The lips of the righteous nourish many,** but fools die for lack of judgment. (Proverbs, 10:20-21)

He who walks righteously and speaks what is right... This is the man who will dwell on the heights, whose refuge will be the mountain fortress. His bread will be supplied, and water will not fail him. (Isaiah, 33:15-16)

These are the things you are to do: **Speak the truth to each other...** (Zechariah, 8:16)

Speaking Wisely and Concisely

The words of a man's mouth are deep waters, but the fountain of wisdom is a bubbling brook. (Proverbs, 18:4)

The wise in heart are called discerning, and pleasant words promote instruction... **A wise man's heart guides his mouth, and his lips promote instruction.** (Proverbs, 16:21, 23)

King Solomon was greater in riches and wisdom than all the other kings of the earth. **The whole world sought audience with Solomon to hear the wisdom God had put in his heart.** (1 Kings, 10:23-24)

A fool shows his annoyance at once... Reckless words pierce like a sword, but **the tongue of the wise brings healing.** (Proverbs, 12:16, 18)

A prudent man keeps his knowledge to himself, but the heart of fools blurts out folly. (Proverbs, 12:23)

A fool's talk brings a rod to his back, but the **lips of the wise protect them.** (Proverbs, 14:3)

The tongue of the wise commends knowledge, but the mouth of the fool gushes folly. (Proverbs, 15:2)

The lips of the wise spread knowledge; not so the hearts of fools. (Proverbs, 15:7)

A man finds joy in giving an apt reply **and how good is a timely word!** (Proverbs, 15:23)

Wisdom is found on the lips of the discerning, but a rod is for the back of him who lacks judgment. Wise men store up knowledge, but the mouth of a fool invites ruin. (Proverbs, 10:13-14)

A man who lacks judgment derides his neighbor, **but a man of understanding holds his tongue.** (Proverbs, 11:12)

A man of knowledge uses words with restraint, and a man of understanding is even-tempered. Even a fool is thought wise if he keeps silent, and discerning if he holds his tongue. (Proverbs, 17:27-28)

An unfriendly man pursues selfish ends; he defies all sound judgment. **A fool finds no pleasure in understanding** but delights in airing his own opinions. (Proverbs, 18:1-2)

Gold there is, and rubies in abundance, but **lips that speak knowledge are a rare jewel.** (Proverbs, 20:15)

He who guards his lips guards his life, but he who speaks rashly will come to ruin. (Proverbs, 13:3)

God gave Solomon wisdom and very great insight, and a breadth of understanding as measureless as the sand on the seashore. Solomon's wisdom was greater than the wisdom of all the men of the East, and greater than all the wisdom of Egypt. He was wiser than any other man... **Men of all nations came to listen to Solomon's wisdom, sent by all the kings of the world, who had heard of his wisdom.** (1 Kings, 4:29-34)

Avoiding Evil Words and Speaking Truthfully

The tongue that brings healing is a tree of life, but a deceitful tongue crushes the spirit. (Proverbs, 15:4)

Pleasant words are a honeycomb, sweet to the soul and healing to the bones. (Proverbs, 16:24)

A gentle answer turns away wrath, but a harsh word stirs up anger. (Proverbs, 15:1)

Through patience a ruler can be persuaded, and a gentle tongue can break a bone. (Proverbs, 25:15)

An anxious heart weighs a man down, but **a kind word cheers him up.** (Proverbs, 12:25)

... I have resolved that **my mouth will not sin.** (Psalms, 17:3)

His mouth is full of curses and lies and threats; trouble and evil are under his tongue. (Psalms, 10:7)

[They] devise evil plans in their hearts and stir up war every day. They make their tongues as sharp as a serpent's; the poison of vipers is on their lips. (Psalms, 140:2-3)

With his mouth the godless destroys his neighbor, but **through knowledge the righteous escape... Through the blessing of the upright a city is exalted**, but by the mouth of the wicked it is destroyed. (Proverbs, 11:9, 11)

They sharpen their tongues like swords and aim their words like deadly arrows. They shoot from ambush at the innocent man; they shoot at him suddenly, without fear... He will turn their own tongues against them and bring them to ruin. (Psalms, 64:3-4, 8)

The heart of the righteous weighs its answers, but the mouth of the wicked gushes evil. (Proverbs, 15:28)

A wicked man listens to evil lips; a liar pays attention to a malicious tongue. (Proverbs, 17:4)

... And he [Joseph] reassured them and **spoke kindly to them.** (Genesis, 50:21)

My heart is stirred by a noble theme... My tongue is the pen of a skillful writer. (Psalms, 45:1)

Preaching Goodness and Forbidding Evil

Do not hate your brother in your heart. **Rebuke your neighbor frankly so you will not share in his guilt.** (Leviticus, 19:17)

She speaks with wisdom, and faithful instruction is on her tongue. (Proverbs, 31:26)

A righteous man is cautious in friendship, but the way of the wicked leads them astray. (Proverbs, 12:26)

Do not be like your forefathers, **to whom the earlier Prophets proclaimed: This is what the Lord Almighty says: "Turn from your evil ways and your evil practices."** But they would not listen or pay attention to Me, declares the Lord. (Zechariah, 1:4)

And [Lot] said, "No, my friends. **Don't do this wicked thing."** (Genesis, 19:7)

Listen now to me and **I will give you some advice, and may God be with you...** (Exodus, 18:19)

... "No, my friends, **don't be so vile...** don't do this disgraceful thing... But to this man, don't do such a disgraceful thing." (Judges, 19:23-24)

There is deceit in the hearts of those who plot evil, but **joy for those who promote peace.** (Proverbs, 12:20)

... forsaking Me and serving other gods, so they are doing to you... but **warn them solemnly...** (1 Samuel, 8:8-9)

[David:] **Turn from evil and do good;** seek peace and pursue it. (Psalms, 34:14)

 [Job:] **But my mouth would encourage you; comfort from my lips would bring you relief.** (Job, 16:5)

Avoiding Idle Talk

All hard work brings a profit, but mere talk leads only to poverty. (Proverbs, 14:23)

... and **not** doing as you please or **speaking idle words,** then you will find your joy in the Lord. (Isaiah, 58:13-14)

Would a wise man answer with empty notions or fill his belly with the hot east wind? **Would he argue with useless words, with speeches that have no value?** (Job, 15:2-3)

Therefore thus said the Lord God; "**Because you have spoken vanity**, and seen lies, therefore, behold, **I am against you,**" said the Lord God. (Ezekiel, 13:8)

... Why then this meaningless talk? (Job, 27:12)

... **He speaks vanity**: His heart gathers iniquity to itself; when he goes abroad, he tells it... (Psalms, 41:6)

... They are prophesying to you false visions, divinations, idolatries and the delusions of their own minds. (Jeremiah, 14:14)

So how can you console me with your nonsense? Nothing is left of your answers but falsehood! (Job, 21:34)

Avoiding Gossip

A perverse man stirs up dissension, and a **gossip separates close friends.** (Proverbs, 16:28)

Without wood a fire goes out; **without gossip a quarrel dies down.** As charcoal to embers and as wood to fire, so is a quarrelsome man for kindling strife. (Proverbs, 26:20-22)

A gossip betrays a confidence; so avoid a man who talks too much. (Proverbs, 20:19)

A gossip betrays a confidence, but a trustworthy man keeps a secret. (Proverbs, 11:13)

Do not go about spreading slander among your people. Do not do anything that endangers your neighbor's life. I am the Lord. (Leviticus, 19:16)

They are all hardened rebels, going about with slanders. They are bronze and iron; they all act corruptly... the Lord has rejected them. (Jeremiah, 6:28, 30)

Other Forms of Speech Recommended

Do not boast about tomorrow, for you do not know what a day may bring forth. **Let another praise you, and not your own mouth; someone else, and not your own lips.** (Proverbs, 27:1-2)

Do not keep talking so proudly or let your mouth speak such arrogance, for the Lord is a God Who knows, and by Him deeds are weighed. (1 Samuel, 2:3)

He who answers before listening—that is his folly and his shame. (Proverbs, 18:13)

He who covers over an offense promotes love, but whoever repeats the matter separates close friends. (Proverbs, 17:9)

... and a flattering mouth works ruin. (Proverbs, 26:28)

A fool's lips bring him strife, and his mouth invites a beating. A fool's mouth is his undoing, and his lips are a snare to his soul. (Proverbs, 18:6-7)

From the fruit of his lips a man is filled with good things as surely as the work of his hands rewards him. (Proverbs, 12:14)

From the fruit of his lips a man enjoys good things, but the unfaithful have a craving for violence. (Proverbs, 13:2)

But you even undermine piety and hinder devotion to God. Your **sin prompts your mouth;** you adopt the tongue of the crafty. Your own mouth condemns you, not mine; your own lips testify against you. (Job, 15:4-6)

An evil man is trapped by his sinful talk, but a righteous man escapes trouble. (Proverbs, 12:13)

May the Lord cut off all flattering lips and every boastful tongue that says, "We will triumph with our tongues; we own our lips—who is our master?" (Psalms, 12:3-4)

THE COMMANDMENTS AND PROHIBITIONS ACCORDING TO THE TORAH THAT ARE COMPATIBLE WITH THOSE IN THE QURAN

Lying Is Prohibited

... **Do not lie... Do not swear falsely by My name.** (Leviticus, 19:11-12)

You shall not give **false testimony against your neighbor.** (Exodus, 20:16; Deuteronomy, 5:20)

Have nothing to do with a false charge and do not put an innocent or honest person to death, for I will not acquit the guilty. (Exodus, 23:7)

Do not spread false reports. Do not help a wicked man by being a malicious witness. Do not follow the crowd in doing wrong. When you give testimony in a lawsuit, do not pervert justice by siding with the crowd... (Exodus, 23:1-2)

... If he finds lost property and **lies about it, or if he swears falsely,** or if he commits any such sin that people may do... he thus **sins and becomes guilty...** (Leviticus, 6:3-4)

The remnant... will do no wrong; **they will speak no lies, nor will deceit be found in their mouths.** They will eat and lie down and no one will make them afraid. (Zephaniah, 3:13)

Theft Is Prohibited

You shall not steal. (Exodus, 20:15; Deuteronomy, 5:19)

Do not steal. Do not lie. Do not deceive one another. (Leviticus, 19:11)

... Thieves break into houses, bandits rob in the streets; but **they do not realize that I remember all their evil deeds.** Their sins engulf them; they are always before Me. (Hosea, 7:1-2)

Will you steal and murder, commit adultery and perjury, burn incense to Baal and follow other gods you have not known, and then come and stand before Me in this house, which bears My Name, and say, "We are safe" -safe to do all these detestable things? (Jeremiah, 7:9-10)

Whoever is an accomplice of a thief is an enemy of his own soul... (Proverbs, 29:24)

Eating Pork Is Prohibited

And **the pig,** though it has a split hoof completely divided, does not chew the cud; **it is unclean for you. You must not eat their meat or touch their carcasses;** they are unclean for you. (Leviticus, 11:7-8)

... [The people] **who eat the flesh of pigs, and whose pots hold broth of unclean meat.** (Isaiah, 65:4)

"... Those who eat the flesh of pigs and rats and other abominable things—they will meet their end together," declares the Lord. (Isaiah, 66:17)

Earning Interest Is Prohibited

Do not charge your brother interest, whether on money or food or anything else that may earn interest. (Deuteronomy, 23:19)

... If you lend money to one of My people among you who is needy, **do not be like a moneylender; charge him no interest.** (Exodus, 22:25)

Do not take interest of any kind from him, but fear your God, so that your countryman may continue to live among you. **You must not lend him money at interest or sell him food at a profit.** (Leviticus, 25:36-37)

... **who lends his money without usury**... He who does these things will never be shaken. (Psalms, 15:5)

I and my brothers and my men are also lending the people

money and grain. But **let the exacting of usury stop!** (Nehemiah, 5:10)

Suppose there is a righteous man who does what is just and right... **He does not lend at usury.** (Ezekiel, 18:5, 8)

Distractions Such as Astrology and Fortune-Telling Are Prohibited

... **Do not practice divination or sorcery.** (Leviticus, 19:26)

Isn't this the cup... uses for **divination? This is a wicked thing you have done.** (Genesis, 44:5)

Let no one be found among you who... **practices divination or sorcery, interprets omens, engages in witchcraft, or casts spells, or who is a medium or spiritist or who consults the dead. Anyone who does these things is detestable to the Lord**, and because of these detestable practices the Lord your God will drive out those nations before you. (Deuteronomy, 18:10-12)

The nations you will dispossess listen to those who practice sorcery or divination. But as for you, the Lord your God has not permitted you to do so. (Deuteronomy, 18:14)

... **They practiced divination and sorcery... do evil in the eyes of the Lord.** (2 Kings, 17:17)

Have you not seen false visions and uttered lying divinations when you say, "The Lord declares," though I have not spoken? Therefore this is what the Sovereign Lord says: "**Be-**

cause of your false words and lying visions, I am against you, declares the Sovereign Lord.** My hand will be against the [false] prophets who see false visions and utter lying divinations... Therefore **you will no longer see false visions or practice divination."** (Ezekiel, 13:7-9, 23)

So do not listen to... your diviners, your interpreters of dreams, your mediums or your sorcerers... (Jeremiah, 27:9)

Despite false visions concerning you and lying divinations about you... whose day has come, whose time of punishment has reached its climax. (Ezekiel, 21:29)

I will destroy your witchcraft and **you will no longer cast spells**. I will destroy your carved images and your sacred stones from among you; you will no longer bow down to the work of your hands. I will take vengeance in anger and wrath upon the nations that have not obeyed Me. (Micah, 5:12-15)

... They are prophesying to you false visions, divinations, idolatries and the delusions of their own minds... I will pour out on them the calamity they deserve. (Jeremiah, 14:14, 16)

Taking Bribes Is Prohibited

Do not pervert justice or show partiality. **Do not accept a bribe,** for a bribe blinds the eyes of the wise and twists the words of the righteous. (Deuteronomy, 16:19, Exodus, 23:8)

Cursed is the man who accepts a bribe to kill an innocent person. (Deuteronomy, 27:25)

He who walks righteously and speaks what is right, who rejects gain from extortion and **keeps his hand from accepting bribes... This is the man who will dwell on the heights,** his bread will be supplied, and water will not fail him. (Isaiah, 33.15:16)

For I know how many are y**our offenses and how great your sins. You oppress the righteous and take bribes** and you deprive the poor of justice in the courts. (Amos, 5:12)

... [He] **does not accept a bribe against the innocent**. He who does these things will never be shaken. (Psalms, 15:5)

Woe to those who... acquit the guilty for a bribe, but deny justice to the innocent. (Isaiah, 5:22-23)

Judge carefully, for with the Lord our God there is no injustice or partiality or bribery. (2 Chronicles, 19:7)

Be careful that no one entices you by riches; **do not let a large bribe turn you aside.** (Job, 36:18)

Cheating Is Prohibited

... **Do not deceive one another...** (Leviticus, 19:11)

Blessed is the man whose sin the Lord does not count against him and in whose spirit is no deceit. (Psalms, 32:2)

A good man obtains favor from the Lord, but the Lord condemns a crafty man. (Proverbs, 12:2)

Murdering Is Prohibited

You shall not murder. (Exodus, 20:13; Deuteronomy, 5:17)

Have nothing to do with a false charge and **do not put an innocent or honest person to death,** for I will not acquit the guilty. (Exodus, 23:7)

Will you steal and murder, commit adultery and perjury, burn incense to Baal and follow other gods you have not known, and then come and stand before Me in this house, which bears My Name, and say, "We are safe"—safe to do all these detestable things? (Jeremiah, 7:9-10)

My son, if sinners entice you, do not give in to them. If they say, "Come along with us; let's lie in wait for someone's blood, let's waylay some harmless soul." (Proverbs, 1:10-11)

Adultery Is Prohibited

You shall not commit adultery. (Exodus, 20:14, Deuteronomy, 5:18)

They will not set their thoughts to return to their God: for **the spirit of fornication is in the midst of them**, and they have not known the Lord. (Hosea, 5:4)

For **a spirit of harlotry has led them astray**, and they have played the harlot, departing from their God. (Hosea, 4:12)

Do not rejoice... Do not be jubilant like the other nations. For you have been unfaithful to your God; **you love the wages of a prostitute** at every threshing floor. (Hosea, 9:1)

The land is full of **adulterers... [they] follow an evil course**. (Jeremiah, 23:10)

But **a man who commits adultery lacks judgment**; whoever does so destroys himself. Blows and disgrace are his lot, and his shame will never be wiped away. (Proverbs, 6:32-33)

The eye of the adulterer watches for dusk; he thinks, "No eye will see me"... They make friends with the terrors of darkness. (Job, 24:15, 17)

Homosexuality Is Prohibited

If a man lies with a man as one lies with a woman, both of them have done what is detestable. (Leviticus, 20:13)

Do not lie with a man as one lies with a woman; that is detestable. (Leviticus, 18:22)

Eating Blood Products Is Prohibited

This is a lasting ordinance for the generations to come, wherever you live: **You must not eat... any blood.** (Leviticus, 3:17)

And wherever you live, **you must not eat the blood** of... animal. (Leviticus, 7:26)

But be sure you **do not eat the blood... You must not eat the blood... Do not eat it,** so that it may go well with you and your children after you, because you will be doing what is right in the eyes of the Lord. (Deuteronomy, 12:23-25)

But **you must not eat the blood.** (Deuteronomy, 15:23)

Eating the Flesh of Dead Animals Is Prohibited

He must not eat anything found dead or torn by wild animals, and so become unclean through it. I am the Lord. The priests are to keep My requirements... (Leviticus, 22:8-9)

The priests **must not eat anything, bird or animal, found dead or torn by wild animals.** (Ezekiel 44:31)

Do not eat anything you find already dead... (Deuteronomy, 14:21)

Anyone, whether native-born or alien, who eats anything found dead or torn by wild animals... will be ceremonially unclean... (Leviticus, 17:15)

RELIGIOUS OBSERVANCES ACCORDING TO THE TORAH THAT ARE COMPATIBLE WITH THE QUR AN

Daily Prayer (Salat)

And the Levites... **stood up and praised the Lord**... with very loud voice. (2 Chronicles, 20:19)

Standing on the stairs were the Levites... who called with loud voices to the Lord their God. And the Levites... said: "**Stand up and praise the Lord your God**, Who is from everlasting to everlasting. Blessed be Your glorious name, and may it be exalted above all blessing and praise." (Nehemiah, 9:4-5)

... "**Do not fear any other gods or worship down to them**, serve them or sacrifice to them. But the Lord, Who brought you up out of Egypt with mighty power and outstretched arm, is the one you must fear. **To Him you shall worship** and to Him offer sacrifices." (2 Kings, 17:35-36)

Then the man **bowed down and worshipped the Lord.** (Genesis, 24:26)

WISDOM AND SOUND ADVICE FROM THE TORAH

... So they sang praises with gladness and **bowed their heads and worshipped.** (2 Chronicles, 29:30)

And **I bowed down and worshiped the Lord**. I praised the Lord... (Genesis, 24:48)

Come, **let us bow down in worship**, let us kneel before the Lord our Maker. (Psalms, 95:6)

... Then **the people bowed down and worshipped...** did just what the Lord commanded Moses and Aaron. (Exodus, 12:27-28)

... They **bowed down and worshipped**. (Exodus, 4:31)

David... **fell on his face to the ground**, and bowed himself three times... (1 Samuel, 20:41)

Ezra praised the Lord, the great God; and all the people lifted their hands and responded, "Amen! Amen!" Then they **bowed down and worshipped the Lord with their faces to the ground.** (Nehemiah, 8:6)

Abram **bowed with his face touching the ground...** (Genesis, 17:3)

When Abraham's servant heard what they said, **he bowed down to the ground before the Lord.** (Genesis, 24:52)

Moses **bowed to the ground at once and worshipped.** (Exodus, 34:8)

When Moses heard this, **he fell facedown.** (Numbers, 16:4)

But Moses and Aaron **bowed to the ground** and cried out, "O God, God of the spirits of all mankind..." (Numbers, 16:22)

Moses and Aaron... **bowed to the ground**... and the glory of the Lord appeared to them. (Numbers, 20:6)

... the oracle of one who hears the words of God, who sees a vision from the Almighty, who **falls prostrate**, and whose eyes are opened. (Numbers, 24:4)

Then Joshua **bowed to the ground in reverence**... (Joshua, 5:14)

When all the people saw this, **they fell prostrate** and cried, "The Lord—He is God! The Lord—He is God!"(1 Kings, 18:39)

... When **I bow down in the house...** The Lord forgive Your servant... (2 Kings, 5:18)

... They bowed low and **fell prostrate before the Lord**. (1 Chronicles, 29:20)

... **They knelt on the pavement with their faces to the ground**, and they worshipped and gave thanks to the Lord... (2 Chronicles, 7:3)

... The king and everyone present with him **knelt down and worshipped...** ordered... to praise the Lord. So they sang praises with gladness and **bowed their heads and worshipped**. (2 Chronicles, 29:29-30)

Then **he fell to the ground in worship** and said: "Naked I came from my mother's womb, and naked I will depart. The Lord gave and the Lord has taken away; may the name of the Lord be praised." (Job, 1:20-21)

All kings will **bow down to Him** and all nations will serve Him. (Psalms, 72:11)

Come, let us bow down in worship, **let us kneel before the Lord** our Maker. (Psalms, 95:6)

Three times a day **he got down on his knees and prayed**. Giving thanks to his God... (Daniel, 6:11)

Then, at the evening sacrifice, **I... fell on my knees** with my hands spread out to the Lord my God. (Ezra, 9:5)

When Solomon had finished all these prayers and supplications to the Lord, he rose from before the altar of the Lord, where **he had been kneeling** with his hands spread out toward heaven. (1 Kings, 8:54)

He [Solomon] stood on the platform and then **knelt down...** and spread out his hands toward heaven. (2 Chronicles, 6:13)

Fasting

So **we fasted** and petitioned our God about this, and He answered our prayer. (Ezra, 8:23)

I... **fasted** and prayed before the God of heavens. (Nehemiah, 1:4)

They fasted that day until evening... (Judges, 20:26)

... On that day **they fasted..** (1 Samuel, 7:6)

... He... put on sackcloth and **fasted.** He lay in sackcloth and went around meekly. (1 Kings, 21:27)

On the twenty-fourth day of the same month... gathered together, **fasting** and wearing sackcloth and threw earth on their heads. (Nehemiah, 9:1)

So you go to the house of the Lord on a **day of fasting** and read to the people from the scroll the words of the Lord... **A time of fasting before the Lord** was proclaimed... (Jeremiah, 36:6, 9)

So I turned to the Lord God and pleaded with Him in prayer and petition, **in fasting**, and in sackcloth and ashes. (Daniel, 9:3)

Declare **a holy fast;** call a sacred assembly. Summon the elders and all who live in the land to the house of the Lord your God, and cry out to the Lord. (Joel, 1:14)

This is what the Lord Almighty says: **"The fasts of the fourth, fifth, seventh and tenth months** will become joyful and glad occasions and happy festivals... Therefore love truth and peace." (Zechariah, 8:19)

Giving Alms (Zakat)

Do not go over your vineyard a second time or pick up the grapes that have fallen. **Leave them for the poor and the alien...** (Leviticus, 19:10)

When you reap the harvest of your land, do not reap to the very edges of your field or gather the gleanings of your harvest. **Leave them for the poor and the alien...** (Leviticus, 23:22)

If one of your countrymen becomes poor and is unable to support himself among you, help him as you would an alien or a temporary resident, so he can continue to live among you. (Leviticus, 25:35)

If **there is a poor man among your brothers** in any of the towns of the land that the Lord your God is giving you, **do not be hardhearted or tightfisted toward your poor brother.** Rather be openhanded and **freely lend him whatever he needs.** Be careful not to harbor this wicked thought: **"The seventh year, the year for canceling debts, is near,"** so that you do not show ill will toward your needy brother and give him nothing. He may then appeal to the Lord against you, and you will be found guilty of sin. **Give generously to him and do so without a grudging heart;** then because of this the Lord your God will bless you in all your work and in everything you put your hand to. There will always be poor people in the land. Therefore I **command you to be openhanded toward your brothers and toward the poor and needy in your land.** (Deuteronomy, 15:7-11)

And you and the Levites and the aliens among you shall rejoice in all the good things the Lord your God has given to you and your household. When you have finished **setting aside a tenth of all your produce in the third year, the year of the tithe, you shall give it to** the Levite, the alien, **the fatherless and the widow,** so that they may eat in your towns and be satisfied. Then say to the Lord your God: "I have removed from my house the sacred portion and have given it to the Levite, the alien, the fatherless and the widow, according to all You commanded. I have not turned aside from Your commands nor have I forgotten any of them." (Deuteronomy, 26:11-13)

WISDOM AND SOUND ADVICE FROM THE TORAH

Ablution (Wudu)

Make a bronze basin, with its bronze stand, **for washing.** Place it between the Tent of Meeting and the altar, and put water in it. Aaron and his sons **are to wash their hands and feet with water from it.** Whenever they enter the Tent of Meeting, they shall wash with water... Also, when they approach the altar to minister by presenting an offering made to the Lord... **they shall wash their hands and feet...** This is to be a lasting ordinance for Aaron and his descendants for the generations to come. (Exodus, 30:18-21)

Bring Aaron and his sons to the entrance to the Tent of Meeting and **wash them with water...** He placed the basin between the Tent of Meeting and the altar and **put water in it for washing,** and Moses and Aaron and his sons **used it to wash their hands and feet. They washed whenever they entered the Tent of Meeting or approached the altar, as the Lord commanded Moses.** (Exodus, 40:12, 30-32)

... **Bring Aaron and his sons to the entrance to the Tent of Meeting and wash them** with water. (Exodus, 29:4)

Harun Yahya (Adnan Oktar)

SOME OF THE BEAUTIES CREATED BY GOD THAT ARE REFERRED TO IN THE TORAH

The Beauty of God

One thing I ask of the Lord, this is what I seek; that I may dwell in the house of the Lord all the days of my life to **gaze upon the beauty of the Lord**[1] and to seek Him in His house. (Psalms, 27:4)

He has made everything beautiful in its time. He has also set eternity in the hearts of men; yet they cannot fathom what God has done from beginning to end. (Ecclesiastes, 3:11)

Who is like You, O Lord? Who is like You—**majestic in holiness, awesome in glory, working wonders?** (Exodus, 15:11)

Dominion and awe belong to God; He establishes order in the heights of heaven. (Job, 25:2)

1- A reference to devout believers' seeing *Jamal* of Allah as a blessing of Paradise.

The Beauty in Objects

They captured fortified cities and fertile land; **they took possession of houses filled with all kinds of good things, wells already dug, vineyards, olive groves and fruit trees in abundance.** They ate to the full and were well-nourished; they reveled in Your great goodness. (Nehemiah, 9:25)

You welcomed him **with rich blessings and placed a crown of pure gold on his head.** (Psalms, 21:3)

Through knowledge its rooms are filled with rare and beautiful treasures. (Proverbs, 24:4)

Beautiful Plants

Consider Assyria, once a cedar in Lebanon, **with beautiful branches overshadowing the forest;** it towered on high, its top above the thick foliage. (Ezekiel, 31:3)

It was majestic in beauty, with its spreading boughs, for its roots went down to abundant waters. (Ezekiel, 31:7)

I made it **beautiful with abundant branches**... (Ezekiel, 31:9)

Its leaves were beautiful, its fruit abundant, and on it was food for all. Under it the beasts of the field found shelter, and the birds of the air lived in its branches; from it every creature was fed. (Daniel, 4:12)

WISDOM AND SOUND ADVICE FROM THE TORAH

Beautiful Foods

Then she handed to her son Jacob **the tasty food and the bread** she had made. (Genesis, 27:17)

And Abraham hastened into the tent unto Sarah, and said: "Make ready quickly **three measures of fine meal, knead it, and make cakes.**" And Abraham ran unto the herd, and **fetched a calf tender and good, and gave it unto the servant;** and he hastened to dress it. And he **took curd, and milk, and the calf which he had dressed**, and set it before them; and he stood by them under the tree, and they did eat. (Genesis, 18:6-8)

And it shall come to pass in that day, that a man shall rear a young cow, and two sheep; and it shall come to pass, for **the abundance of milk that they shall give, he shall eat curd; for curd and honey shall every one eat** that is left in the midst of the land. (Isaiah, 7:21-22)

He made him ride on the high places of the earth, and **he did eat the fruitage of the field; and he made him to suck honey out of the crag, and oil out of the flinty rock**. (Deuteronomy, 32:13)

And their father Israel said unto them: "If it be so now, do this: **take of the choice fruits of the land in your vessels, and carry down the man a present, a little balm, and a little honey, spicery and ladanum, nuts, and almonds**". (Genesis, 43:11)

... At dusk **ye shall eat flesh**, and in the morning ye shall be filled with bread; and ye shall know that I am the Lord your God. (Exodus, 16:12)

... [They] **brought beds, and basins, and earthen vessels, and wheat, and barley, and meal, and parched corn, and beans, and lentils, and parched pulse, and honey, and curd, and sheep, and cheese of kine**, for David, and for the people that were with him, to eat ... (2 Samuel, 17:28-29)

Beautiful Places

Splendor and majesty are before Him; strength and **glory are in His house.** (Psalms, 96:6)

Otherwise, when you eat and are satisfied, **when you build fine houses and settle down...** (Deuteronomy, 8:12)

... **How beautiful are your tents.** (Numbers, 24:5)

Let me go over and see **the good land** beyond the Jordan— **that fine hill country** and Lebanon. (Deuteronomy, 3:25)

The pleasant fields, for the fruitful vines... for all houses of joy in the joyous city... (Isaiah, 32:12-13)

When the Lord your God brings you into the land... **a land with large, flourishing cities** you did not build, houses filled with all kinds of good things you did not provide, wells you did not dig, and vineyards and olive groves you did not plant... (Deuteronomy, 6:10-11)

... this good land, which the Lord your God has given you... (Joshua, 23:13)

... from the good land He [the Lord your God] has given you... (Joshua, 23:16)

Beautiful Scents

Perfume and incense bring joy to the heart, and the earnest counsel of one's friend is sweet to the soul. (Proverbs, 27:9)

... They exchanged wrought iron, **cassia and calamus** for your wares. (Ezekiel, 27:19)

While the king was at his table, **my spikenard spread its fragrance.** (Song of Songs, 1:12)

Also the food I provided for you—the fine flour, olive oil and honey I gave you to eat—**you offered as fragrant incense before them.** That is what happened, declares the Sovereign Lord. (Ezekiel, 16:19)

Nard and saffron, calamus and cinnamon, with every kind of incense tree, with myrrh and aloes and all the finest spices. (Song of Songs, 4:14)

Eleazar son of Aaron... is to have charge of the oil for the light, **the fragrant incense,** the regular grain offering and the anointing oil. He is to be in charge of the entire tabernacle and everything in it, including its holy furnishings and articles. (Numbers, 4:16)

Olive oil for the light; **spices** for the anointing oil and **for the fragrant incense.** (Exodus, 25:6)

Aaron must **burn fragrant incense** on the altar every morning when he tends the lamps. (Exodus, 30:7)

Take the following fine spices: 500 shekels of liquid myrrh, half as much (that is, 250 shekels) **of fragrant cinnamon, 250 shekels of fragrant cane.** (Exodus, 30:23)

Make these into a sacred anointing oil, a fragrant blend, the work of a perfumer. It will be the sacred anointing oil. (Exodus, 30:25)

Then the Lord said to Moses, **"Take fragrant spices—gum resin, onycha and galbanum—and pure frankincense,** all in equal amounts. (Exodus, 30:34)

And make a fragrant blend of incense, the work of a perfumer... (Exodus, 30:35)

And the anointing oil and **fragrant incense for the holy place.** They are to make them just as I commanded you. (Exodus, 31:11)

They also brought **spices and olive oil for the light and for the anointing oil and for the fragrant incense.** (Exodus, 35:28)

WISDOM AND SOUND ADVICE FROM THE TORAH

They also made **the sacred anointing oil and the pure, fragrant incense—the work of a perfumer.** (Exodus, 37:29)

... Then they brought the tabernacle to Moses: ... the gold altar, the anointing oil, **the fragrant incense**, and the curtain for the entrance to the tent; the bronze altar with its bronze grating, its poles and all its utensils; the basin with its stand. (Exodus, 39:33, 38-39)

And burned fragrant incense on it, as the Lord commanded him. (Exodus, 40:27)

Beautiful Words

"So then, don't be afraid. I will provide for you and your children." **And he reassured them and spoke kindly to them.** (Genesis, 50:21)

An anxious heart weighs a man down, **but a kind word cheers him up.** (Proverbs, 12:25)

A man finds joy in giving an apt reply—**and how good is a timely word!** (Proverbs, 15:23)

He who loves a pure heart and **whose speech is gracious** have the king for his friend. (Proverbs, 22:11)

My heart has uttered a good word... my tongue is the pen of a skillful writer. (Psalms, 45:1)

What advice You have offered to one without wisdom! **And how plentifully You have declared sound knowledge!** (Job, 26:3)

THE ORDER IN THE UNIVERSE AND CREATION ACCORDING TO THE TORAH

The Creation of the Heavens and the Earth

In the beginning **God created the heavens and the earth.** Now the earth was form-less and empty, darkness was over the surface of the deep... (Genesis, 1:1-2)

And God said, "Let there be an expanse between the waters to separate water from water." So **God made the expanse** and separated the water under the expanse from the water above it. And it was so. God called the expanse "sky"... (Genesis, 1:6-8)

... **When the Lord God made the earth and the heavens**... (Genesis, 2:4-5)

You alone are the Lord. **You made the heavens, even the highest heavens, and all their starry host, the earth and all that is on it, the seas and all that is in them...**
the multitudes of heaven worship You.
(Nehemiah, 9:6)

And God said, **"Let the water under the sky be gathered to one place, and let dry ground appear."** And it was so. **God called the dry ground "land," and the gathered waters He called "seas"**... (Genesis, 1:9-10)

Thus the heavens and the earth were completed in all their vast array. (Genesis, 2:1)

Praise the Lord, O my soul. O Lord my God, You are very great; are clothed with splendor and majesty... **He set the earth on its foundations; it can never be moved.** (Psalms, 104:1, 5)

The Creation of Light

And God said, "Let there be light," and there was light... He separated the light from the darkness. (Genesis, 1:3-4)

The Creation of Night and Day

God called the light "day," and the darkness He called "night." And there was evening, and there was morning... (Genesis, 1:5)

As long as the earth endures, seedtime and harvest, cold and heat, summer and winter, **day and night will never cease.** (Genesis, 8:22)

The Creation of Celestial Bodies

And God said, **"Let there be lights in the expanse of the sky to separate the day from the night,** and let them serve as signs to mark seasons and days and years, and let them be lights in the expanse of the sky to give light on the earth." And it was so. **God made two great lights—the greater light to govern the day and the lesser light to govern the night. He also made the stars.** God set them in the expanse of the sky to give light on the earth. (Genesis, 1:14-17)

O Lord, our Lord, how majestic is Your name in all the earth! **You have set Your glory above the heavens... When I consider Your heavens... the Moon and the stars, which You have set in place,** what is man...? (Psalms, 8:1-4)

The Creation of the Heavens Within an Order

This is what the Lord says, **He Who appoints the Sun shine by day, Who decrees the Moon and stars** to shine by night, stirs up the sea so that its waves roar—the Lord Almighty is His name... (Jeremiah, 31:35-36)

Lift your eyes and look to the heavens: Who created all these? **He Who brings out the starry host one by one**, and calls them each by name. Because of His great power and mighty strength, **not one of them is missing**. (Isaiah, 40:26)

Can you bring forth the constellations in their seasons or lead out the bear with its cubs? Do you know the laws of the heavens?... (Job, 38:32-33)

The Earth's Position in Space

He spreads out the northern skies over empty space; **He suspends the earth over nothing.** (Job, 26:7)

The Course of the Sun

The Sun rises and the Sun sets, **hurries back to where it rises.** (Ecclesiastes, 1:5)

The Movement of the Winds Within an Order

The wind blows to the south and turns to the north; **round and round it goes, ever returning on its course.** (Ecclesiastes, 1:6)

The Order and Cycle in the Waters

How great is God... **He draws up the drops of water, which distill as rain to the streams;** the clouds pour down their moisture and abundant showers fall on mankind. (Job, 36:26-28)

When He established the force of the wind and **measured out the waters, when He made a decree for the rain** and a path for the thunderstorm... (Job, 28:25-26)

As the rain and the snow come down from heaven, and do not return to it without watering the earth, and making it bud and flourish, so that it yields seed for the sower and bread for the eater... (Isaiah, 55:10)

When He established the clouds... when **He gave the sea its boundary so the waters would not overstep His command,** and when He marked out the foundations of the earth. (Proverbs, 8:29)

They flowed over the mountains, **they went down into the valleys, to the place You assigned** for them. **You set a boundary they cannot cross;** never again will they cover the earth. (Psalms, 104:8-9)

All streams flow into the sea, yet the sea is never full. To the place the streams come from, there they return again. (Ecclesiastes, 1:7)

The Protective Nature of the Atmosphere

... He stretches out the heavens like a canopy, spreads them out like a tent... (Isaiah, 40:22)

The Creation of Animals

And God said, "Let the water teem with living creatures, and let birds fly above the earth across the expanse of the sky." **So God created the great creatures of the sea and every living and moving thing with which the water teems, according to their kinds, and every winged bird according to its kind...** God blessed them and said, "Be fruitful and increase in number and fill the water in the seas, and let the birds increase on the earth." (Genesis, 1:20-22)

And God said, "Let the land produce living creatures according to their kinds: livestock, creatures that move along the ground, and wild animals, each according to its kind." And it was so. **God made the wild animals according to their kinds, the livestock according to their kinds, and all the creatures that move along the ground according to their kinds...** (Genesis, 1:24-25)

You made him [man] ruler over Your works; You put everything under his feet: **all flocks and herds, and the beasts of the field, the birds of the air, and the fish of the sea, all that swim the paths of the seas,** O Lord, our Lord, how majestic is Your name in all the earth! (Psalms, 8:6-9)

The Creation of Plants

Then God said, "Let the land produce vegetation: seed-bearing plants and trees on the land that bear fruit with seed in it, according to their various kinds." And it was so. The land produced vegetation: plants bearing seed according to their kinds and trees bearing fruit with seed in it according to their kinds... (Genesis, 1:11-12)

Then God said, "I give you every seed-bearing plant on the face of the whole earth and every tree that has fruit with seed in it. They will be yours for food. And to all the beasts of the earth and all the birds of the air and all the creatures that move on the ground—everything that has the breath of life in it—I give every green plant for food." And it was so. (Genesis, 1:29-30)

The Creation of Man

The Lord God formed the man from the dust of the ground and breathed into... [him] the breath of life (He breathed His spirit), and the man became a living being. (Genesis, 2:7)

Then God said, "Let... them [men] rule over the fish of the sea and the birds of the air, over the livestock, over all the earth, and over all the creatures that move along the ground." So... **male and female He created them.** (Genesis, 1:26-27)

He created them male and female and blessed them. And when they were created, He called them "man". (Genesis, 5:2)

I will attach tendons to you and make flesh come upon you and cover you with skin; I will put breath in you, and you will come to life. Then you will know that I am the Lord. (Ezekiel, 37:6)

[Did You not] clothe me with skin and flesh and knit me together with bones and sinews? You gave me life and showed me kindness... (Job, 10:11-12)

... you will eat your food until you return to the ground, since from it you were taken; **for dust you are and to dust you will return.** (Genesis, 3:19)

As you do not know... how the body is formed in a mother's womb, so you cannot understand the work of God, the Maker of all things. (Ecclesiastes, 11:5)

This is what the Lord says—He Who made you, Who formed you in the womb, and Who will help you... (Isaiah, 44:2)

The Heretical Darwinist Idea of "Mother Nature"

They say to wood, 'You are my father,' and to stone, 'You gave me birth.' They have turned their backs to Me not their faces... (Jeremiah, 2:27)

The Positive Effect on Health of Moral Virtue

... fear the Lord and shun evil. This will bring health to your body and nourishment to your bones. (Proverbs, 3:7-8)

A heart at peace gives life to the body, but envy rots the bones. (Proverbs, 14:30)

The fear of the Lord adds length to life... (Proverbs, 10:27)

He who pursues righteousness and love finds life, prosperity and honor. (Proverbs, 21:21)

Humility and the fear of the Lord bring wealth and honor and **life.** (Proverbs, 22:4)

Pleasant words are a honeycomb, sweet to the soul and healing to the bones. (Proverbs, 16:24)

A cheerful heart is good medicine, but a crushed spirit dries up the bones. (Proverbs, 17:22)

A cheerful look brings joy to the heart, and good news gives health to the bones. (Proverbs, 15:30)

ART AND ARCHITECTURE ACCORDING TO THE TORAH

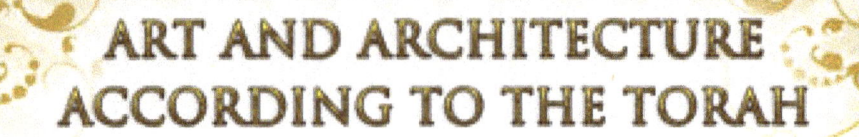

Gold Veneer

... He [Solomon] **overlaid the inside with pure gold**. (2 Chronicles, 3:4)

He paneled the main hall with pine and **covered it with fine gold** and decorated it with palm tree and chain designs. (2 Chronicles, 3:5)

He overlaid the ceiling beams, doorframes, walls and doors of the house with gold... (2 Chronicles, 3:7)

He also made two pine doors, each having two leaves that turned in sockets. He carved cherubim, palm trees and open flowers on them and **overlaid them with gold hammered evenly over the carvings**. (1 Kings, 6:34-35)

Then the king [Solomon] **made a great throne** inlaid with ivory and **overlaid with fine gold.** (1 Kings, 10:18)

They overlaid the frames with gold and made gold rings to hold the crossbars. **They also overlaid the**

crossbars with gold... They made four posts of acacia wood for it and overlaid them with gold. They made gold hooks for them and cast their four silver bases. For the entrance to the tent they made a curtain of blue, purple and scarlet yarn and finely twisted linen—the work of an embroiderer; and they made five posts with hooks for them. They overlaid the tops of the posts and their bands with gold and made their five bases of bronze. (Exodus, 36:34-38)

Have them make a chest of acacia wood... **Overlay it with pure gold, both inside and out**... Then **make poles** of acacia wood and **overlay them with gold.** (Exodus, 25:10-13)

Make a table of acacia wood—two cubits[1] long, a cubit wide and a cubit and a half high. **Overlay it with pure gold and make a gold molding around it.** (Exodus, 25:23-24)

Make the **poles** of acacia wood, **overlay them with gold** and carry the table with them. (Exodus, 25:28)

Overlay the frames with gold and make gold rings to hold the crossbars. Also overlay the crossbars with gold. (Exodus, 26:29)

Make gold hooks for this curtain **and five posts** of acacia wood **overlaid with gold**. And cast five bronze bases for them. (Exodus, 26:37)

He overlaid it with pure gold, both inside and out, and made a gold molding around it. He cast four gold rings for it and fastened them to its four feet,

---

1- 1 cubit = 45.72 centimeters

with two rings on one side and two rings on the other. Then he made **poles** of acacia wood and **overlaid them with gold.** (Exodus, 37:2-4)

Then they overlaid it with pure gold and made a gold molding around it. (Exodus, 37:11)

The poles for carrying the table were made of acacia wood and were **overlaid with gold**. (Exodus, 37:15)

Timber Panelling

So he built the house, and finished it; and **he covered the house with beams and planks of cedar.** (1 Kings, 6:9)

He built the walls of the house within with boards of cedar: from the floor of the house to the walls of the ceiling, he covered them on the inside with **wood**; and **he covered the floor of the house with boards of fir**. (1 Kings, 6:15)

And he built twenty cubits on the sides of the house, **both the floor and the walls with boards of cedar.** (1 Kings, 6:16)

There was cedar on the house within, carved with buds and open flowers: **all was cedar;** there was no stone seen. (1 Kings, 6:18)

The inmost place was twenty cubits long, twenty wide and twenty high. He overlaid the inside with pure gold, and he also **overlaid the altar of cedar.** (1 Kings, 6:20)

And he built the inner courtyard of three courses of dressed stone and one course of trimmed **cedar beams.** (1 Kings, 6:36)

He built the throne hall, the Hall of Justice, where he was to judge, and he **covered it with cedar from floor to ceiling**. (1 Kings, 7:7)

The Art of Carving and Relief Work

For the entrance of the oracle **he made doors of olivewood**: the lintel and door-posts were a fifth part of the wall. And **on the two olive wood doors he carved cherubim, palm trees and open flowers...** (1 Kings, 6:31-32)

The inside of the house **was cedar, carved with gourds and open flowers**. Everything was cedar; no stone was to be seen. (1 Kings, 6:18)

In the same way he made four-sided jambs of olive wood for the entrance to the main hall. He also made two pine doors, each having two leaves that turned in sockets. **He carved... palm trees and open flowers on them and overlaid them with gold hammered evenly over the carvings. (1 Kings, 6:33-35)

So that the face of a man was towards the palm-tree on the one side, and the face of a young lion towards the palm-tree on the other side... **From the ground to above the door were cherubim and palm-trees made,** and on the wall of the house... Both the outer house and the Most Holy Place had double doors.... And on the doors... were carved cherubim and **palm trees like those carved on the walls**, and there was a wooden overhang on the front of the portico. **On the sidewalls of the portico were narrow windows with palm trees carved on each side**. The side rooms... also had overhangs. (Ezekiel, 41:19-26)

... Every precious stone adorned you: ruby, topaz and emerald, chrysolite, onyx and jasper, sapphire, turquoise and beryl. **Your settings and mountings were made of gold**; on the day you were created they were prepared. (Ezekiel, 28:13)

... to cut and **set stones, to work in wood**, and to engage in all kinds of craftsmanship. (Exodus, 31:5)

... and **onyx stones and other gems** to be mounted on the ephod and breastpiece. (Exodus, 25:7)

The Use of Decorative Plant Motifs

And on the lampstand were four cups shaped like almond flowers with buds and blossoms. (Exodus, 37:20)

They made the lampstand of pure gold and hammered it out, base and shaft; **its flowerlike cups, buds and blossoms** were of one piece with it. Six branches extended from the sides of the lampstand—three on one side and three on the other. **Three cups shaped like almond flowers with buds and blossoms were on one branch**, three on the next branch and the same for all six branches extending from the lampstand. (Exodus, 37:17-19)

This is how the lampstand was made: It was made of hammered gold—**from its base to its blossoms.** The lampstand was made exactly like the pattern the Lord had shown Moses. (Numbers, 8:4)

Make a lampstand of pure gold and hammer it out, base and shaft; **its flowerlike cups, buds and blossoms** shall be of one piece with it. Six branches are to extend from the sides of the lampstand—three on one side and three on the other. **Three cups shaped like almond flowers with buds and blossoms are to be on one branch,** three on the next branch, and the same for all six branches extending from the lampstand. And on the lampstand **there are to be four cups shaped like almond flowers with buds and blossoms**. (Exodus, 25:31-34)

They made pomegranates of blue, purple and scarlet yarn and finely twisted linen around the hem of the robe. (Exodus, 39:24)

A network of interwoven chains festooned the capitals on top of the pillars, seven for each capital. **He made pomegranates in two rows** encircling each network to decorate the capitals on top of the pillars... **The capitals on top of the pillars in the portico were in the shape of lilies**, four cubits high. On the capitals of both pillars, above the bowl-shaped part next to the network, were **the two hundred pomegranates in rows** all around. (1 Kings, 7:17-20)

The **four hundred pomegranates for the two sets of network, two rows of pomegranates for each network,** decorating the bowl-shaped capitals on top of the pillars. (1 Kings, 7:42)

Below the rim, gourds encircled it—ten to a cubit. **The gourds were cast in two rows in one piece with the Sea**. (1 Kings, 7:24)

The inside of the house **was cedar, carved with gourds and open flowers**. Everything was cedar; no stone was to be seen. (1 Kings, 6:18)

He carved all the walls of the house round about with **carved figures of cherubim and palm-trees and open flowers,** inside and outside... And on the two olive wood doors he **carved cherubim, palm trees and open flowers**, and overlaid the cherubim and palm trees with beaten gold. (1 Kings, 6:29-35)

He paneled the main hall with pine and covered it with fine gold and **decorated it with palm tree** and chain designs. (2 Chronicles, 3:5)

He made interwoven chains and put them on top of the pillars. He also made **a hundred pomegranates** and attached them to the chains. (2 Chronicles, 3:16)

...the two pillars; the two bowl-shaped capitals on top of the pillars; the two sets of network decorating the two bowl-shaped capitals on top of the pillars. And **the four hundred pomegranates** for the two networks; **two rows of pomegranates** for each network, to cover the two bowls of the capitals that were on the pillars. (2 Chronicles, 4:12-13)

Each of the pillars was eighteen cubits high... The bronze capital on top of the one pillar was five cubits high and was decorated with **a network and pomegranates of bronze all around.** The other pillar, with its pomegranates, was similar. (Jeremiah, 52:21-22)

There were ninety-six pomegranates on the sides; **the total number of pomegranates above the surrounding network was a hundred.** (Jeremiah, 52:23)

The alcoves and the projecting walls inside the gateway were surmounted by narrow parapet openings all around, as was the portico; the openings all around faced inward. **The faces of the projecting walls were decorated with palm trees.** (Ezekiel, 40:16)

Its openings, its portico and **its palm tree decorations** had the same measurements as those of the gate facing east. Seven steps led up to it, with its portico opposite them; it had **palm tree decorations** on the faces of the projecting walls on each side. (Ezekiel, 40:22-26)

Make pomegranates of blue, purple and scarlet yarn around the hem of the robe, with gold bells between them. (Exodus, 28:33)

Decorative Gold Objects

The lampstands of pure gold with their lamps, to burn in front of the inmost room as prescribed; **the gold floral work and lamps and tongs. They were solid gold. The pure gold wick trimmers, sprinkling bowls, dishes and censers; and the gold doors**... to the Most Holy Place. (2 Chronicles, 4:20-22)

And they made from pure gold the articles for the table—its

plates and dishes and bowls and its pitchers for the pouring out of drink offerings. They made the lampstand of pure gold and hammered it out, base and shaft; its flowerlike cups, buds and blossoms were of one piece with it. (Exodus, 37:16-17)

Solomon also made all the furnishings that were in the Lord's house: the golden altar; the golden table...; **the lampstands of pure gold (five on the right and five on the left, in front of the innermost room the gold floral work and lamps and tongs; the pure gold basins, wick trimmers, sprinkling bowls, dishes and censers; and the gold sockets for the doors of the innermost room, the Most Holy Place...** (1 Kings, 7:48-50)

And he made the **ten candlesticks of gold** according to the ordinance concerning them; and he set them in the temple, five on the right hand, and five on the left. He made also ten tables ... five on the right side, and five on the left. And he made a **hundred basins of gold**. (2 Chronicles, 4:7-8)

You shall make **settings of gold, and two chains of pure gold;**

you make them like cords shall, of braided work: and you shall put the braided chains on the settings. (Exodus, 28:13-14)

All King Solomon's **goblets were gold**, and all the household articles in the Palace of the Forest of Lebanon were **pure gold**. Nothing was made of silver... (1 Kings, 10:21)

The buds and branches shall all be of one piece with the **lampstand, hammered out of pure gold**. Then make its seven lamps and set them up on it so that they light the space in front of it. **Its wick trimmers and trays are to be of pure gold.** A talent[2] of pure gold is to be used for the lampstand and all these accessories. (Exodus, 25:36-39)

Have them make a **chest of acacia wood**—two and a half cubits long, a cubit and a half wide, and a cubit and a half high. **Overlay it with pure gold, both inside and out, and make a gold molding around it.** (Exodus, 25:10-11)

And make its **plates and dishes of pure gold, as well as its pitchers and bowls for the pouring out of offerings.** (Exodus, 25:29)

2- 1 talent = 30 kgs. (66 pounds)

Make a lampstand of pure gold... base and shaft... The buds and branches shall all be of one piece with the **lampstand, hammered out of pure gold... Its wick trimmers and trays are to be of pure gold.** A talent of pure gold is to be used for the lampstand and all these accessories. (Exodus, 25:31-39)

For the breastpiece **make braided chains of pure gold.** Make two gold rings for it and fasten them to two corners of the breastpiece. Fasten the two gold chains to the rings at the corners of the breastpiece. (Exodus, 28:22-24)

And they **made bells of pure gold** and attached them around the hem between the pomegranates. The bells and pomegranates alternated around the hem of the robe to be worn for ministering, as the Lord commanded Moses. (Exodus, 39:25-26)

They made the lampstand of pure gold and hammered it out, base and shaft; its flowerlike cups, buds and blossoms were of one piece with it... The buds and the branches were all of **one piece with the lampstand, hammered out of pure gold**. They made its seven lamps, as well as **its wick trimmers and trays, of pure gold**. They made the lampstand and all its accessories from one talent of pure gold. (Exodus, 37:17-24)

Cast four gold rings for it and fasten them to its four feet, with two rings on one side and two rings on the other. (Exodus, 25:12)

Then make **fifty gold clasps** and use them to fasten the curtains together so that the tabernacle is a unit. (Exodus, 26:6)

You welcomed him with rich blessings and placed a **crown of pure gold on his head.** (Psalms, 21:3)

The Use of Silver

Hang it with gold hooks on four posts of **acacia wood** overlaid with gold and **standing on four silver bases**. (Exodus, 26:32)

With twenty posts and twenty bronze bases and **with silver hooks** and bands on the posts. (Exodus, 27:10)

All the posts around the courtyard are to have **silver bands and hooks**, and bronze bases. (Exodus, 27:17)

With twenty posts and twenty bronze bases, **and with silver hooks and bands on the posts**. (Exodus, 38:10)

The north side was also a hundred cubits long and had twenty posts and twenty bronze bases, **with silver hooks and bands on the posts**. The west end was fifty cubits wide and had curtains, with ten posts and ten bases, **with silver hooks and bands on the posts.** (Exodus, 38:11-12)

Thick Beams

And he made the porch of pillars: the length thereof was fifty cubits, and the breadth thereof thirty cubits; and a porch before them; and pillars and **thick beams** before them. (1 Kings, 7:6)

... There were **thick beams of wood** upon the face of the porch without. And there were narrow windows and palm-trees on the one side and on the other side, on the sides of the porch; there were also the brackets of the house, and the **thick beams**. (Ezekiel, 41:25-26)

Decorated Baths

He made the Sea of cast metal, circular in shape, measuring ten cubits from rim to rim and five cubits high. It took a line of thirty cubits to measure around it. Below the rim, gourds encircled it—ten to a cubit. The gourds were cast in two rows in one piece with the Sea. **The Sea stood on twelve bulls,** three facing north, three facing west, three facing south and three facing east. The Sea rested on top of them, and their hindquarters were toward the center. It was a handbreadth in thickness, and **its rim was like the rim of a cup, like a lily blossom**. It held two thousand baths. (1 Kings, 7:23-26)

The Sea and the twelve bulls under it; the pots, shovels and sprinkling bowls. All these objects that Huram made for King Solomon for the house of the Lord were of burnished bronze. (1 Kings, 7:44-45)

He made the Sea of cast metal, circular in shape, measuring ten cubits from rim to rim and five cubits high. It took a line of thirty cubits to measure around it. Below the rim, figures of bulls encircled it—ten to a cubit. The bulls were cast in two rows in one piece with the Sea. The Sea stood on twelve bulls, three facing north, three facing west, three facing south and three facing east. The Sea rested on top of them, and their hindquarters were toward the center. It was a handbreadth in thickness, and its rim was like the rim of a cup, like a lily blossom. It held three thousand baths. (2 Chronicles, 4:2-5)

I made reservoirs **to water groves of** flourishing **trees**. (Ecclesiastes, 2:6)

Windows

And for the house he made **windows of narrow lights**. (1 Kings 6:4)

Its windows were placed high in sets of three, facing each other. All the doorways had rectangular frames; they were in the front part in sets of three, facing each other. (1 Kings, 7:4-5)

The alcoves and the projecting walls inside the gateway were surmounted by **narrow parapet openings all around,** as was the portico; the openings all around faced inward. The faces of the projecting walls were decorated with palm trees. (Ezekiel, 40:16)

As well as the thresholds and the **narrow windows** and galleries around the three of them—everything beyond and including the threshold was covered with wood. **And the windows were covered**. On the sidewalls of the portico were **narrow windows with palm trees carved on each side**. (Ezekiel, 41:16,26)

Ivory Decorations

Then the king made a great throne inlaid with ivory and overlaid with pure gold. The throne had six steps, and a footstool of gold was attached to it. On both sides of the seat were **armrests, with a lion standing beside each of them**. Twelve lions stood on the six steps, one at either end of each step. Nothing like it had ever been made for any other kingdom. (2 Chronicles, 9:17-19)

Moreover the king made a great throne of ivory, and overlaid it with the finest gold. The throne had six steps, and its back had a rounded top. On both sides of the seat were armrests, with a lion standing beside each of them. Twelve lions stood on the six steps, one at either end of each step. Nothing like it had ever been made for any other kingdom. (1 Kings, 10:18-20)

Columns

He built the Palace of the Forest of Lebanon a hundred cubits long, fifty wide and thirty high, with four rows of cedar columns supporting trimmed cedar beams. **It was roofed with cedar above the beams that rested on the columns**—forty-five beams, fifteen to a row... **He made a colonnade** fifty cubits long and thirty wide. In front of it was a portico, and **in front of that were pillars and an overhanging roof**. (1 Kings, 7:2-6)

He cast two bronze pillars, each eighteen cubits high and twelve cubits around, by line. He also made **two capitals of cast bronze to set on the tops of the pillars**; each capital was five cubits high. **A network of interwoven chains festooned the capitals on top of the pillars, seven for each capital.** He made pomegranates in two rows encircling each network to decorate the capitals on top of the pillars. He did the same for each capital. **The capitals on top of the pillars in the portico were in the shape of lilies**, four cubits high. On the capitals of both pillars, above the bowl-shaped part next to the network, were the two hundred pomegranates in rows all around. (1 Kings, 7:15-20)

The garden had hangings of white and blue linen, fastened with cords of white linen and purple material to silver rings **on marble pillars**. There were couches of gold and silver on a mosaic pavement of porphyry, marble, mother-of-pearl and other costly stones. (Esther, 1:6)

The two pillars; the two bowl-shaped capitals on top of the pillars; the two sets of network decorating the two bowl-shaped capitals on top of the pillars; the four hundred pomegranates for the two sets of network; two rows of pomegranates for each network, decorating the bowl-shaped capitals on top of the pillars... were of burnished bronze. (1 Kings, 7:41-42, 45)

Also he made before the house two pillars of thirty-five cubits high, and the capital that was on the top of each of them was five cubits. **He made interwoven chains and put them on top of the pillars.** He also made a hundred pomegranates and attached them to the chains. (2 Chronicles, 3:15-16)

... They carried all the bronze to Babylon. The pots also, and the shovels, and the snuffers, and the basins, and the spoons, and all the vessels of brass with which they ministered, took they away... The bronze from **the two pillars**, the Sea and the twelve bronze bulls under it, and the movable stands, which King Solomon had made in the house of the Lord, was more than could be weighed. Each of the pillars was eighteen cubits high and twelve cubits in circumference; each was four fingers thick, and hollow. The bronze capital on top of the one pillar was five cubits high and was decorated with a network and pomegranates of bronze all around. **The other pillar, with its pomegranates**, was similar. There were ninety-six pomegranates on the sides; the total number of pomegranates above the surrounding network was a hundred. (Jeremiah 52:17-23)

The portico was twenty cubits wide, and twelve cubits from front to back. It was reached by a flight of stairs, and **there were pillars on each side of the jambs**. (Ezekiel, 40:49)

Courtyards

Make a courtyard for the tabernacle. The south side shall be a hundred cubits long and is to have curtains of finely twisted linen. (Exodus, 27:9)

The great courtyard was surrounded by a wall of three courses of dressed stone and one course of trimmed cedar beams... (1 Kings, 7:12)

He made the courtyard of the priests, and **the large court** and the doors for the court, and overlaid the doors with bronze. (2 Chronicles, 4:9)

For the entrance to the courtyard, provide a curtain twenty cubits long, of blue, purple and scarlet yarn and finely twisted linen—the work of an embroiderer—with four posts and four bases. **All the posts around the courtyard are to have silver bands and hooks, and bronze bases.** The courtyard shall be a hundred cubits long and fifty cubits wide, with curtains of finely twisted linen five cubits high, and with bronze bases. **All the other articles used in the service of the tabernacle, whatever their function, including all the tent pegs for it and those for the courtyard, are to be of bronze.** (Exodus, 27:16-19)

Curtains

For the entrance to the tent **make a curtain of blue, purple and scarlet yarn and finely twisted linen—the work of an embroiderer**. Make gold hooks for this curtain and five posts of acacia wood overlaid with gold. And cast five bronze bases for them. (Exodus, 26:36-37)

... **curtains of finely twisted linen and blue, purple and scarlet yarn... worked into them by a skilled craftsman.** All the curtains are to be the same size—twenty-eight cubits long and four cubits wide. Join five of the curtains together, and do the same with the other five. **Make loops of blue material along the edge of the end curtain** in one set, and do the same with the end curtain in the other set. (Exodus, 26:1-4)

Make a curtain of blue, purple and scarlet yarn and finely twisted linen... worked into it by a skilled craftsman. Hang it with gold hooks on four posts of acacia wood overlaid with gold... (Exodus, 26:31-32)

Make a courtyard for the tabernacle. The south side shall be a hundred cubits long and is to have **curtains of finely twisted linen**, with twenty posts and twenty bronze bases and with silver hooks and bands on the posts. The north side shall also be a hundred cubits long and is to have curtains, with twenty posts and twenty bronze bases and with silver hooks and bands on the posts... For the entrance to the courtyard, **provide a curtain twenty cubits long, of blue, purple and scarlet yarn and finely twisted linen—the work of an embroiderer**—with four posts and four bases...The courtyard shall be a hundred cubits long and fifty cubits wide, **with curtains of finely twisted linen** five cubits high, and with bronze bases. (Exodus, 27:9-18)

All the skilled men among the workmen made the tabernacle with ten **curtains of finely twisted linen and blue, purple and scarlet yarn... worked into them by a skilled craftsman. All the curtains were the same size**—twenty-eight cubits long and four cubits wide. They joined five of the curtains together and did the same with the other five. Then they made **loops of blue material** along the edge of the end curtain in one set, and the same was done with the end curtain in the other set... **Then they made fifty gold clasps and used them to fasten the two sets of curtains together** so that the tabernacle was a unit. (Exodus, 36:8-13)

They made the curtain of blue, purple and scarlet yarn and finely twisted linen... worked into it by a skilled craftsman. They made four posts of acacia wood for it and overlaid them with gold. They made gold hooks for them and cast their four silver bases. For the entrance to the tent they **made a curtain of blue, purple and scarlet yarn and finely twisted linen—the work of an embroiderer;** and they made five posts with hooks for them. They overlaid the tops of the posts and their bands with gold and made their five bases of bronze. (Exodus, 36:35-38)

Next they made the courtyard. The south side was a hundred cubits long and **had curtains of finely twisted linen**, with twenty posts and twenty bronze bases, and with silver hooks and bands on the posts... **All the curtains around the courtyard were of finely twisted linen... The curtain** for the entrance to the courtyard **was of blue, purple and scarlet yarn and finely twisted linen—the work of an embroiderer.** It was twenty cubits long and, like the curtains of the courtyard, five cubits high. (Exodus, 38:9-18)

Embroidered Garments

Tell all the skilled men to whom I have given wisdom in such matters that they are to make garments for Aaron... These are the garments they are to make: a breastpiece, an ephod[3], a

---
3- Ephod: A sleeveless garment.

robe, **a woven tunic**, a turban and a sash... **Have them use gold, and blue, purple and scarlet yarn, and fine linen.** (Exodus, 28:3-5)

For Aaron and his sons, they made **tunics of fine linen—the work of a weaver- and the turban of fine linen, the linen headbands** and the trousers of finely twisted linen. **The sash was of finely twisted linen and blue, purple and scarlet yarn—the work of an embroiderer**—as the Lord commanded Moses. (Exodus, 39:27-29)

Fashion a breastpiece for making decisions—**the work of a skilled craftsman**. Make it like the ephod: **of gold, and of blue, purple and scarlet yarn, and of finely twisted linen**... Then mount four rows of precious stones on it. In the first row there shall be **a ruby, a topaz and a beryl**; in the second row **a turquoise, a sapphire and an emerald**; in the third row **a jacinth, an agate and an amethyst**; in the fourth row **a chrysolite, an onyx and a jasper**. **Mount them in gold filigree settings**. (Exodus, 28:15-20)

For the breastpiece make **braided chains of pure gold, like a rope**. Make two gold rings for it and fasten them to two corners of the breastpiece. Fasten the **two gold chains** to the rings at the corners of the breastpiece. (Exodus, 28:22-24)

Make the robe of the ephod entirely of blue cloth... **Make pomegranates of blue, purple and scarlet yarn around the hem of the robe,**

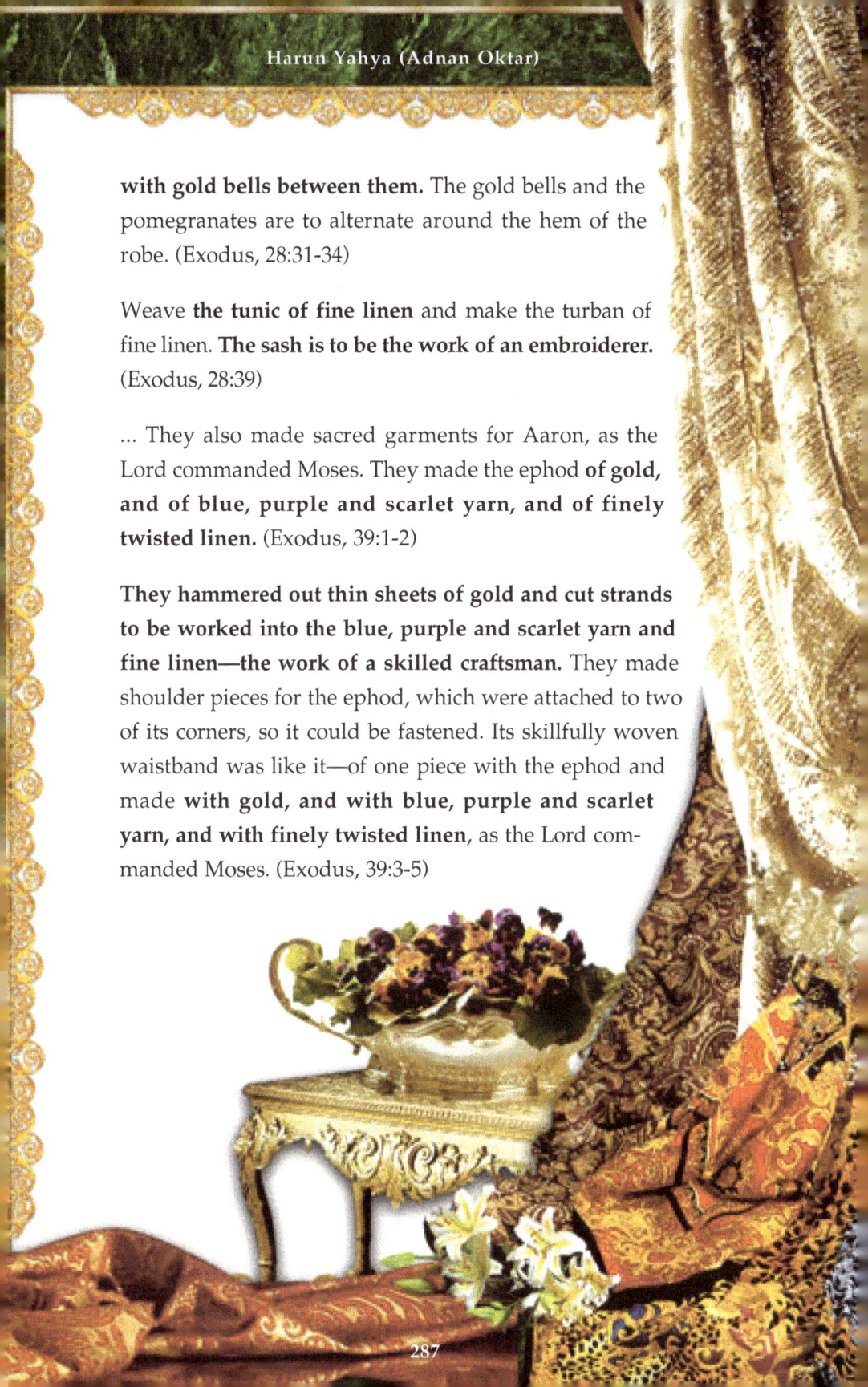

with gold bells between them. The gold bells and the pomegranates are to alternate around the hem of the robe. (Exodus, 28:31-34)

Weave **the tunic of fine linen** and make the turban of fine linen. **The sash is to be the work of an embroiderer.** (Exodus, 28:39)

... They also made sacred garments for Aaron, as the Lord commanded Moses. They made the ephod **of gold, and of blue, purple and scarlet yarn, and of finely twisted linen.** (Exodus, 39:1-2)

They hammered out thin sheets of gold and cut strands to be worked into the blue, purple and scarlet yarn and fine linen—the work of a skilled craftsman. They made shoulder pieces for the ephod, which were attached to two of its corners, so it could be fastened. Its skillfully woven waistband was like it—of one piece with the ephod and made **with gold, and with blue, purple and scarlet yarn, and with finely twisted linen**, as the Lord commanded Moses. (Exodus, 39:3-5)

Decoration with Precious Stones

With all my resources I have provided for the house of my God—gold for the gold work, silver for the silver, bronze for the bronze, iron for the iron and wood for the wood, as well as onyx for the settings, **turquoise, stones of various colors, and all kinds of fine stone** and marble—all of these in large quantities. (1 Chronicles, 29:2)

He adorned the house with precious stones... (2 Chronicles, 3:6)

... There were couches of gold and silver on **a mosaic pavement of porphyry, marble, mother-of-pearl and other costly stones**. (Esther, 1:6)

They fashioned the breastpiece—the work of a skilled craftsman. They made it like the ephod: of gold, and of blue, purple and scarlet yarn, and of finely twisted linen. It was square—a span long and a span wide—and folded double. Then **they mounted four rows of precious stones on it. In the first row there was a ruby, a topaz and a beryl; in the second row a turquoise, a sapphire and an emerald; in the third row a jacinth, an agate and an amethyst; in the fourth row a chrysolite, an onyx and a jasper. They were mounted in gold filigree settings.** There were twelve stones... (Exodus, 39:8-14)

... Every precious stone adorned you: **ruby, topaz and emerald, chrysolite, onyx and jasper, sapphire, turquoise and beryl.** Your settings and mountings were made of gold; on the day you were created they were prepared. (Ezekiel, 28:13)

... **onyx stones and other gems** to be mounted on the... breastpiece. (Exodus, 25:7)

Then mount four rows of precious stones on it. **In the first row there shall be a ruby, a topaz and a beryl; in the second row a turquoise, a sapphire and an emerald; in the third row a jacinth, an agate and an amethyst; in the fourth row a chrysolite, an onyx and a jasper. Mount them in gold filigree settings.** There are to be twelve stones... (Exodus, 28.17-21)

An Understanding of Art and Beauty as a Blessing from God

Then the Lord said to Moses, "**... I have filled him with the Spirit of God, with skill, ability and knowledge in all kinds of crafts—to make artistic designs for work in gold, silver and bronze, to cut and set stones, to work in wood, and to engage in all kinds of craftsmanship**... Also I have given skill to all the craftsmen to make everything I have commanded you." (Exodus, 31:1-6)

Then Moses said to the Israelites, See, **the Lord... has filled him with the Spirit of God, with skill, ability and knowledge in all kinds of crafts— to make artistic designs for work in gold, silver and bronze, to cut and set stones, to work in wood and to engage in all kinds of artistic craftsmanship.** And He has given... the ability to teach others. **He has filled them with skill to do all kinds of work as craftsmen, designers, embroiderers in blue, purple and scarlet yarn and fine linen, and weavers—all of them master craftsmen and designers.** (Exodus, 35:30-35)

SIMILAR PASSAGES FROM THE QUR AN AND THE TORAH

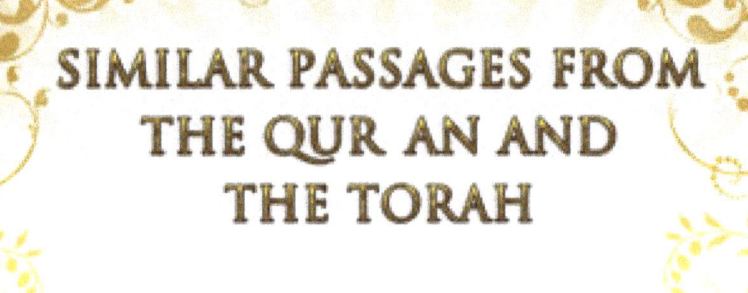

Everything Is Written in a Book

TORAH: My frame was not hidden from You when I was made in the secret place. When I was woven together in the depths of the earth, Your eyes saw my unformed body. **All the days ordained for me were written in Your book before one of them came to be.** (Psalms, 139:16)

QURAN: You do not engage in any matter or recite any of the Qur'an or do any action without Our witnessing you while you are occupied with it. **Not even the smallest speck eludes your Lord, either on earth or in heaven. Nor is there anything smaller than that, or larger, which is not in a Clear Book.** (Surah Yunus, 61)

God Is Always with Believers

TORAH: Have I not commanded you? Be strong and courageous. Do not be terrified; do not be discouraged, **for the Lord your God will be with you wherever you go**." (Joshua, 1:9)

QURAN: He said, **"Have no fear. I will be with you, All-Hearing and All-Seeing**." (Surah Ta Ha, 46)

Even if the Faithful Are Few in Numbers, They Will Still Emerge Victorious

TORAH: Were not the Cushites and Libyans a mighty army with great numbers of chariots and horsemen? Yet when you relied on the Lord, He delivered them into your hand. (2 Chronicles, 16:8)

QURAN: ... **How many a small force has triumphed over a much greater one by Allah's permission!** Allah is with the steadfast. (Surat al-Baqara, 249)

A Thousand Years Is Like One Day in the Sight of God

TORAH: For a thousand years in your sight are like a day that has just gone by, or like a watch in the night. (Psalms, 90:4)

QURAN: A day with your Lord is equivalent to a thousand years in the way you count. (Surat al-Hajj, 47)

Sinners Can Be Known from Their Faces

TORAH: The look on their faces testifies against them; they parade their sin like Sodom; they do not hide it. Woe to them! They have brought disaster upon themselves. (Isaiah, 3:9)

QURAN: The evildoers will be recognised by their mark and seized by their forelocks and their feet. (Surat ar-Rahman, 41)

Human Beings Are Tested

TORAH: "I the Lord search the heart and examine the mind, to reward a man according to his conduct, according to what his deeds deserve."** (Jeremiah, 17:10)

QURAN: Every self will taste death. **We test you with both good and evil as a trial.** And you will be returned to Us. (Surat al-Anbiya', 35)

Unbelievers' Mockery of the Messengers

TORAH: But they mocked God's messengers, **despised His words** and scoffed at His prophets... (2 Chronicles, 36:16)

QURAN: We sent Messengers before you among the disparate groups of previous peoples. **No Messenger came to them without their mocking him.** (Surat Al-Hijr, 10-11

God Is Close to Believers and Answers Prayers

TORAH: The Lord is near to all who call on Him, to all who call on Him in truth. He fulfills the desires of those who fear

Him; He hears their cry and saves them. The Lord watches over all who love Him... (Psalms, 145:18-20)

QURAN: If My servants ask you about Me, I am near. I answer the call of the caller when he calls on Me. They should therefore respond to Me and believe in Me so that hopefully they will be rightly guided. (Surat al- Baqara, 186)

People's True Duty Is to Serve God

TORAH: ... Fear God and keep His commandments, for this is the whole duty of man. (Ecclesiastes, 12:13)

QURAN: I only created jinn and man **to worship Me.** (Surat Adh-Dhariyat, 56)

The Hardening of Hearts

TORAH: They made their hearts as hard as flint and would not listen to the law or to the words that the Lord Almighty had sent by His Spirit through the earlier Prophets. Therefore came a great wrath from the Lord of hosts. (Zechariah, 7:12)

QURAN: Then your hearts became hardened after that, so they were like rocks or even harder still. There are some rocks from which rivers gush out, and others which split open and water pours out, and others which crash down from fear of Allah. Allah is not unaware of what you do. (Surat al-Baqara, 74)

Believers Think Deeply About God's Creation

TORAH: I will meditate on all Your works and consider all Your mighty deeds. (Psalms, 77:12)

QURAN: Those who remember Allah, standing, sitting and lying on their sides, and reflect on the Creation of the heavens and the earth: 'Our Lord, You have not created this for nothing. Glory be to You! So safeguard us from the punishment of the Fire. (Surah Al Imran, 191)

How Unbelievers Killed Prophets

TORAH: ... "But they were disobedient and rebelled against You; they put Your law behind their backs. **They killed Your Prophets, who had admonished them in order to turn them back to You...** (Nehemiah, 9:26)

QURAN: ... They brought down anger from Allah upon themselves. **That was because they rejected Allah's Signs and killed the Prophets without any right to do so**. That was because they rebelled and went beyond the limits. (Surat al- Baqara, 61)

Nobody Can Alter God's Laws

TORAH: I know that everything God does will endure forever; **nothing can be added to it and nothing taken from it.** (Ecclesiastes, 3:14)

QURAN: The Words of your Lord are perfect in truthfulness and justice. No one can change His Words. He is the All-Hearing, the All-Knowing. (Surat al- An'am,115)

Worldly Riches Are of No Avail in the Hereafter

TORAH: Neither on the day of the Lord's wrath. **Neither their silver nor their gold will be able to save them...** He will make a sudden end of all who live in the earth. (Zephaniah, 1:18)

QURAN: As for those who disbelieve, their wealth and children will not help them against Allah in any way. They are fuel for the Fire. (Surah Al-Imran, 10)

How the Number of God's Blessings Cannot Be Counted

TORAH: Many, O Lord my God, are the wonders You have done. The things You planned for us no one can recount to You; **were I to speak and tell of them, they would be too many to declare.** (Psalms, 40:5)

QURAN: If **you tried to number Allah's blessings, you could never count them.** Allah is Ever-Forgiving, Most Merciful. (Surat An-Nahl, 18)

God Elevates or Lowers Whomsoever He Chooses

TORAH: But it is God Who judges: **He brings one down, he exalts another.** (Psalms, 75:7)

QURAN: Do you not see those who claim to be purified? **No, Allah purifies whoever He wills.** They will not be wronged by so much as the smallest speck. (Surat an-Nisa', 49)

TORAH: The Lord sends poverty and wealth; He humbles and He exalts... [T]he foundations of the earth are the Lord's. (1 Samuel, 2:7-8)

QURAN: Say, "O Allah! Master of the Kingdom! **You give sovereignty to whoever You will You take sovereignty from whoever You will. You exalt whoever You will You abase whoever You will. All good is in Your hands.** You have power over all things." (Surah Al 'Imran, 26)

People Are Punished for Their Own Evil Deeds

TORAH: **What has happened to us is a result of our evil deeds and our great guilt,** and yet, our God, you have punished us less than our sins have deserved... (Ezra, 9:13)

QURAN: **Any disaster that strikes you is through what your own hands have earned** and He (Allah) pardons much. (Surat ash-Shura, 30)

How the Morally Corrupt Communicate by Means of Ignorant Facial Expressions

TORAH: A scoundrel and villain, who goes about with a corrupt mouth, **who winks with his eye, signals with his feet and motions with his fingers,** who plots evil with deceit in his heart—he always stirs up dissension. (Proverbs, 6:12)

QURAN: Woe to every faultfinding backbiter. (Surat al Humaza, 1)

Unbelievers' Eyes and Ears Are Insensitive

TORAH: He said, "Go and tell this people: **'Be ever hearing, but never understanding; be ever seeing, but never perceiving.'"** (Isaiah, 6:9)

The word of the Lord came to me: "Son of man, you are living among a rebellious people. **They have eyes to see but do not see and ears to hear but do not hear,** for they are a rebellious people. (Ezekiel, 12:1-2)

QURAN: We created many of the jinn and mankind for Hell. They have hearts they do not understand with. **They have eyes they do not see with. They have ears they do not hear with.** Such people are like cattle. No, they are even further astray! They are the unaware. (Surat al-A'raf, 179)

TORAH: "Hear, you deaf; look, you blind, and see! You have seen many things, but have paid no attention; your ears are open, but you hear nothing." (Isaiah, 42:18, 20)

QURAN: Can you make **the dead hear or guide the blind and those who are patently misguided?** (Surat az-Zukhruf, 40)

Believers' Responding to Evil with Good

TORAH: If your enemy is hungry, give him food to eat; if he is thirsty, give him water to drink. In doing this, you will heap burning coals on his head, and the Lord will reward you. (Proverbs, 25:21-22)

QURAN: A good action and a bad action are not the same. Repel the bad with something better and, if there is enmity between you and someone else, he will be like a bosom friend. (Surah Fussilat, 34)

It Is God Who Bestows Sustenance

TORAH: The eyes of all look to You, and **You give them their food at the proper time. You... satisfy the desires of every living thing.** (Psalms, 145:15-16)

QURAN: There is no creature on the earth which is not dependent upon Allah for its provision.** He knows where it lives and where it dies. They are all in a Clear Book. (Surah Hud, 6)

Those Who Do Good and Evil Will Be Recompensed

TORAH: Tell the righteous it will be well with them, **they will enjoy the fruit of their deeds.** Woe to the wicked! **Disaster is upon them! They will be paid back for what their hands have done.** (Isaiah, 3:10-11)

QURAN: Those who do good will have the best and more! Neither dust nor debasement will darken their faces. They are the Companions of the Garden, remaining in it timelessly, for ever. But as for those who have earned bad actions–**a bad action will be repaid with one the like of it.** Debasement will darken them. They will have no one to protect them from Allah. It is as if their faces were covered by dark patches of the night. Those are the Companions of the Fire, remaining in it timelessly, for ever. (Surah Yunus, 26-27)

Nothing Can Be Hidden from God

TORAH: He reveals deep and hidden things; He knows what lies in darkness, and light dwells with Him. (Daniel, 2:22)

For God will bring every deed into judgment, including every hidden thing, whether it is good or evil. (Ecclesiastes, 12:14)

You know my folly, O God; **my guilt is not hidden from You.** (Psalms, 69:5)

QURAN: Everything in the heavens and everything on the earth and everything in between them and everything under the ground belongs to Him. Though you speak out loud, **He knows your secrets and what is even more concealed.** (Surah Ta Ha, 6-7)

Our Lord! You know what we keep hidden and what we divulge. **Nothing is hidden from Allah either on the earth or in heaven.** (Surah Ibrahim, 38)

Whether you keep your words secret or say them out loud **He knows what the heart contains.** (Surat al-Mulk, 13)

Nobody Can Assume Responsibility for Another's Sins

TORAH: ... **The son will not share the guilt of the father, nor will the father share the guilt of the son.** The righteousness of the righteous man will be credited to him, and the wickedness of the wicked will be charged against him. (Ezekiel, 18:20)

QURAN: Whoever is guided is only guided to his own good. Whoever is misguided is only misguided to his detriment. **No burden-bearer can bear another's burden.** We never punish until We have sent a Messenger. (Surat al-Isra', 15)

If the Guilty Were Punished at Once, There Would Be Nobody Left on Earth

TORAH: Out of the depths I cry to you, O Lord; O Lord... **If You, O Lord, kept a record of sins, O Lord, who could stand?** (Psalms, 130:1-3)

QURAN: If Allah were to punish people for their wrong actions, not a single creature would be left upon the earth, but He defers them till a predetermined time. When their specified time arrives, they cannot delay it for a single hour nor can they bring it forward. (Surat an-Nahl, 61)

An Example of Those Who Do not Put Their Trust in God

TORAH: Such is the destiny of all who forget God; so perishes the hope of the godless. What he trusts in is fragile; what he relies on is a spider's web. **He leans on his web, but it gives way; he clings to it, but it does not hold.** (Job, 8:13)

QURAN: The metaphor of those who take protectors besides Allah is that of a spider which builds itself a house; **but no house is flimsier than a spider's house, if they only knew.** (Surat al-'Ankabut, 41)

The Oneness of God

TORAH: So that all the peoples of the earth may know that **the Lord is God and that there is no other.** (1 Kings, 8:60)

QURAN: Your God is One God. There is no deity but Him, the All-Merciful, the Most Merciful. (Surat Al-Baqara, 163)

God Being the Generous and Loving

TORAH: ... The Lord, the Lord, the compassionate and gracious God... maintaining love to thousands, and forgiving wickedness, rebellion and sin. (Exodus, 34:6-7)

The Lord is compassionate and gracious... abounding in love. (Psalms, 103:3-8)

QURAN: Ask your Lord for forgiveness and then repent to Him. My Lord is **Most Merciful, Most Loving.**' (Surah Hud, 90)

He is the **Ever-Forgiving, the All-Loving.** (Surat al-Buruj, 14)

God Leads Those on His Path to Success

TORAH: And observe what the Lord your God requires: **Walk in His ways, and keep His decrees and commands, His laws and requirements... so that you may prosper in all you do and wherever you go.** (1 Kings 2:3)

QURAN: As **for those who make Allah their friend, and His Messenger and those who believe: it is the party of Allah who are victorious!** (Surat al-Maida, 56)

God Is the Creator of the Earth and the Heavens and All Between

TORAH: The Maker of **heaven and earth, the sea, and everything in them...** (Psalms, 146:6-7)

QURAN: Allah is He Who created **the heavens and the earth and everything between** them in six days and then established Himself firmly upon the Throne. You have no protector or intercessor apart from Him. So will you not pay heed? (Surat as-Sajda, 4)

Believers' Placing Their Hopes in God

TORAH: Let your hope be in the Lord; be strong and take heart and wait for the Lord. (Psalms, 27:14)

No one whose hope is in You will ever be put to shame... Show me Your ways, O Lord, teach me Your paths; guide me in Your truth and teach me, for You are God my Savior, and **my hope is in You all day long**. (Psalms, 25:3-5)

QURAN: Say: 'My servants, you who have transgressed against yourselves, **do not despair of the mercy of Allah**.' (Surat az-Zumar, 53)

What of him who spends the night hours in prayer, prostrating and standing up, mindful of the Hereafter, hoping for the mercy of his Lord? Say: 'Are they the same – those who know and those who do not know?' It is only people of intelligence who pay heed. (Surat az-Zumar, 9)

He is the Creator of Ears and Eyes

TORAH: Ears that hear and eyes that see—the Lord has made them both. (Proverbs, 20:12)

QURAN: It is He Who has created hearing, sight and hearts for you. What little thanks you show! (Surat Al-Muminun, 78)

WISDOM AND SOUND ADVICE FROM THE TORAH

Everything Being Simultaneously Under God's Command

TORAH: For He spoke, and it came to be; He commanded, and it stood firm. (Psalms, 33:9)

QURAN: The Originator of the heavens and earth. **When He decides on something, He just says to it, 'Be!' and it is.** (Surat al-Baqara, 117)

It is God Who Leads to Salvation

TORAH: Acknowledge In all your ways acknowledge Him, and **He will make your paths straight.** (Proverbs, 3:6)

QURAN: The way should lead to Allah, but there are those who deviate from it. If He had wished He could have guided every one of you. (Surat An-Nahl, 9)

God is He in Whom Shelter Is Sought

TORAH: He said: "The Lord is my strength, **my fortress** and my deliverer."... He is a **shield for all who take refuge in Him.** (2 Samuel, 22:2, 31)

The Lord is good, a **refuge** in times of trouble. He **cares for those who trust in Him.** (Nahum, 1:7)

QURAN: Recite what has been revealed to you of your Lord's Book. No one can change His words. **You will never find any safe haven apart from Him.** (Surat al-Kahf, 27)

Say: 'No one can protect me from Allah **and I will never find any refuge apart from Him.** (Surat al-Jinn, 22)

How the Earth Will Be Flattened on the Judgment Day

TORAH: Every valley shall be raised up, every mountain and hill made low; **the rough ground shall become level, the rugged places a plain.** And the glory of the Lord will be revealed... For... the Lord has spoken. (Isaiah, 40:4-5)

QURAN: On the Day We make the mountains move and **you see the earth laid bare** and We gather them together, not leaving out a single one of them. (Surat al-Kahf, 47)

It is God Who Bestows Life and Kills

TORAH: See now that I Myself am He! There is no god besides Me. **I put to death and I bring to life,** I have wounded and I will heal... (Deuteronomy, 32:39)

The Lord kills and makes alive. (1 Samuel, 2:6)

QURAN: It is He Who gives life and causes to die and His is the alternation of the night and day. So will you not use your intellect? (Surat al-Muminun, 80)

That it is He Who brings about both **death and life**. (Surat An-Najm, 44)

How God Gives All Living Things to Man as a Blessing

TORAH: Then God said, "I give you every seed-bearing plant on the face of the whole earth and every tree that has fruit with seed in it. They will be yours for food." (Genesis, 1:29)

Everything that lives and moves will be food for you. **Just as I gave you the green plants, I now give you everything.** (Genesis, 9:3)

QURAN: And He created livestock. There is warmth for you in them, and various uses and some you eat. (Surat an-Nahl, 5)

And also the things of varying colours He has created for you in the earth. There is certainly a sign in that for people who pay heed. **It is He Who made the sea subservient to you so that you can eat fresh flesh from it...** (Surat an-Nahl, 13-14)

God Raises, Lowers and Bestows Goods on Whom He Pleases

TORAH: But it is God Who judges: **He brings one down, He exalts another.** (Psalms, 75:7)

The Lord sends poverty and wealth; He humbles and He exalts... For the foundations of the earth are the Lord's... (1 Samuel, 2:7-8)

QURAN: Say, 'O Allah! Master of the Kingdom! **You give sovereignty to whoever You will You take sovereignty from whoever You will.** You exalt whoever You will You abase whoever You will. All good is in Your hands. You have power over all things. (Surah Al 'Imran, 26)

Do you not see those who claim to be purified? No, **Allah purifies whoever He wills.** They will not be wronged by so much as the smallest speck. (Surat an-Nisa', 49)

Believers' Fearing None Other Than God

TORAH: Be strong and take heart, and have no fear of them: for **it is the Lord your God Who is going with you; He will not take away His help from you.** (Deuteronomy, 31:6)

It is the Lord Who goes before you and will be with you; He will never leave you nor forsake you. Do not be afraid; do not be discouraged. (Deuteronomy, 31:8)

"Be strong and courageous. Do not be afraid or discouraged because of the king of Assyria and the vast army with him, **for there is a greater power with us than with him**. (2 Chronicles, 32:7)

QURAN: They said, 'Our Lord, we are afraid that he might persecute us or overstep the bounds.' **He said, 'Have no fear. I will be with you, All-Hearing and All-Seeing.** (Surah Ta Ha, 45-46)

WISDOM AND SOUND ADVICE FROM THE TORAH

The angels descend on those who say, 'Our Lord is Allah,' and then go straight: **'Do not fear and do not grieve but rejoice in the Garden you have been promised.** (Surah Fussilat, 30)

How God Shapes Man

TORAH: ... O foolish and unwise people? Is He not your Creator, **Who made you and formed you?** (Deuteronomy, 32:6)

Quran: When I have formed him and breathed My spirit into him, fall down in prostration in front of him!' (Surat Al-Hijr, 29)

Quran: It is **He Who forms you in** the womb **however He wills**. There is no deity but Him, the Almighty, the All-Wise. (Surah Al 'Imran, 6)

The Order in the Heavens

TORAH: Lift your eyes and look to the heavens: Who created all these? He Who brings out the starry host one by one, and calls them each by name. Because of his great power and mighty strength, **not one of them is missing.** (Isaiah 40:26)

Quran: He Who created the seven heavens in layers. **You will not find any flaw** in the Creation of the All-Merciful. **Look again** – do you see any gaps? **Then look again and again.** Your sight will return to you dazzled and exhausted! (Surat al-Mulk, 3-4)

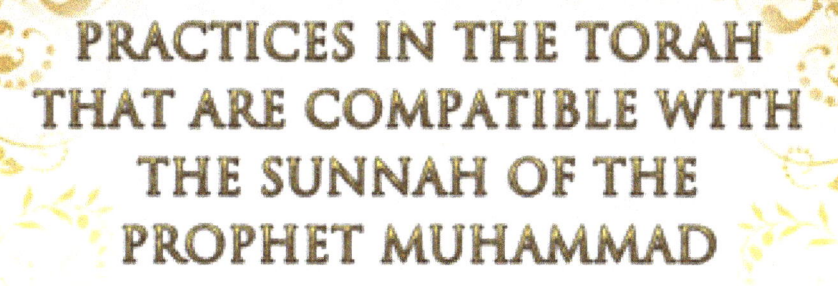

PRACTICES IN THE TORAH THAT ARE COMPATIBLE WITH THE SUNNAH OF THE PROPHET MUHAMMAD (MAY GOD BLESS HIM AND GRANT HIM PEACE)

Through their superior virtues all the prophets sent ever since the time of the Prophet Adam (pbuh) have lived in a way that sets an example for all. How the prophets spent their days, what foods they liked, how they ate them, the kinds of clothes they wore, the way they wore their hair, the attention they paid to cleanliness, their conversation, and how they treated other people are all valuable information for believers to know. According to Prophet Muhammad (may God bless him and grant him peace), all messengers are blessed individuals on whom our Lord has bestowed moral virtues, grandeur, wisdom, the ability to influence others, nobility and radiance. The lives of these blessed individuals, their habits and behavior that guided their communities, are their Sunnah.

In the hadith, Prophet Muhammad (may God bless him and grant him peace) tells us that the Sunnah of all the prophets and messengers are very similar to one another.

God reveals in the Qur'an that all the prophets have been descended from the same family line, and have had the same belief and moral virtues:

This is the argument We gave to Abraham against his people. We raise in rank anyone We will. Your Lord is All-Wise, All-Knowing. We gave him Isaac and Jacob, each of whom We guided. And before him We had guided Noah. And among his descendants were David and Solomon, and Job, Joseph, Moses and Aaron. That is how We recompense the good-doers. And Zachariah, John, Jesus and Elijah. All of them were among the righteous. And Ishmael, Isaiah, Jonah and Lot. All of them We favored over all beings. And some of their forebears, descendants and brothers; We chose them and guided them to a straight path. That is Allah's guidance. He guides by it those of His servants He wills. If they had associated others with Him, nothing they did would have been of any use. They are the ones to whom We gave the Book, Judgment and prophethood. If these people reject it We have already entrusted it to a people who did not. (Surat al-An'am, 83-89)

Those are some of the prophets Allah has blessed, from the descendants of Adam and from those We carried with Noah, and from the descendants of Abraham and Israel and from those We guided and chose. When the signs of the All-Merciful were recited to them they fell on their faces, weeping, in prostration. (Surah Maryam, 58)

When the Torah revealed to the Prophet Moses (pbuh) is examined in detail, it can be seen to contain important information, in terms of the lives, moral values and Sunnah of the prophets and messengers who lived in the past.

In this section of the book, you will see the similarities between prophets who were sent as beacon for the worlds.

Forms of Dress Recommended in the Torah

Wearing the skullcap:

> *He (the Prophet Muhammad [may God bless him and grant him peace]) would wear the skullcap. He sometimes wore it under his turban, and sometimes on its own. He would sometimes remove it and place a shawl over his head and brow.[1]*
>
> *Most of the blessed one's clothes were white. He wore a turban over his skullcap. He began donning his shirt from the right. He had a special costume he wore on Fridays.[2]*
>
> *The Messenger of God (may God bless him and grant him peace) wore a striped skullcap.[3]*

Make tunics, sashes and **headbands** for Aaron's sons, to give them dignity and honor. (Exodus, 28:40)

And **put headbands** on them... The priesthood is theirs by a lasting ordinance. In this way you shall ordain Aaron and his sons. (Exodus, 29:9)

Then he brought Aaron's sons forward, put tunics on them, tied sashes around them and **put headbands on them,** as the Lord commanded Moses. (Leviticus, 8:13)

Wearing a shirt:

> *Al-Ghazali says in his Ihya' al-'Ulum: "The Messenger of God (may God bless him and grant him peace) would wear all kinds of clothing prepared for him. Shirts, jackets, shawls etc.[4]*
>
> *He would tie it over his shirt, sometimes opening it at the daily prayer and outside the daily prayer.[5]*
>
> *He began donning his shirt from the right.[6]*

Weave the tunic of fine linen and make the turban of fine linen. The sash is to be the work of an embroiderer. (Exodus, 28:39)

Bring his sons and **dress them in tunics.** (Exodus, 29:8)

He put the tunic on Aaron, tied the sash around him, clothed him with the robe and put the ephod* on him. (Leviticus, 8:7)

* Ephod: A garment worn over the robe.

Using clothes made of linen:

> *In his book Manaqib, Ibn Shahr Ashub relates: "He (the Prophet Muhammad [may God bless him and grant him peace]) would wear clothes of woven linen and cotton. Most of the blessed one's clothes were white.[7]*
>
> *The Makarim al-Akhlaq relates: "Linen was one of the prophets' clothes."[8]*

For Aaron and his sons, **they made tunics of fine linen**—the work of a weaver—and the turban of fine linen, the linen headbands and the **undergarments of finely twisted linen.** The sash was of finely twisted linen and blue, purple and scarlet yarn—the work of an embroiderer—as the Lord commanded Moses. (Exodus, 39:27-29)

"**Make linen undergarments... reaching from the waist to the thigh.** Aaron and his sons must wear them whenever they enter the Tent of Meeting or approach the altar to minister in the Holy Place..." **This is to be a lasting ordinance for Aaron and his descendants.** (Exodus, 28:40-43)

They are to wear **linen turbans on their heads and linen undergarments around their waists.** They must not wear anything that makes them perspire. (Ezekiel, 44:18)

He is to put on the **sacred linen tunic, with linen undergarments** next to his body; he is to **tie the linen sash around him and put on the linen turban.** These are sacred garments; so he must bathe himself with water before he puts them on. (Leviticus, 16:4)

Using the turban:

> *He (the Prophet Muhammad [may God bless him and grant him peace]) would wear the turban over his skull-cap.[9]*
>
> *According to the account, the Prophet (may God bless him and grant him peace) would wind his turban around him three or five times.[10]*
>
> *He had a turban referred to as al-sahab, and he gave this to the blessed Ali, when Ali came wearing this turban God's Messenger (may God bless him and grant him peace) said, "Ali has come to you inside al-sahab."[11]*

Then I said, **"Put a clean turban on his head."** So **they put a clean turban on his head and clothed him,** while the angel of the Lord stood by. (Zechariah, 3:5)

These are the garments they are to make: a breast piece, an ephod, a robe, a woven tunic, **a turban** and a sash. (Exodus, 28:4)

They are to wear **linen turbans on their heads** and linen undergarments around their waists. They must not wear anything that makes them perspire. (Ezekiel, 44:18)

Wearing a robe and kaftan:

> *On days of battle and on normal days he (the Prophet Muhammad [may God bless him and grant him peace]) wore lined clothes. He had a green silk robe, and it was worth seeing when the blessed one wore this and it contrasted with his white skin...*
>
> *The garment he wore on top of his clothes was dyed with saffron. He sometimes led the community in prayer dressed in this single garment. Sometimes he wore just a single robe...*
>
> *He sometimes donned a striped Yemeni cloak, and sometimes a robe made of wool over his garments. In the same way, he wore clothes woven from cotton and linen.*[12]

They made the **robe of the ephod*** entirely of blue cloth—the work of a weaver—with an opening in the center of the robe like the opening of a collar, and a band around this opening, so that it would not tear. They made pomegranates of blue, purple and scarlet yarn and finely twisted linen around the hem of the robe. (Exodus, 39:22-24)

* Ephod: A garment worn over the robe.

Then bring Aaron and his sons to the entrance to the Tent of Meeting and wash them... **Take the garments** and dress Aaron with the tunic, **the robe of the ephod, the ephod itself and the breast piece.** Fasten the ephod on him by its skillfully woven waistband. (Exodus, 29:4-5)

He put the tunic on Aaron, tied the sash around him, clothed him with the robe and **put the ephod on him.** He also tied the ephod to him by its skillfully woven waistband. (Leviticus, 8:7)

Tell all the skilled men to whom I have given wisdom in such matters that they are to **make garments** for Aaron, for his consecration, so he may serve Me as priest. **These are the garments they are to make: a breast piece, an ephod, a robe, a woven tunic,** a turban and a sash. They are to make these sacred garments for your brother Aaron and his sons, so they may serve Me as priests. Have them use gold, and blue, purple and scarlet yarn, and fine linen. (Exodus, 28:3-5)

The Importance Attached to Cleanliness According to the Torah

> *They wove two jackets for the blessed one (the Prophet Muhammad [may God bless him and grant him peace]), and these he wore only for the daily prayer. He would encourage and command his community to be clean.[13]*
>
> *When we, the Ahl al-Bayt, wish to sleep we abide by ten things: To be clean...[14]*
>
> *It is reported by the son of Omar ibn Hattab that, "I never saw a more generous, braver and cleaner person than the Messenger of God (may God bless him and grant him peace)."[15]*
>
> *The Messenger of God (may God bless him and grant him peace) said: "Islam is clean and unsullied. You, too, must be clean, clean yourselves, because the clean enter Paradise."[16]*

And the Lord said to Moses, "Go to the people and consecrate them today and tomorrow. **Have them wash their clothes.**" (Exodus, 19:10)

After Moses had gone down the mountain to the people, he consecrated them, and **they washed their clothes.** (Exodus, 19:14)

"My father, if the prophet had told you to do some great thing, would you not have done it? How much more, then, when he tells you, **'Wash and be cleansed'!**" (2 Kings, 5:13)

They washed whenever they entered the Tent of Meeting or approached the altar, **as the Lord commanded Moses.** (Exodus, 40:32)

Then David got up from the ground. **After he had washed,** put on lotions and changed his clothes, he went into the house of the Lord and worshiped. (2 Samuel, 12:20)

"You must keep the believers separate from things that make them unclean, so they will not die in their uncleanness for defiling My dwelling place, which is among them." (Leviticus, 15:31)

... [He] must wash his clothes and bathe himself with water; afterward he may come into the camp. (Leviticus, 16:28)

He shall bathe himself with water in a holy place and put on his regular garments. (Leviticus, 16:24)

... [They] purified themselves and washed their clothes. (Numbers, 8:21)

He is to put on the sacred linen tunic, with linen undergarments next to his body; he is to tie the linen sash around him and put on the linen turban. These are sacred garments; **so he must bathe himself with water before he puts them on.** (Leviticus, 16:4)

Wash and make yourselves clean. Take your evil deeds out of My sight! (Isaiah, 1:16)

You must distinguish between the holy and the common, **between the unclean and the clean.** (Leviticus, 10:10)

Wearing good smell:

> *The Messenger of God (may God bless him and grant him peace) had a box containing musk. He would take this and anoint himself with it after every ritual purification. This delightful scent would spread all around whenever he left his house.[17]*
>
> *When the Messenger of God (may God bless him and grant him peace) was given scent he would rub it on himself. "It smells good and is easy to carry," he would say. If he had an excuse not to, he would have made to with touching it with the tip of his finger.[18]*
>
> *The Prophet's (may God bless him and grant him peace) grandson, the blessed Hasan, stated his views regarding his pleasant smell: "The Prophet commanded us to wear the best clothes we could find and the most pleasant scents we could find."[19]*
>
> *His body was clean and he smelt very pleasant. Whether or not he had used scent, his skin smelt more pleasant than the finest perfume. When anyone had close contact with him (shaking hands or enjoying his conversation, friendship and affection), he would perceive that lovely smell all day, and if he touched the head of a child with his blessed hand, that child would be distinguished among the other children.[20]*

Then David got up from the ground. After he had washed, **put on lotions** and changed his clothes... (2 Samuel, 12:20)

Wash and **perfume yourself,** and put on your best clothes. Then go down to the threshing floor... (Ruth, 3:3)

Places of worship smelling pleasant:

The Prophet Muhammad (may God bless him and grant him peace), who attached meticulous attention to cleanliness, wished Muslims to remain in clean places and liked beauties and beautiful scents as a manifestation of God commanded Muslims to keep the mosques clean. The Prophet Muhammad (may God bless him and grant him peace) wanted mosques to have a fragrant odor and a comfortable environment that would give relief to Muslims. For this end, he also made Muslims to incense the mosques. Incensing for the purpose of fragrant odor is also mentioned in the Torah. Below are the related accounts and explanations in the Torah:

> *Camphor (an oil obtained from the camphor tree) or other incense was burned in the Prophet's (may God bless him and grant him peace) general assemblies, and the community would thus be called to rest. On Fridays he commanded pleasant scents to be used.[21]*
>
> *The Messenger of God (may God bless him and grant him peace) would give a pleasant aroma with "Awd al-Gumari" (a species of plant that gives off a pleasant smell when placed over fire).[22]*

... And fragrant incense for the Holy Place. They are to make them just as I commanded you. (Exodus, 31:11)

And burned fragrant incense on it, as the Lord commanded him. (Exodus, 40:27)

Perfume and incense bring joy to the heart. (Proverbs, 27:9)

Aaron must burn fragrant incense on the altar every morning when he tends the lamps. **He must burn incense again** when he lights the lamps at twilight so **incense will burn regularly** before the Lord **for the generations to come.** (Exodus, 30:7-9)

From the basket of bread made without yeast, which is before the Lord, take a loaf, and a cake made with oil, and a wafer. Put all these in the hands of Aaron and his sons and wave them before the Lord as a wave offering. Then take them from their hands and **burn them on the altar along with the burnt offering for a pleasing aroma** to the Lord, an offering made to the Lord by fire. (Exodus, 29:23-25)

The Lord said to Moses, "Tell the believers to bring me an offering. You are to receive the offering for Me from each man whose heart prompts him to give... olive oil for the light; **spices for the anointing oil and for the fragrant incense.**" (Exodus, 25:2, 6)

The cleanliness of places of worship:

One hot day, business owners and workers came to the mosque in their work clothes, and since the mosque was small the air inside became heavy and unpleasant. At this the Messenger of God (may God bless him and grant him peace) said; "It would have been better if you had washed and then come." After that, it became a custom to wash on Fridays.[23]

The Messenger of God's (may God bless him and grant him peace) mosque would be carefully scrubbed and cleaned.[24]

Neither shall he leave the house of his God nor **desecrate it** because he has been dedicated by the anointing oil of his God... **He must not... desecrate My house.** I am the Lord, Who makes them holy. So Moses told this to Aaron and his sons and to all the Israelites. (Leviticus, 21:12, 23-24)

I gave orders to purify the rooms, and then I put back into them the equipment of the house of God, with the grain offerings and the incense. (Nehemiah, 13:9)

The priests went into the house of the Lord to purify it. They brought out to the courtyard of the Lord's house everything unclean that they found in the house of the Lord... (2 Chronicles, 29:16)

On the seventh day **wash your clothes and you will be clean. Then you may come into the camp.** (Numbers, 31:24)

After that, **the priest must wash his clothes and bathe himself with water...** (Numbers, 19:7)

The importance attached to bodily cleanliness:

> *The Prophet Muhammad [may God bless him and grant him peace): "Surely, Islam is pure, therefore be pure, because he can never enter Paradise who is not pure."[25]*
>
> *The Messenger of God (may God bless him and grant him peace) combed his hair and set it right with water, and he then said, "Water is enough for a believer to smell pleasant."[26]*
>
> *Ibn Shuba says in his book Tuhaf al-Uqul, "Cleanliness is one of the virtues of the prophets."[27]*

Naaman's servants went to him and said, "My father, if the prophet had told you to do some great thing, would you not have done it? How much more, then, when he tells you, **'Wash and be cleansed'!"** (2 Kings, 5:13)

... If **I washed myself with soap** and my hands with washing soda. (Job, 9:30)

Wash and make yourselves clean. Take your evil deeds out of my sight! Stop doing wrong. (Isaiah, 1:16)

Make a bronze basin, with its bronze stand, for washing. Place it between the Tent of Meeting and the altar, and put water in it. (Exodus, 30:18)

Depart, depart, go out from there! **Touch no unclean thing! Come out from it and be pure...** (Isaiah, 52:11)

... **His teeth whiter than milk.** (Genesis, 49:12)

Attention to hair and dress:

> *Aisha (ra) relates "When the Messenger of God (may God bless him and grant him peace) combed and oiled his hair..."[28]*
>
> *Tabarsi reports in the Makarim al-Akhlaq: "The Messenger of God (may God bless him and grant him peace) would comb his hair with a special comb known as "madari"... He would usually comb his hair twice a day." He also related that, "After combing his hair, he would leave his comb under his bed."[29]*
>
> *The Prophet (may God bless him and grant him peace) once intended to go to his companions and so he put on his turban and dressed his hairs... He said: "Yes, God loves the actions of His servant who refines his body in order to meet his friends and brothers."[30]*
>
> *The Prophet's (may God bless him and grant him peace) grandson, the blessed Hasan, expressed his views on the subject of clothing: "The Prophet (may God bless him and grant him peace) commanded us to wear the best clothes we had and to use the finest perfumes."[31]*

They (priests) must not shave their heads or let their hair grow long, but they are to keep the **hair of their heads trimmed.** (Ezekiel, 44:20)

Then Moses said to Aaron and his sons Eleazar and Ithamar, **"Do not let your hair become unkempt, and do not tear your clothes."** (Leviticus, 10:6)

The high priest, the one among his brothers who has had the

anointing oil poured on his head and who has been ordained to wear the **priestly garments,** must not let his hair become unkempt or tear his clothes. (Leviticus, 21:10)

Your clothes were of fine linen and **costly fabric and embroidered cloth.** (Ezekiel, 16:13)

For Aaron and his sons, they made tunics of fine linen—**the work of a weaver**—and the turban of fine linen, **the linen** headbands and the undergarments of finely twisted linen. The sash was of finely twisted linen and **blue, purple and scarlet yarn—the work of an embroiderer**—as the Lord commanded Moses. (Exodus, 39:27-29)

Oiling the hair and body:

> *The Messenger of God (may God bless him and grant him peace) would oil his body with many different oils, during which time he would oil his head before his beard and say, "The head comes before the beard."[32]*
>
> *The blessed one would generally oil his body with violet oil and said, "This is the best of all oils."[33]*
>
> *When the Prophet (may God bless him and grant him peace) wish to oil himself he would first oil his eyebrows, then his moustache and then smell, and finally oil his blessed head.[34]*

He poured some of the **anointing oil on Aaron's head** and anointed him to consecrate him. (Leviticus, 8:12)

It is like precious oil poured on the head, running down on the beard, running down on Aaron's beard, down upon the collar of his robes. (Psalm, 133:2)

You prepare a table before me in the presence of my enemies. **You anoint my head with oil...** (Psalm, 23:5)

Let a righteous man strike me—it is a kindness; let him rebuke me—**it is oil on my head.** My head will not refuse it. Yet my prayer is ever against the deeds of evildoers. (Psalm, 141:5)

Foods and Drinks Noted in the Torah

Stew:

> *It is reported in the Makarim that: "The Messenger of God (may God bless him and grant him peace) would generally eat helim (a kind of soup made from cracked wheat, meat and water.) He sometimes preferred to eat helim for the sahr meal."[35]*
>
> *Some of the foods eaten by the Prophet (may God bless him and grant him peace) may be listed as follows: the meat from the foreleg and back of the sheep, chops, kebabs, chicken, bustard, meat soup, sippet, courgettes, olive oil, melon, halwa, honey, dates, chard, fish..."[36]*

While the company of the prophets was meeting with him, Elisha said to his servant, **"Put on the large pot and cook some stew for these men."** (2 Kings, 4:38)

Once when Jacob was cooking some stew, Esau came in from the open country... (Genesis, 25:29)

Meat:

> *Meat was the best food in the sight of the blessed one (the Prophet Muhammad [may God bless him and grant him peace]). He would eat it in gravy... He would eat game... He liked the shoulder, leg and wrist parts of the sheep.* [37]
>
> *In the Makarim it is reported of the Prophet (may God bless him and grant him peace) that: "Meat was the blessed one's favorite food... He would reach for that among the foods on the table and ate chicken and other poultry and birds..."* [38]
>
> *Some of the foods eaten by the Prophet (may God bless him and grant him peace) may be listed as follows: the meat from the foreleg and back of the sheep, chops, kebabs, chicken, bustard, meat soup, sippet, courgettes, olive oil, melon, halwa, honey, dates, chard, fish..."* [39]
>
> *Meat was his favorite food.* [40]

Jacob said to his father, "I am Esau your firstborn. **I have done as you told me. Please sit up and eat some of my game** so that you may give me your blessing." (Genesis, 27:19)

Moses also said, "You will know that it was the Lord when He gives you **meat to eat in the evening** and all the bread you want in the morning. (Exodus, 16:8)

Then he said, "My son, **bring me some of your game to eat,** so that I may give you my blessing." (Genesis, 27:25)

He (Esau) too **prepared some tasty food and brought it to his father.** Then he said to him, "My father, sit up and **eat some of my game,** so that you may give me your blessing." (Genesis, 27:31)

Tell them, "At twilight you will **eat meat,** and in the morning you will be filled with bread. Then you will know that I am the Lord your God." (Exodus, 16:12)

Dates:

> *In the Makarim it is reported that: "When he (the Prophet Muhammad [may God bless him and grant him peace]) fasted, if the time coincided with that of "fresh dates," he would eat only those as iftar... The blessed one's meals generally consisted of dates and water."*[41]
>
> *He loved the Ajwah date best of all dates.*[42]
>
> *Aisha (ra) tells us that: "God's Messenger (may God bless him and grant him peace) ate watermelon with fresh dates."*[43]
>
> *The blessed Jabir relates that: "He would often eat fresh dates and melon, and would say 'These are delicious fruits.'"*[44]

Then they came to Elim, where there were twelve springs and seventy **palm trees,** and they camped there near the water. (Exodus, 15:27)

Then (David) he gave a loaf of bread, **a cake of dates**... and a cake of raisins to each person in the whole crowd of Israelites, both men and women. And all the people went to their homes. (2 Samuel, 6:19)

On the first day you are to take choice fruit from the trees, and **palm fronds,** leafy branches and poplars, and rejoice before the Lord your God for seven days. (Leviticus, 23:40)

Bread:

> *Abu Hazim relates: "I asked whether the people had a sieve in the time of the Prophet (may God bless him and grant him peace). 'I never saw a sieve up to the death of the Messenger,' he said. 'In that case, how did you eat barley bread that had not been sieved?' I asked. He answered, 'We would blow on it, and the husks would fly away. The remaining (bran) we would soften with water and knead.'"[45]*
>
> *According to Ummi Ayman (ra): "The Messenger of God (may God bless him and grant him peace) said, 'Put the bran you have removed back with the rest (the flour), then knead it (and make bread).'"[46]*
>
> *Anas (ra) relates: "The Messenger of God (may God bless him and grant him peace) ate 'nourishing' foods and wore starched clothes. Hasen (who narrated the above from Anas) was asked, 'What is 'nourishing' food?' He answered: 'Rough-milled barley, such that anyone placing it in his mouth could only swallow it with water.'"[47]*
>
> *Ibn 'Abbas relates: "The Messenger of God's (may God bless him and grant him peace) favorite food was sippet made from bread and sippet made from hays (a well-known Arab dish.)"[48]*

Solomon's daily provisions were **thirty cores of fine flour and sixty cores of meal,** ten head of stall-fed cattle, twenty of pasture-fed cattle and a hundred sheep and goats, as well as deer, gazelles, roebucks and choice fowl. (1 Kings, 4:22-23)

Moses also said, "You will know that it was the Lord when He gives you meat to eat in the evening and **all the bread you want in the morning."** (Exodus, 16:8)

From the **basket of bread made without yeast,** which is before the Lord, take a loaf, and a cake made with oil, and a wafer. Put all these in the hands of Aaron and his sons. (Exodus, 29:23)

At twilight you will eat meat, and in the morning you will be **filled with bread.** Then you will know that I am the Lord your God. (Exodus, 16:12)

So he did what the Lord had told him... The ravens brought him **bread** and meat in the morning and bread and meat in the evening, and he drank from the brook. (1 Kings, 17:5-6)

But he insisted so strongly that they did go with him and entered his house. He prepared a meal for them, **baking bread without yeast,** and they ate. (Genesis, 19:3)

Take **wheat** and **barley,** beans and lentils, millet and spelt; put them in a storage jar and use them to **make bread for yourself. You are to eat it** during the 390 days you lie on your side. Weigh out twenty shekels of food to eat each day and eat it at set times. (Ezekiel, 4:9-10)

Moses said to Aaron and his remaining sons, Eleazar and Ithamar, "Take the grain offering left over from the offerings made to the Lord by fire and **eat it** prepared without yeast **beside the altar, for it is most holy."** (Leviticus, 10:12)

Along with his fellowship offering of thanksgiving he is to present an offering with **cakes of bread made with yeast.** (Leviticus, 7:13)

Grapes and grape molasses:

> *Narrated from Ibn Omar: They asked, "What is grape essence?" "Drink," he (the Prophet Muhammad [may God bless him and grant him peace]) said. "That is what they call the essence: They boil the must, two out of three parts disappear, and one part remains."*[49]
>
> *Ibn Zayd relates: "The blessed Prophet (may God bless him and grant him peace) loved grapes and melon among fruits."*[50]

If you follow My decrees and are careful to obey My commands, I will send you rain in its season, and the ground will yield its crops and the trees of the field their fruit. Your threshing will continue until grape harvest and **the grape harvest will continue until planting,** and **you will**

eat all the food you want and live in safety in your land. (Leviticus, 26:3-5)

For the Lord your God is bringing you into a good land—a land with streams and pools of water, with springs flowing in the valleys and hills; a land with wheat and barley, **vines** and fig trees, pomegranates, olive oil and honey. (Deuteronomy, 8:7-8)

When they reached the Valley of Eshcol, **they cut off a branch bearing a single cluster of grapes.** Two of them carried it on a pole between them, along with some pomegranates and figs. (Numbers, 13:23)

Honey:

> *Haysama ibn Aswad relates from 'Abd God: "The Prophet (may God bless him and grant him peace) said, 'Draw health from the Qur'an and from honey.'"[51]*
>
> *He loved sweet things and honey.[52]*
>
> *The Prophet (may God bless him and grant him peace) loved such drinks as honey sherbet, and date and dried-grape must.[53]*
>
> *Of all sherbets he loved honey sherbet the best.[54]*

Then their father Israel said to them, "If it must be, then do this: Put some of the **best products of the land** in your bags and take them down to the man as a gift—a little balm and a little **honey,** some spices and myrrh, some pistachio nuts and almonds. (Genesis, 43:11)

... They also brought wheat and barley, flour and roasted grain, beans and lentils, **honey** and curds, sheep, and cheese from cows' milk for David and his people to eat. For they said, "The people have become hungry and tired and thirsty in the desert." (2 Samuel, 17:28-29)

And I am come down... to bring them up out of that land into a good and spacious land, **a land flowing with** milk and **honey...** (Exodus, 3:8)

... The children of Israel gave in abundance... oil and **honey** and all that the fields produced. They brought a great amount, a tithe of everything. (2 Chronicles, 31:5)

Milk:

> *The Prophet Muhammad [may God bless him and grant him peace]: "Whenever God gives someone milk to drink, let that person pray 'My Lord, make this milk plentiful for us and give us more milk.' I know of no fitter food and drink than milk."[55]*
>
> *Of all drinks, he loved milk the best.[56]*

He asked for water, and she **gave him milk**... (Judges, 5:25)

... She **opened a skin of milk, gave him a drink,** and covered him up. (Judges, 4:19)

... **A land flowing with milk** and honey, **the most beautiful of all lands...** (Ezekiel, 20:6)

Pomegranates:

> *It is related in the Makarim that: "The blessed one's (the Prophet Muhammad [may God bless him and grant him peace]) favorite fruits were melon and pomegranate... He often ate pomegranates one by one."*[57]
>
> *Al-Kulayni reports Omar ibn Aban al-Kulayni as saying: "I heard that Imam Baqir and Imam Sadiq said 'The Prophet (may God bless him and grant him peace) loved the pomegranate best of all the fruits of the earth.'"*[58]

When they reached the Valley of Eshcol, they cut off a branch bearing a single cluster of grapes. Two of them carried it on a pole between them, along with some **pomegranates** and figs. (Numbers, 13:23)

Is there yet any seed left in the barn? Until now, the vine and the fig tree, the **pomegranate** and the olive tree have not borne fruit. "From this day on I will bless you." (Haggai, 2:19)

The use of olive oil:

> *The Prophet Muhammad (may God bless him and grant him peace): "Eat and use olive oil. Because that oil is blessed.*[59]

WISDOM AND SOUND ADVICE FROM THE TORAH

... Your food was fine flour, honey and **olive oil.** You became very beautiful and rose to be a queen. (Ezekiel, 16:13)

This is what you are to do to consecrate them, so they may serve Me as priests: Take a young bull and two rams without defect. And from fine wheat flour, without yeast, make bread, and cakes mixed **with oil,** and wafers spread **with oil.** (Exodus, 29:1-2)

If he offers it as an expression of thankfulness, then along with this thank offering he is to offer cakes of bread made without yeast and mixed **with oil,** wafers made without yeast and **spread with oil,** and cakes of fine flour well-kneaded and mixed with oil. (Leviticus, 7:12)

If your grain offering is prepared on a griddle, it is to be made of fine flour mixed with oil, and without yeast. Crumble it and **pour oil on it;** it is a grain offering. If your grain offering is cooked in a pan, it is to be made of fine flour and **oil.** (Leviticus, 2:5-7)

Other Practices in the Qur'an Compatible with the Sunnah of the Prophet Muhammad (May God Bless Him and Grant Him Peace)

The use of carnelian:

> *The Prophet (may God bless him and grant him peace) used a seal, on which were written the words "Muhammad, the Messenger of God," in three lines, to sign the bottom of the letters he sent to the rulers of neighboring states. The words were carved onto carnelian stone held in a silver clasp. The Prophet (may God bless him and grant him peace) wore this on his finger in the form of a ring. He would remove it in order to seal official documents he dictated, and he would replace it on his finger once the papers had been sealed.* ⁶⁰

They fashioned the breast piece—the work of a skilled craftsman. They made it like the ephod: of gold, and of blue, purple and scarlet yarn, and of finely twisted linen. It was square—a span long and a span wide—and folded double. Then they mounted four rows of precious stones on it. In the first row there was a ruby, a topaz and a beryl; in the second row a turquoise, a sapphire and an emerald; in the third row a jacinth, an **agate** and an amethyst; in the fourth row a chrysolite, an **onyx** and a jasper. They were mounted in gold filigree settings... so that the breast piece would not swing out from the ephod—**as the Lord commanded Moses.** (Exodus, 39:8-13, 21)

Fashion a breast piece for making decisions—the work of a skilled craftsman. Make it like the ephod: of gold, and of blue, purple and scarlet yarn, and of finely twisted linen. It is to be square—a span long and a span wide—and folded double. Then mount four rows of precious stones on it. In the first row there shall be a ruby, a topaz and a beryl; in the second row a turquoise, a sapphire and an emerald; in the third row a jacinth, an **agate** and an amethyst; in the fourth row a chrysolite, an **onyx** and a jasper. Mount them in gold filigree settings... Make two more gold rings and attach them to the bottom of the shoulder pieces on the front of the ephod, close to the seam just above the waistband of the ephod. (Exodus, 28:15-20, 27)

The use of a signet ring:

> *Anas Malik (ra) says: "The Prophet (may God bless him and grant him peace) had a ring made of silver and its (inlaid) gem was also of silver. When the Prophet (may God bless him and grant him peace) wanted to write to the leaders of foreign states, he ordered a seal-ring to be made, the brightness of which is still before my eyes. The inscription engraved on the ring of the Prophet (may God bless him and grant him peace) was 'Muhammad Rasul God,' of which in the first line was engraved 'Muhammad,' in the second line 'Rasul,' and in the third line 'God'."*[61]

A stone was brought and placed over the mouth of the den, and the king **sealed it with his own signet ring** and with the rings of his nobles, so that Daniel's situation might not be changed. (Daniel, 6:17)

So the king took **his signet ring** from his finger and gave it to Haman... These were written in the name of King Xerxes himself and **sealed with his own ring.** (Esther, 3:10, 12)

Now write another decree in the king's name... and **seal it with the king's signet ring**—for no document written in the king's name and **sealed with his ring** can be revoked. (Esther, 8:8)

PASSAGES FROM THE PSALMS AND THE PROVERBS

Psalms

Blessed is the man who does not go in the company of the wicked, or take his place in the way of sinners, or sit in the seat of mockers. But **whose delight is in the law of the Lord, and whose mind is on His law day and night.** He shall be like a tree planted by the streams of water that brings forth its fruit in its season, whose leaf also does not wither. **Whatever he does shall prosper.** The wicked are not so, but are like the chaff which the wind drives away. Therefore the wicked shall not stand in the judgment, nor sinners in the congregation of the righteous. **For the Lord watches over the way of the righteous,** but the way of the wicked will perish. (Psalms, 1:1-6)

Why do the nations rage, and the peoples plot a vain thing? The kings of the earth set themselves, and the rulers take counsel together, against the Lord... Now therefore be wise, you kings. Be instructed, you judges of the earth. **Give worship to the Lord with fear, and rejoice with trembling.** (Psalms, 2:1-2,10-11)

Lord, how many are my foes? How many rise up against me! Many are saying of me, 'There is no salvation for him in God. And **You, O God, are a shield for me,** my honor, and lifter up of my head. I cried to the Lord with my voice, and He heard me... I took my rest in sleep, and then again I was awake; for the **Lord was my support.** I will not fear the tens of thousands drawn up against me on every side... **Save me, my God!... Salvation comes from the Lord; Your blessing is on Your people**[1] . (Psalms, 3:1-8)

Hear me when I call, O my righteousness God: Give me relief from my distress. Have mercy on me, and hear my prayer. You sons of men, how long... will you love vanity, and seek after falsehood?... Stand in awe, and don't sin. Search your own heart on your bed... **Put your trust in God. Let the light of Your face**[2] **shine on us.** You have put gladness in my heart... I will take my rest on my bed in peace, because **You only, Lord, keep me safe**. (Psalms, 4:1-8)

Hear my words, O Lord, consider my sighing. My voice will come to You in the morning, O Lord; in the morning will I send my prayer to You, and wait in expectation... Neither shall the wicked dwell near You. The arrogant cannot stand in Your presence... bloodthirsty and deceitful men the Lord dislikes and He is not pleased with them. But as for me, I will come into Your house [a place where God is worshipped], in reverence will I bow down toward Your inmost room... **Lead me, O Lord, in Your righteousness... make straight Your way before me.** Not a word from their mouth

---

1. Those who believe.
2. *Jamal* of Allah; *Noor* (Light) of Allah.

can be trusted; their heart is filled with destruction. Their throat is an open tomb. They flatter with their tongue... **O Lord; let their evil designs be the cause of their fall;** let them be forced out by all their sins; because they have gone against Your authority. But **let all who take refuge in You be glad; let them ever sing for joy. Spread Your protection over them, that those who love Your name may rejoice in You.** For surely, **O Lord, You bless the righteous; You surround them with Your favor as with a shield.** (Psalms 5:1-12)

Oh Lord... do not discipline me in Your wrath. **Have mercy on me,** O Lord, for I am weak: heal me, O Lord, for my bones are troubled. My soul is in anguish... And **save me for Your loving kindness' sake.** (Psalms, 6:1-4)

O Lord my God, I take refuge in You; save and deliver me from all who pursue me... **The Lord will be judge[3] of the peoples;** judge me, O Lord, because of my righteousness, according my integrity. O let the evil of the evildoer come to an end, but give strength to the upright: for men's minds and hearts are tested by God by righteousness. **My shield is with God, Who saves the upright in heart. God is a righteous judge...** Behold, he travails with iniquity; yes, he has conceived mischief and brought forth falsehood. He made a pit, and dug it, and is fallen into the ditch which he made. His wrongdoing will come back to him, and his violent behavior will come down on his head. **I will praise the Lord according to His righteousness: and will sing praise to the name of Lord the Most High.** (Psalms, 7:1, 7-11, 14-17)

O Lord, how majestic is Your name in all the earth, You have set Your glory above the heavens! When I consider Your heavens,

---

3. Allah's attribute of *al-Adl* (the Utterly Just) is meant here.

the work of Your fingers[4], the Moon and the stars, which You have ordained. What is man, that you keep him in mind? The son of man that you take into account?... crowned him with glory and honor. You have made him ruler over the works of Your hands [Your Creations]; You have put all things under his feet; all sheep and oxen, and all the beasts of the field; the birds of the air and the fish of the sea, and whatever goes through the deep waters of the seas. **O Lord our Lord, how excellent is Your name in all the earth!** (Psalms, 8:1-9)

I will give You praise, O Lord, with all my heart; I will make clear all the wonder of Your works. I will be glad and have delight in You: I will make a song of praise to Your name, O Most High... You gave approval to my right and my cause... **judging in righteousness...** Their cities You have destroyed. You have put an end to their name for ever and ever. But **the Lord shall endure for ever:** He has prepared his throne for judgment. And **He will be the judge of the world in righteousness,** giving true decisions for the peoples. The Lord will be a high tower[5] for those who are crushed down, a high tower in times of trouble; **and those who have knowledge of Your name will put their faith in You; because You, Lord, have ever given Your help to those who were waiting for You**. Make songs of praise to the Lord: make His doings clear to the people... He doesn't forget the cry of the afflicted. Have mercy on me, O Lord... So that I may make clear all Your praise... **I will be glad because of Your salvation.** The nations have gone down into the pit they have dug; in their secret net is

---
4. Allah's title of *Sani* (The Artist, He Who creates infinite beauties in His artistry) is described by use of simile.
5. One of the glorious names of Allah is *Malja* (He in Whom refuge is sought). A reference to the manifestation of Allah's title of *Malja*.

their foot taken. **The Lord is known by His justice;** the wicked are ensnared by the work of their hands. The wicked shall be turned into the underworld [sheol, hell], and all the nations that forget God. **For the poor will not be forgotten to the end; the hopes of those in need will not be crushed forever.** (Psalms, 9:1-18)

O Lord!... The wicked man... boasts of the cravings of his heart... In his pride the wicked does not seek Him [God]. His ways are firm at all times; Your judgments are far above out of his sight... He says to himself, "Nothing will shake me; I will... never have trouble." His mouth is full of curses and lies and threats; trouble and evil are under his tongue. He lies in wait near the villages. From ambushes, he murders the innocent. His eyes are secretly set against the helpless. He keeps himself in a secret place like a lion in his hole, waiting to put his hands on the poor man, and pulling him into his net... But You, O God, do see trouble and grief; You consider it to take it in hand. **The poor commits himself to You; You are the helper of the child who has no father... You hear, O Lord, the desire of the afflicted: You encourage them, and You listen to their cry, defending the fatherless and the oppressed, in order that man, who is of the earth, may terrify no more.** (Psalms, 10:1-18)

In the Lord I take refuge... His eyes are watching and testing the children of men. The Lord examines the righteous, but the wicked and him **who loves violence He dislikes and is not pleased**. On the evil-doer He will send down fire and flames, and a burning wind; with these will their cup be full. **For the Lord is upright; He is a lover of righteousness: the upright will see His face.**[6] (Psalms, 11:1-7)

---

6. A reference to devout believers' seeing Allah's beauty as a blessing of paradise.

Help, Lord, for there is no saint; there is no more faith among the children of men. Everyone lies to his neighbor: their flattering lips speak with deception. May the Lord silence all flattering lips and every boastful tongue. They have said, with our tongues will we overcome; our lips are ours: Who is master over us?... **The words of the Lord are true words**: like silver tested by fire and burned clean seven times. **You will keep them, O Lord, You will keep them safe from this generation for ever.** The wicked freely strut bout when what is vile is honored among men. (Psalms, 12:1-8)

Look on me... **O Lord... I trust in Your loving-kindness; my heart will be glad in Your salvation...** I will sing to the Lord, because He has been good to me. (Psalms, 13:3-6)

... He **who goes on his way uprightly, doing righteousness,** and saying **what is true in his heart**; **whose tongue is not false,** who **does no evil** to his friend, and **does not take away the good name of his neighbor. Who gives honor to those who have the fear of the Lord,** turning away from Him who has not the Lord's approval. He who takes an oath against himself, and makes no change. He **who does not put out his money at interest**, or for payment give false decisions against men **who have done no wrong**. **He who does these things will never be shaken.** (Psalms, 15:1-5)

Keep me safe, O God: for you I take refuge. I said to the Lord, **You are my Lord: I have no good but You.** Their sorrows will be increased who go after other gods: I will not... take their names on my lips. Lord, You have assigned my portion and my cup; **You are the supporter of my right.** Fair are the places marked out for me; I have a noble heritage. I will give praise to the Lord Who has been my guide; even at night my heart instructs me. **I have set the Lord always before me. Because He is at my right[7], I will not be shaken.** Because of this **my heart is glad, and my glory is full of joy; my body also will rest secure, because You will not abandon my soul in the underworld [sheol, hell]** nor will you let your faithful one see decay... **You have made known to me the path of life [paradise]; you will fill me with joy in your presence, with eternal pleasures at your right hand.**[8] (Psalms, 16:1-11)

---

7. A description of Allah being the Protector by way of simile.
8. Allah's blessings, His bestowal of joy, peace and security on believers, are described by way of simile.

Hear my prayer—it does not rise from deceit lips. May my vindication come from You; may Your eyes see what is right. You have put my heart to the test, searching me in the night; You have put me to the test and seen no evil purpose in me; I have purposed that my mouth shall not transgress. As for the works of men, by Your words I have kept myself from the ways of the violent. **My steps have held to Your paths; my feet have not slipped I call on You, O God,** for You will answer me... **Show the wonder of Your great love,** You Who save by your right hand those who take refuge in You from their foes. Keep me as the apple of the eye; hide me under the shadow of Your wings[9] from the wicked evildoers who assail me, from my mortal enemies who surround me. They are shut up in their fat: with their mouths they say words of pride. They have tracked me down, they now surround me with eyes alert, to throw me to the ground. He is like a lion that is greedy of its prey, and as a young lion lurking in secret places. **O Lord... save me from the wicked...** whose portion is in this life. (Psalms, 17:1-5)

I love You, O Lord, my strength. The Lord is my firmament, my fortress, and my savior; my Lord, my firmament, in Whom I take refuge. He is my shield and the strength of my salvation, my stronghold. In my distress I called to the Lord; I cried to my God for help... He heard my voice... Then the earth shook and trembled and the bases of the mountains were moved and shaking... He took me, pulling me out of great waters. He delivered me from... them that hated me; for they were too mighty for me. They came on me in the day of my trouble; but **the Lord was my support.** He took me out into a wide place; **He was my savior be-**

---

9. A description of Allah being the Protector by way of simile.

WISDOM AND SOUND ADVICE FROM THE TORAH

cause He had delight in me. **The Lord gives me the reward of my righteousness, because my hands are clean before Him.** For I have kept the ways of the Lord; I have not done evil by turning from my God. **For all His decisions were before me, and I did not put away His laws from me.** And I was upright before Him, and I kept myself from sin. Because of this the Lord has given me the reward of my righteousness, because my hands are clean in His eyes. On him who has mercy You will have mercy... **For You are the savior of those who are in trouble;** but eyes full of pride will be made low. **You, O Lord, will be my light;** by You, the dark will be made bright for me... As for Lord, His way is completely good; the word of the Lord is tested; **He is a shield [protector] for all those who take refuge in Him.** For who is God but the Lord? Or who is God but our God? God puts a strong band about me, guiding me in a straight way. He makes my feet like roes' feet, and puts me on high places... You have made my steps wide under me, so that my feet are kept from slipping... The Lord is living; **praise be to my God and let God of my salvation be honored...** He rescues me from my enemies. You lift me up above those who rise up against me. You deliver me from the violent man. Because of this **I will give You praise, O Lord,** among the nations, and will make a song of praise to Your name. Great salvation does He give to His king. (Psalms, 18:1-49)

The heavens declare the glory of God; the arch of the sky makes clear the work of His hands[10]. Day after day it sends out its word, and night after night it gives knowledge... It [the Sun] rises at one end of the heavens and makes its circuit to the other; nothing is

---

10. Allah's title of Sani (The Artist, He Who creates infinite beauties in His artistry) is described by use of simile.

hidden from its heat. **The law of the Lord is good, giving new life to the soul: the statutes of the Lord are trustworthy,** making wise the simple. The orders of the Lord are right, making glad the heart: **the rule of the Lord is holy, giving light to the eyes. The fear of the Lord is clean, and has no end; the decisions of the Lord are true and full of righteousness.** More to be desired are they than gold, even than much shining gold; sweeter than the dropping honey. By them is Your servant made conscious of danger, and in keeping them there is great reward. Who has full knowledge of his errors? Make me clean from secret evil. Keep Your servant back from sins of pride; let them not have rule over me: then will I be upright and innocent from the great transgression. **Let the words of my mouth and the thoughts of my heart be pleasing before You, O Lord, my strength and my salvation.** (Psalms, 19:1-14)

May the Lord answer you when you are in distress... protect you. May He send you help... Some trust in chariots, and some in horses; but **we will make mention of the name of God our God.** They are bent down and made low; but we have been lifted up... **Lord... Answer us when we call!** (Psalms, 20:1-9)

The king will be glad in **Your strength, O Lord... You have granted him the desire of his heart... You welcomed him with rich blessings...** For the king has faith in the Lord, and through the mercy of the Most High he will not be moved... their thoughts were bitter against You: they had an evil design in their minds, which they were not able to put into effect... **Be exalted, O Lord, in Your strength; we will sing and praise Your might.** (Psalms, 21:1-13)

Our fathers had **faith in You:** they had faith and You were their saviour. **They cried to You and were saved; they trusted in You,** and were not put to shame... But it was You Who took care of me from the day of my birth: You gave me faith even in my mother's arms. From birth I was cast upon You; from my mother's womb You have been my God... **O Lord: O my strength**... Be my saviour from the lion's mouth; let me go free from the horns of the wild oxen. (Psalms, 22:4-21)

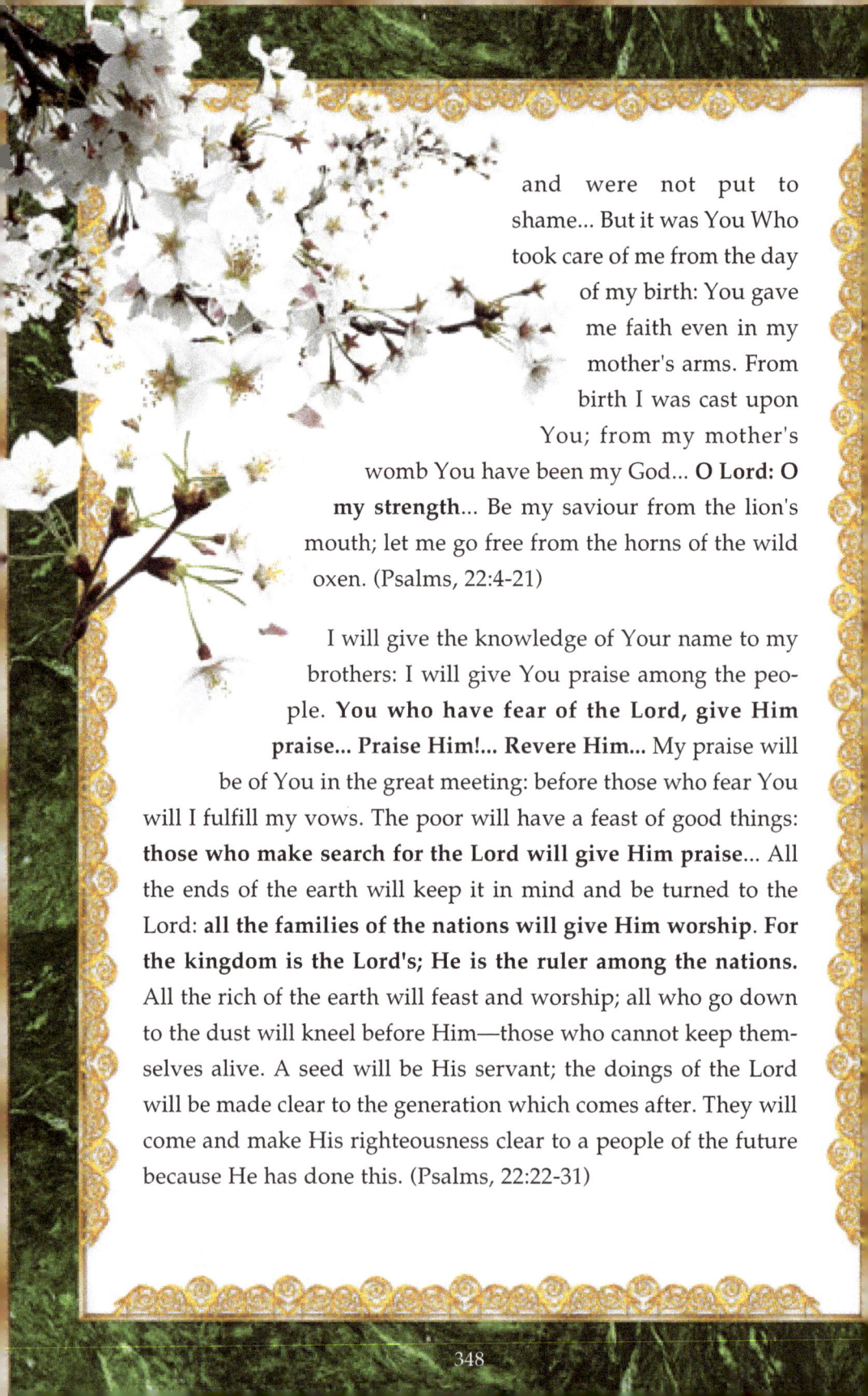

I will give the knowledge of Your name to my brothers: I will give You praise among the people. **You who have fear of the Lord, give Him praise... Praise Him!... Revere Him...** My praise will be of You in the great meeting: before those who fear You will I fulfill my vows. The poor will have a feast of good things: **those who make search for the Lord will give Him praise**... All the ends of the earth will keep it in mind and be turned to the Lord: **all the families of the nations will give Him worship**. **For the kingdom is the Lord's; He is the ruler among the nations.** All the rich of the earth will feast and worship; all who go down to the dust will kneel before Him—those who cannot keep themselves alive. A seed will be His servant; the doings of the Lord will be made clear to the generation which comes after. They will come and make His righteousness clear to a people of the future because He has done this. (Psalms, 22:22-31)

The Lord takes care of me[11]; I will not be without any good thing. He makes a resting-place for me in the green fields: He is my guide by the quiet waters. **He gives new life to my soul: He is my guide in the ways of righteousness because of His name.** Yes, though I go through the valley of deep shade, **I will have no fear of evil; for You are with me...** Truly, blessing and mercy will be with me all the days of my life; and **I will have a place in the house of the Lord all my days.** (Psalms, 23:1-6)

The earth is the Lord's, with all its wealth; the world and all the people living in it. For **He founded it upon the seas and established it upon the waters.** (Psalms, 24:1-2)

He who has clean hands and a true heart; whose desire has not gone out to foolish things, who has not taken a false oath. He will have blessing from the Lord, and righteousness from the God of his salvation. (Psalms, 24:4-5)

To You, O Lord, my soul is lifted up. **O my God, I have put my faith in You...** Let no servant of Yours be put to shame; may those be shamed who transgress without cause. Make Your steps clear to me, **O Lord; give me knowledge of Your ways.** Be my guide and teacher in the true way; for **You are the God of my salvation;** I am waiting for Your word all the day. O Lord... Remember not the sins of my youth and my rebellious ways[12]; **let Your memory of me be full of mercy, O Lord, because of Your righteousness.** Good and upright is the Lord: so He will be the teacher of sinners in the way. He guides the humble in what is right and teaches

---

11. Allah is He Who shows the way to His servants and bestows salvation on them.
12. In the sense of believers praying to Allah "for their evils to be hidden and their errors forgiven."

them his way. All the ways of the Lord are mercy and good faith for those who keep His agreement and His witness. Because of Your name, O Lord, let me have forgiveness for my sin... **If a man has the fear of the Lord, He shall instruct him in the way that He shall choose. His soul will be full of good things... The secret of the Lord is with those in whose hearts is the fear of Him**; He will make His agreement clear to them. My eyes are turned to the Lord at all times; for He will take my feet out of the net. Be turned to me, and have mercy on me; for I am troubled and have no helper... O take me out of my sorrows... and take away all my sins. O keep my soul, and take me out of danger... for **I have put my faith in You.** For my clean and upright ways keep me safe, because **my hope is in You**. (Psalms, 25:1-21)

O Lord, be my judge, for my behaviour has been upright: I have trusted in the Lord without wavering. Put me in the scales, O Lord, so that I may be tested; try my heart and my mind. For **Your mercy is before my eyes;** and **I have gone in the way of Your good faith.** I do not sit with deceitful men, nor do I consort with hypocrites. I abhor the assembly of evildoers and refuse to sit with the wicked... O Lord; That I may give out the voice of praise, and make public all the wonders which You have done. **Lord... the resting place of Your glory has been dear to me.** Do not take away my soul along with sinners, my life with bloodthirsty men, in whose hands are wicked schemes, whose right hands are full of bribes. But as for me, I will go on in my upright ways: **be my saviour, and have mercy on me.** I have a safe resting-place for my feet; in the great assembly **I will praise the Lord.** (Psalms, 26:1-12)

The Lord is my light and my salvation; who is then a cause of fear to me? **The Lord is the strength of my life;** who is a danger to me? When evil-doers, even my haters, came on me to put an end to me, they were broken and put to shame. Even if an army came against me with its tents, my heart would have no fear: if war was made on me, my faith would not be moved. **One prayer have I made to the Lord, and this is my heart's desire; that I may have a place in the House of the Lord all the days of my life, looking on His glory, and getting wisdom...** For in the time of trouble **He will keep me safe...** He will keep me from men's eyes; high on a rock He will put me. I will make offerings of joy in His tent[13]; I will make a song, truly I will make a song of praise to the Lord... O **Lord; be merciful to me and answer me.** When You said, make search for My face[14], my heart said to You, for Your face will I make my search. Let not Your face be covered from me [do not withhold Your approval from me]. **You have been my help: do not give me up or take Your support from me, O God of my salvation.** Though my father and mother forsake me, the Lord will receive me. Make Your way clear to me, O Lord, guiding me by the right way, because of my haters. Do not turn me over to the desire of my foes, for false witnesses rise up against me, breathing out violence. I am still confident of this: I will see the goodness of the Lord in the land of the living. **Let your hope be in the Lord: take heart and be strong; yes, let your hope be in the Lord.** (Psalms, 27:1-14)

To you I call, **O Lord my strength...** Hear my cry for mercy as I call to You for help... Do not drag me away with the wicked, with

---

13. A place where Allah is worshiped.
14. Allah's approval, Allah's pleasure.

WISDOM AND SOUND ADVICE FROM THE TORAH

those who do evil, who speak cordially with their neighbors but harbor malice in their hearts. Repay them for their deeds and for their evil work; repay them for what their hands have done and bring back upon them what they deserve. Since they show no regard for the works of the Lord... He will tear them down and never build them up again. **Praise be to the Lord, for He has heard my cry for mercy. The Lord is my strength and my shield [my]; my heart trusts in Him, and I am helped.** My heart leaps for joy and I will give thanks to Him in song. **The Lord is the strength of His people...** (Psalms, 28:1-8)

Ascribe to the Lord... give to the Lord glory and strength. Ascribe to the Lord the glory due His name; worship the Lord in the splendor of His Holiness... The voice of the Lord is powerful; the voice of the Lord is majestic... in the House of God, all cry, **"Glory!"**... (Psalms, 29:1-9)

I will exalt You, O Lord, for You lifted me out of the depths and did not let my enemies gloat over me. O Lord my God, I called to You for help and **You healed me.** O Lord... You spared me from going down into the pit [hell]. Sing to the Lord, you saints of His; praise His Holy name... When I felt secure, I said, "I will never be shaken." O Lord, when You favored me, You made my mountain stand firm... **be merciful to me O Lord, be my help**." You turned my wailing into dancing; **You removed my sackcloth and clothed me with joy, that my heart may sing to You and not be silent.** O Lord my God, I will give You thanks forever... (Psalms, 30:1-12)

In You, O Lord, I have taken refuge; let me never be put to shame; deliver me in Your righteousness... come quickly to my rescue... save me. Since You are my strength and my fortress, for the sake of Your name lead and guide me. Free me from the trap that is set for me, for You are my refuge. Into Your ways I commit my spirit; redeem me, O Lord, God of truth. I dislike those who cling to worthless idols; **I trust in the Lord. I will be glad and rejoice in Your love,** for You saw my affliction and knew the anguish of my soul. You have not handed me over to the enemy but have set my feet in a spacious place... **But I trust in You, O Lord;** I say, "**You are my God.**" My times are in Your hands [in Your approval, Your might]; deliver me from my enemies and from those who pursue me. Let Your face [Your light] shine on Your servant; save me in your unfailing love. Let me not be put to shame, O Lord, for I have cried out to you; Let the wicked be ashamed, and let them be silent in the grave [sheol, hell]. Let their lying lips be silenced, for with pride and contempt they speak arrogantly against the righteous. **How great is Your goodness,** which You have for those who fear You, which You bestow in the sight of men on those who take refuge in You. In the shelter of Your presence You hide them from the intrigues of men; in Your dwelling You keep them safe from accusing tongues. **Praise be to the Lord, for He showed His wonderful love to me** when I was in a besieged city... **Love the Lord,** all His saints! The Lord preserves the faithful, but the proud He pays back in full. Be strong and take heart, **all you who hope in the Lord.** (Psalms, 31:1-24)

Blessed is he whose transgressions are forgiven, whose sins are covered. Blessed is the man whose sin the Lord does not count against him and in whose spirit is no deceit... You are my hiding place; **You will protect me from trouble and surround me with songs of deliverance**... Many are the woes of the wicked, but the **Lord's unfailing love surrounds the man who trusts in Him. Rejoice in the Lord and be glad, you righteous;** sing, all you who are upright in heart! (Psalms, 32:1-11)

Sing joyfully to the Lord, You righteous; it is fitting for the upright to praise Him. **Praise the Lord** with the harp; make music to Him on the ten-stringed lyre. Sing to Him a new song; play skillfully, and shout for joy. For the word of the Lord is right and true; And all His work is in faithfulness. **The Lord loves righteousness and justice; the earth is full of His unfailing love**. By the word of the Lord were the heavens made... He gathers the waters of the sea together as a heap; He puts the deep into storehouses. **Let all the earth fear the Lord; let all the people of the world revere Him.** For He spoke, and it came to be; He commanded, and it stood firm. The Lord foils the plans of the nations; He thwarts the purposes of the peoples. But the plans of the Lord stand firm forever... Blessed is the nation whose God is the Lord... Lord... sees all mankind... **He Who forms the hearts of all, Who considers everything they do.** No king is saved by the size of his army; no warrior escapes by His great strength. A horse is a vain hope for deliverance; despite all its great strength it cannot save. **But the eyes of the Lord[15] are on those who fear Him, on those whose hope is in His unfailing love,** to deliver them from death and keep them alive in famine. **We wait in hope for the Lord; He is our help and our shield [protector].** In Him our hearts rejoice, for we trust in His Holy name. **May Your unfailing love rest upon us, O Lord, as we put our hope in You.** (Psalms, 33:1-22)

I will extol the Lord at all times; His praise will always be on my lips. My soul will boast in the Lord; let the afflicted hear and rejoice. **Glorify the Lord with me; let us exalt His name together.** I sought the Lord, and He answered me; He delivered me from all my fears. Those who look to Him are radiant; their faces are never covered with shame. This poor man called, and the

---

15. A description by way of simile of the grace of Allah, His protection of believers.

Lord heard him; He saved him out of all his troubles. The angel of the Lord encamps around those who fear Him, and He delivers them... **the Lord is good;** blessed is the man who takes refuge in Him. **Fear the Lord... for those who fear Him lack nothing.** The lions may grow weak and hungry, but those who seek the Lord lack no good thing. Come, my children, listen to me; I will teach you the fear of the Lord. Whoever of you loves life and desires to see many good days, keep your tongue from evil and your lips from speaking lies. Turn from evil and do good; seek peace and pursue it. The eyes of the Lord are on the righteous and His ears[16] listen to their cry. Lord is against those who do evil, to cut off the memory of them from the earth. The righteous cry out, and the Lord hears them; **He delivers them from all their troubles...** Evil will slay the wicked; the foes of the righteous will be condemned. **The Lord redeems His servants; no one will be condemned who takes refuge in Him.** (Psalms, 34:1-22)

My soul will rejoice in the Lord and delight in his salvation. My whole being will exclaim, "Who is like You, O Lord? You rescue the poor from those too strong for them, the poor and needy from those who rob them."... **I will give You thanks in the great assembly; among throngs of people I will praise You...** They do not speak peaceably, but devise false accusations against those who live quietly in the land. (Psalms, 35:9-20)

The sin of the evil-doer says in his heart, there is no fear of God before his eyes. For in his own eyes he flatters himself too much to detect or hate his sin. The words of his mouth are wicked and deceitful; he has ceased to be wise and to do good. Even on his bed he plots evil; he commits himself to a sinful course and does not reject what is wrong. **Your love, O Lord, reaches to the heav-**

---

16. A description by way of simile of the grace of Allah, His protection of believers.

ens, Your faithfulness to the skies. Your righteousness is like the mighty mountains, Your justice like the great deep. O Lord, You preserve both man and animal. **How priceless is Your unfailing love!** Both high and low among men find refuge in the shadow of Your wings.[17] They feast on the abundance of Your house; You give them drink from Your river of delights. **For with you is the fountain of life; in Your light we see light.** Continue Your love to those who know You, Your righteousness to the upright in heart. May the foot of the proud not come against me, nor the hand of the wicked drive me away. (Psalms, 36:1-11)

Do not fret because of evil men or be envious of those who do wrong; for like the grass they will soon wither, like green plants they will soon die away. Trust in the Lord and do good; dwell in the land and enjoy safe pasture. **Delight yourself in the Lord and He will give you the desires of your heart. Commit your way to the Lord; trust in Him and He will do this: He will make your righteousness shine like the dawn, the justice of your cause like the noonday sun.** Be still before the Lord and wait patiently

---

17. A description by way of simile of the grace of Allah, His protection of believers.

WISDOM AND SOUND ADVICE FROM THE TORAH

for Him; do not fret when men succeed in their ways, when they carry out their wicked schemes. **Refrain from anger and turn from wrath; do not fret—it leads only to evil.** For evil men will be cut off, but those who hope in the Lord will inherit the land. A little while, and the wicked will be no more; though you look for them, they will not be found. But **the meek will inherit the land and enjoy great peace**. The wicked plot against the righteous and gnash their teeth at them... Better the little that the righteous have than the wealth of many wicked; for the power of the wicked will be broken, but the Lord upholds the righteous. **The days of the blameless are known to the Lord, and their inheritance will endure forever. In times of disaster they will not wither; in days of famine they will enjoy plenty.** But the wicked will perish: **The Lord's enemies will be like the beauty of the fields, they will vanish—vanish like smoke.** The wicked borrow and do not repay, but the righteous give generously... If the Lord delights in a man's way, He makes his steps firm; though he stumble, he will not fall, for the Lord upholds him. I was young and now I am old, yet I have never seen the righteous forsaken or their children begging bread. He is ever merciful and lending; and his seed is for a blessing. Turn from evil and do good; then you will dwell in the land forever. **For the Lord loves the just and will not forsake His faithful ones. They will be protected forever... The mouth of the righteous man utters wisdom, and his tongue speaks what is just. The law of God is in his heart; his feet do not slip.** The wicked lie in wait for the righteous, seeking their very lives; but the Lord will not leave them in their power... Wait for the Lord and keep His way... I have seen a wicked and ruthless man flourishing like a green tree in its native soil, but he soon passed away and was no more; though I looked for him, he could not be found.

Consider the blameless, observe the upright; there is a future for the man of peace... **The salvation of the righteous comes from the Lord; He is their strength in the time of trouble.** The Lord helps them and delivers them; **He delivers them from the wicked and saves them, because they take refuge in Him.** (Psalms, 37:1-40)

All my longings lie open before you, O Lord; my sighing is not hidden from you. I wait for you, O Lord; You will answer, O Lord my God. Those who repay my good with evil slander me when I pursue what is good... O Lord, do not forsake me; be not far from me, O God. Come quickly to help me, O Lord my savior. (Psalms, 38:9-22)

I said, "**I will watch my ways and keep my tongue from sin...**" My substance is as nothing before You. **Each man's life is but a breath.** Truly, every man goes on his way like an image; he is troubled for no purpose: he makes a great store of wealth, and has no knowledge of who will get it. And now, Lord, what am I waiting for? **My hope is in You.** Make me free from all my sins... truly every man is but a breath. Hear my prayer O Lord, listen to my cry for help... (Psalms, 39:1-12)

I waited patiently for the Lord; and He inclined unto me, and heard my cry. He brought me up also out of the pit of destruction, out of the miry clay; and He set my feet upon a rock, He established my goings. And He put a new song in my mouth, even praise unto our God; many shall see, and fear, and shall trust in the Lord. **Happy is the man who has faith in the Lord, and does not give honour to the men of pride or to those who are turned away to deceit.** Many things You have done, **O Lord my God,** even Your wonderful works, and Your thoughts toward us; there is none to be compared unto You! If I would declare and speak of them, they are more than can be told... Then said I: '... **I delight to do Your will, O my God; truly, Your law is in my inmost parts.**' I have preached righteousness in the great congregation, I did not refrain my lips; O Lord, You have knowledge. I have not hidden Your righteousness within my heart; I have declared Your faithfulness and Your salvation; I have not concealed Your mercy and Your truth from the great congregation. O Lord, don't withhold Your compassions from me; let Your mercy and Your truth continually preserve me. For innumerable evils have compassed me about... Be pleased, O Lord, to deliver me; O Lord,... help me... Let all those who seek You rejoice and be glad in You; let such as love Your salvation say continually: 'The Lord be magnified.'... You are my help and my deliverer; O my God... (Psalms, 40:1-17)

Blessed is he that considers the poor: the Lord will deliver him in time of trouble. The Lord will preserve him, and keep him alive; and he shall be blessed upon the earth: and You will not deliver him unto the will of his enemies. **The Lord will sustain him on his sickbed, and restore him from his bed of illness.** I said, "Lord, be merciful unto me: heal my soul"... You uphold me in my integrity, and set me in Your presence for ever. Blessed be the Lord... from everlasting, and to everlasting. Amen, and Amen. (Psalms, 41:1-13)

As the deer pants for the water brooks, so pants my soul after You, O God. My soul thirsts for God, for the living God: 'When shall I come and appear before God?'[18]... **Hope in God; for I shall yet praise Him for the salvation of His countenance...** By day

---

18. A description by way of simile of earning Allah's approval, mercy and paradise.

the Lord will command His lovingkindness, and in the night His song shall be with me, even a prayer unto the God of my life... Hope in God; for I shall yet praise Him, the salvation of my countenance, and my God. (Psalms, 42:1-11)

... **O deliver me from the deceitful and unjust man.** For You are the God of my strength... **O send out Your light and Your truth; let them lead me**... Then will I go unto the altar of God, unto God, my exceeding joy; and praise You upon the harp, O God, my God... Hope in God; for I shall yet praise Him, the salvation of my countenance, and my God. (Psalms, 43:1-5)

... Neither did their own arm save them; but Your right hand, and Your arm, and the light[19] of Your countenance, because You had pleasure in them... **But You have saved us from our adversaries, and have put them to shame that hate us.** In God have we gloried all the day, and we will give thanks unto Your name for ever... **He knows the secrets of the heart.** (Psalms, 44:3-21)

God is our refuge and strength, a very present help in trouble. Therefore will we not fear, though the earth do change, and though the mountains be moved into the heart of the seas; Though the waters thereof roar and foam, though the mountains shake at the swelling thereof... **The Lord of hosts is with us**... (Psalms, 46:1-7)

O clap your hands, all you peoples; shout unto God with the voice of triumph. For the Lord is most high... Sing praises to God, sing praises... **For God is the King of all the earth**... **God reigns over the nations**... (Psalms, 47:1-2, 6-8)

---

19. A description by way of simile of Allah's glory and His being the Light of the world.

Great is the Lord, and highly to be praised... As is Your name, O God, so is Your praise unto the ends of the earth; **Your right hand is full of righteousness**... For this God is our God, for ever and ever; **He will guide us eternally**. (Psalms, 48:1, 10-14)

Hear this, all you peoples; give ear, all you inhabitants of the world, both men of low and high, rich and poor together. My mouth shall speak wisdom, and in the thoughts of my heart will be knowledge. I will incline my ear to a parable... Of them that trust in their wealth, and boast themselves in the multitude of their riches; **No man can by any means redeem his brother, nor give to God a ransom for him**... **But man despite its riches, does not endure; he is like the animals that perish.** This is the way of them that are foolish, and of those who after them approve their sayings. Like sheep they are appointed for the under-world [sheol, hell]... and the upright shall have dominion over them in the morning; and their form shall be for the underworld [sheol, hell] to wear away, that there be no habitation for it. But God will redeem my soul from the power of the underworld [sheol, hell]; for He shall receive me. Don't be afraid when one is made rich, when the wealth of his house is increased; **for when he dies he shall carry nothing away; his wealth shall not descend after him**. Though while he lived he counted himself blessed—and men praise you when you prosper—he will join the generation of his fathers, who will never see the light of life . A man who has riches without understanding is like the beasts that perish. (Psalms, 49:1-20)

The Mighty One, God, the Lord, has spoken, and called the earth from the rising of the Sun unto the going down thereof... perfect of beauty, God has shined forth... And the heavens declare His righteousness; for God, He is judge. '... I am God, your God... **Every beast of the forest is Mine, and the cattle upon a thousand hills. I know all the fowls of the mountains; and the wild beasts of the field are Mine...** And **call upon Me in the day of trouble; I will deliver you**, and you will honour Me.' But unto the wicked, God says: '... Seeing you hate instruction, and cast My words behind you. When you saw a thief, you had company with him, and with adulterers was your portion. You use your mouth for evil, and your tongue to deceit... I will accuse you to your face... **To him that orders his way aright will I show the salvation of God**.' (Psalms, 50:1-23)

Be gracious unto me, O God, according to Your mercy; according to the multitude of Your compassions **blot out my transgressions. Wash me thoroughly from my iniquity, and cleanse me from my sin**... You desire truth in the inward parts; **make me, therefore, to know wisdom in my inmost heart. Purge me [of my sins]...** and I shall be clean; wash me, and I shall be whiter than snow... **Create me a clean heart, O God; and renew a steadfast spirit within me. Cast me not away from Your presence; and take not Your holy spirit from me. Restore unto me the joy of Your salvation; and let a willing spirit uphold me.** Then will I teach transgressors Your ways; and sinners shall return unto You. Deliver me from bloodguiltiness, O God, You God of my salvation; so shall my tongue sing aloud of Your righteousness. O Lord, open my lips; and my mouth shall declare Your praise... The sacrifices of God are a broken spirit; a broken and a contrite heart, O God, You will not despise. (Psalms, 51:1-17)

Why do you boast of evil, mighty man? The mercy of God endures continually. Your tongue plots destruction; like a sharp razor, you who practice deceit. You love evil more than good; falsehood rather than speaking righteousness. You love all devouring words, the deceitful tongue... The righteous also shall see, and fear, and shall... say: "Here now is the man—who did not make God his stronghold—but trusted in his great wealth and grew strong by destroying others!" But as for me... **I trust in the mercy of God for ever and ever. I will give You thanks for ever, because You have done it; and I will wait for Your name,** for it is good, in the presence of Your saints. (Psalms, 52:1-9)

The fool has said in his heart: 'There is no God'; **they have dealt corruptly, and have done abominable iniquity; there is none who does good...** Everyone has turned away, they have together become corrupt; there is none who does good, no, not one... **They don't call on God. There are they in great fear, where there was no fear... You have put them to shame...** (Psalms, 53:1-5)

O God, save me by Your name, and vindicate me by Your might... Strangers are risen up against me, and ruthless men have sought my life; they have not set God before them. Behold, **God is my helper; the Lord is for me as the upholder of my soul**... **With a freewill-offering will I sacrifice unto You; I will give thanks unto Your name, O Lord, for it is good. For He has delivered me out of all trouble**... (Psalms, 54:1-7)

Destroy, O Lord, and divide their tongue; for I have seen violence and strife in the city. Day and night they go about it upon the walls thereof; iniquity also and mischief are in the midst of it. Wickedness is in the midst thereof; oppression and guile depart not from her broad place... As for me, **I will call upon God; and the Lord shall save me**... They don't fear God. My companion attacks his friends; he violates his covenant. Smoother than cream were the speeches of his mouth, but his heart was war; his words were softer than oil, yet were they keen-edged swords. **Cast your burden upon the Lord, and He will sustain you; He will never suffer the righteous to be moved.** But You, O God, will bring the wicked down into the pit of corruption [sheol, hell]; bloodthirsty and deceitful men will not live out half their days; but as for me, **I trust in You**. (Psalms, 55:9-23)

In the day that I am afraid, I will put my trust in You. In God— I will praise His word—**in God do I trust, I will not be afraid; what can flesh do unto me?** All the day they trouble my affairs; all their thoughts are against me for evil. They gather themselves together, they hide themselves, they mark my steps; according as they have waited for my soul... This I know, that God is for me. In God— I will praise His word— in the Lord— I will praise His word— **In God do I trust, I will not be afraid; what can man do unto me?... For You have delivered my soul from death; have You not delivered my feet from stumbling** that I may walk before God in the light of the living? (Psalms, 56:3-13)

Be gracious unto me, O God, be gracious unto me, for **in You has my soul taken refuge**; yes, in the shadow of Your wings[20] will I take refuge, until calamities be overpast. **I will cry unto God Most High; unto God Who accomplishes it for me**... Be You exalted, O God, above the heavens; Your glory be above all the earth... They have digged a pit before me, they are fallen into the midst thereof themselves. My heart is steadfast, O God, my heart is steadfast; I will sing, yes, I will sing praises... I will give thanks unto You, O Lord, among the peoples; I will sing praises unto You among the nations. For Your mercy is great unto the heavens, and Your truth unto the skies. Be You exalted, O God, above the heavens; Your glory be above all the earth. (Psalms, 57:1-11)

Do you indeed speak as a righteous company? Do you judge with equity the sons of men? No, in heart you work wickedness; you weigh out in the earth the violence of your hands. (Psalms, 58:1-2)

Deliver me from my enemies, O my God; set me on high from them that rise up against me. Deliver me from the workers of iniquity, and save me from the men of blood... You therefore, O Lord God of hosts... I will wait for You; for God is my high tower [my shelter]. The God of my mercy will come to meet me... O Lord our shield... I will sing of Your strength; yes, I will sing aloud of Your mercy in the morning; for **You have been my high**

---

20. A reference by way of simile to Allah's shelter and protection.

tower [my shelter], and a refuge in the day of my distress. O my strength, unto You will I sing praises; for God is my high tower [my shelter], the God of my mercy. (Psalms, 59:1-17)

That Your beloved may be delivered, save with Your right hand, and answer me... **Give us help against the adversary**; for vain is the help of man. **Through God we shall do valiantly**... (Psalms, 60: 5, 11-12)

... O God... For **you have been a refuge for me, a support of strength in the face of the enemy**. I will dwell in Your Tent[21] for ever; I will take refuge in the covert of Your wings[22]. For You, O God, have heard my vows; **You have granted the heritage of those that fear Your name**... Appoint mercy and truth... So will I sing praise unto Your name for ever... (Psalms, 61:1-8)

Only for God does my soul wait in stillness; from Him comes my salvation. For He is my God and my saviour: He is my protector, I shall not be greatly moved... **My soul, wait in silence for God alone, For my expectation is from Him.** For He is my God and my saviour: **He is my helper**, I shall not be moved. **In God is my salvation and my glory**: He is the God of my help, and **my hope is in God**. Trust in Him at all times, O people... **God is a refuge for us...** Trust not in oppression... that strength belongs unto God; also unto You, O Lord, belongs mercy; for **You render to every man according to his work**. (Psalms, 62:1-12)

O God, You are my God, earnestly will I seek You; my soul thirsts for You, my flesh longs for You, in a dry and weary land, where

---

21. A description by way of simile of Allah's Presence.
22. A description of Allah being the Protector by way of simile.

no water is... **Your loving-kindness is better than life**; my lips shall praise You. **So will I bless You as long as I live; in Your name will I lift up my hands.** My soul is satisfied as with marrow and fatness; and **my mouth praises You with joyful lips; When I remember You upon my couch, and meditate on You in the night-watches**. For You have been my help, and in the shadow of Your wings[23] do I rejoice. My soul cleaves unto You; Your right hand holds me fast... The king shall rejoice in God; every one that swears by Him shall glory; for the mouth of them that speak lies shall be stopped. (Psalms, 63:1-11)

Hide me from the council of evil-doers; from the tumult of the workers of iniquity; they sharpen their tongues like swords and aim their words like deadly arrows; they shoot from ambush at the innocent man; they shoot at him suddenly, without fear. They encourage each other in evil plans, they talk about hiding their snares; they say, "Who will see them?" They plot injustice and say, "We have devised a perfect plan!"... So they make their own tongue a stumbling unto themselves... **The righteous shall be glad in the Lord, and shall take refuge in Him; and all the upright in heart shall glory.** (Psalms, 64:2-10)

... O God... O You Who hear prayer, unto You will all flesh come. When we were overwhelmed by sins, You forgave our transgressions. **Blessed are those You choose and bring near to live in Your courts!** We are filled with the good things of Your house... **You answer us in righteousness**, O God of our salvation; **You the confidence of all the ends of the earth, and of the far distant seas; Who by Your strength set fast the mountains, Who is gird-**

---

23. A description of Allah being the Protector by way of simile.

ed about with might; **Who stilled the roaring of the seas, the roaring of their waves, and the tumult of the peoples**; those living far away fear Your wonders; where morning dawns and evening fades You call forth songs of joy. You have the earth, and watered her, greatly enriching her, with the river of God that is full of water; You prepare them corn, for so You prepare her. Watering her ridges abundantly, settling down the furrows thereof, You make her soft with showers; You bless the growth thereof. You crown the year with Your goodness; and Your paths drop fatness. The pastures of the wilderness do drop; and the hills are girded with joy. The meadows are clothed with flocks; the valleys also are covered over with corn; they shout for joy, yes, they sing. (Psalms, 65:1-13)

Shout with joy to God, all the earth; Sing praises unto the glory of His name; make His praise glorious. Say unto God: '**How tremendous is Your work! Through the greatness of Your power shall Your enemies dwindle away before You. All the earth shall worship You, and shall sing praises unto You; they shall sing praises to Your name.**' Come, and see the works of God; He is awesome in His doing toward the children of men. He turned the sea into dry land; they went through the river on foot; there let us rejoice in Him! **Who rules by His might for ever; His eyes keep watch upon the nations;**[24] let not the rebellious exalt themselves. Bless our God, O peoples, and make the voice of His praise to be heard; **He has preserved our lives and kept our feet from slipping.** For you, O God, tested us; You refined us like silver... Come, and hear, all you who fear God, and I will declare what He has done for my soul. I cried unto Him with my mouth, and He

---

24. A description by way of simile of Allah being Omniscient, All-Knowing.

was extolled with my tongue. If I had regarded iniquity in my heart, the Lord would not hear; But verily God has heard; He has attended to the voice of my prayer. **Blessed be God, Who has not turned away my prayer, nor His mercy from me.** (Psalms, 66:1-10, 16-20)

God be gracious unto us, and bless us; may He cause His face to shine[25] toward us; That **Your way may be known upon earth, Your salvation among all nations**. Let the peoples give thanks unto You, O God; let the peoples give thanks unto You, all of them. O let the nations be glad and sing for joy; for **You will judge the peoples with equity, and lead the nations upon earth**. Let the peoples give thanks unto You, O God; let the peoples give thanks unto You, all of them. The earth has yielded her increase; may God, our own God, bless us. May God bless us; and let all the ends of the earth fear Him. (Psalms, 67:1-7)

But let the righteous be glad, let them exult before God; yes, let them rejoice with gladness. Sing unto God, sing praises to His name...**God makes the solitary to dwell in a house; He brings out the prisoners into prosperity**; the rebellious dwell but in a parched land... Praise be to the Lord, to God our Savior, Who daily bears our burdens. **Our God is a God Who saves; from the Sovereign Lord comes escape from death [hell]...** Praise God in the great congregation; praise the Lord in the assembly... O God... Scatter the peoples that delight in war!... Sing unto God, you kingdoms of the earth; O sing praises unto the Lord... Proclaim the power of God... You are awesome, O God... **He gives strength and power unto the people**; blessed be God. (Psalms, 68:3-35)

---

25. A reference to Allah's title of "*Noor*" (Light).

But as for me, let my prayer be unto You, **O Lord, in an acceptable time; O God, in the abundance of Your mercy, answer me with the truth of Your salvation**. Rescue me from the mire, do not let me sink; deliver me from those who hate me, from the deep waters. Do not let the floodwaters engulf me or the depths swallow me up or the pit close its mouth over me. **Answer me, O Lord, for Your mercy is good**; according to the multitude of Your compassions turn unto me [do not deprive me of Your Mercy]. And hide not Your face from Your servant [do not keep me away from Your Mercy]; for I am in distress; answer me speedily. Draw near unto my soul, and redeem it; ransom me because of my enemies... let Your salvation, O God, set me up on high. I will praise the name of God with a song, and will magnify Him with thanksgiving... The humble shall see it, and be glad; you who seek after God, let your heart revive. For the Lord hears the needy... Let heaven and earth praise Him, the seas, and every thing that moves therein. (Psalms, 69:13-18, 29-34)

Let all those that seek You rejoice and be glad in You; and let such as love Your salvation say continually: 'Let God be magnified'... You are my help and my deliverer; O Lord... (Psalms, 70:4-5)

In You, O Lord, have I taken refuge... Deliver me in Your righteousness, and rescue me... and save me. Be to me a sheltering rock [my shelter], where unto I may continually resort, which You have appointed to save me; for You are my rock [my shelter] and my fortress. O my God, rescue me out of the hand of the wicked, out of the grasp of the unrighteous and ruthless man. **For You are my hope; O Lord God, my trust from my youth. Upon**

You have I stayed myself from birth; You are He Who took me out of my mother's womb; my praise is continually of You. I am as a wonder unto many; but **You are my strong refuge**. My mouth shall be filled with Your praise, and with Your glory all the day... I will hope continually, and will praise You yet more and more. My mouth shall tell of Your righteousness, and of Your salvation all the day... I will come and proclaim your mighty acts, O Sovereign Lord; I will proclaim Your righteousness, Yours alone. **O God, You have taught me from my youth**; and until now do I declare Your wondrous works... Your righteousness also, O God, which reaches unto high heaven; You Who have done great things... **You... will quicken me again, and bring me up again from the depths of the earth.** You will increase my greatness, and turn and comfort me. I also will give thanks unto You... even unto Your truth, O my God; I will sing praises unto You with the harp... My lips shall greatly rejoice when I sing praises unto You; and my soul, which You have redeemed. My tongue also shall tell of Your righteousness all the day... (Psalms, 71:1-24)

Blessed be the Lord God... Who only does wondrous things; And blessed be His glorious name for ever; and let the whole earth be filled with His glory. Amen, and Amen. (Psalms, 72:18-19)

Surely God is good... to those who are pure in heart... For they [wicked ones] have no pain; their bodies are fat and strong. They are not in trouble as other men; neither are they plagued like other men. Therefore pride is as a chain about their neck; violence covered them as a garment... They scoff and speak with malice. In arrogance, they threaten oppression. They have set their mouth against the heavens, and their tongue walk through the earth... And when I tried to understand this, it was too painful for me;

until I entered into the house of God, and considered their end. Surely You set them in slippery places. You throw them down to destruction... **Nevertheless I am continually with You: You have held me by my right hand.**[26] **You will guide me with Your counsel, and afterward receive me to glory. Whom have I in heaven but You? And there is none upon earth that I desire besides You.** My flesh and my heart fails, But **God is the strength of my heart and my portion forever**... But as for me, **it is good for me to draw near to God: I have put my trust in the Lord, that I may declare all your works**. (Psalms, 73: 1-28)

You opened up spring and stream. You dried up mighty rivers. The day is Yours, the night also is Yours; You have prepared the Moon and the Sun: You have set all the borders of the earth; You have made summer and winter. (Psalms, 74: 15-17)

Unto You we give thanks, O God, we give thanks; and Your name is near: Your marvelous works declare it. **"When the right time has come, I will be the judge in righteousness." says the Lord.** When the earth and all the inhabitants thereof are dissolved, I Myself establish the pillars of it.' I said unto the arrogant, Deal not arrogantly; and to the wicked, Lift not up the horn. Lift not up your horn on high: speak not with a stiff neck. For neither from the east, nor from the west, nor yet from the south, comes exaltation. But **God is the judge.**[27] **He puts down one, and lifts up another**... But as for me, I will declare forever... I will sing praises to God. All the horns of the wicked also will I cut off; but the horns of the righteous shall be lifted up. (Psalms: 75:1-10)

---

26. Allah's help, His salvation is expressed by the way of smile.
27. Allah's attribute of *al-Adl* (the Utterly Just) is meant here. Allah is the most auspicious of those who make justice.

You, You are to be feared... Vow to the Lord your God and fulfill them. (Psalms: 76:7-11)

I cried to the Lord with my voice... **In the day of my trouble I seek the Lord... I will remember the works of the Lord**: surely I will remember Your wonders of old... **I will make mention of the deeds of the Lord**; yes, I will remember Your wonders of old. O God, Your way is holy... **You are the God Who does wonders. You have made Your strength known among the peoples.** (Psalms: 77:1-14)

... We will not hide from their children, **telling to the generation to come the praises of Lord, and His strength, and His wondrous works that He has done**... That **they might put their confidence in God, and not forget the works of God, but keep His commandments**; and might not be as their fathers, a stubborn and rebellious generation; a generation that set not their heart aright, and whose spirit was not steadfast with God... They kept not the covenant of God, and refused to walk in His law; and they forgot His doings, and His wondrous works that He had shown them. Marvelous things did He in the sight of their fathers... He cleaved the sea, and caused them to pass through; and He made the waters to stand as a heap. By day also He led them with a cloud, and all the night with a light of fire. He cleaved rocks in the wilderness, and gave them drink abundantly as out of the great deep. He brought streams also out of the rock, and caused waters to run down like rivers. Yet went they on still to sin against Him, to rebel against the Most High [God] in the desert. And they tried God [surely God is beyond that] in their heart by asking food for their craving. Yes, they spoke against God; they said: 'Can God prepare a table in the wilderness? Behold, He smote the rock, that waters gushed out, and streams overflowed; can He give bread also? Or will He provide flesh for His people?' When the Lord heard them, He was very angry[28]... Because they believed not in God, and trusted not in His salvation. Yet He commanded the clouds from above, and opened the doors of heaven... He sent them all the food they could eat... He sent He caused the east wind to set forth in heaven; and by His power He brought on the south wind... He gave them their own desire... For all this they sinned still, and believed not in His wondrous works. Therefore He ended their days as a breath, and their years in terror. When He killed them, then **they would inquire after Him, and turn back and seek God earnestly**. And **they remembered that God was their helper, and the Most High God their redeemer**. But they acted ignobly towards Him with their mouth, and lied to Him with their tongue. For their heart was not steadfast with Him, neither were they faithful in His covenant. But **He, being full of compassion, forgave iniquity, and did not destroy them**... How often did they rebel against Him in the desert... They remembered not His hand[29] nor the day when He redeemed them from the adversary. How He set His signs in Egypt and His

---

28. Allah is the One Who is exalted far above rage. What is meant here is the manifestation of Allah's attribute of *al-Muntaqim* (the Avenger).
29. A description of Allah being the Protector by way of simile.

wonders... And turned their rivers into blood, so that they could not drink their streams. He sent among them swarms of flies, which devoured them; and frogs, which destroyed them. He gave also their increase unto the caterpillar, and their labor unto the locust. He destroyed their vines with hail, and their sycamore trees with frost. He gave over their cattle also to the hail, and their flocks to fiery bolts... He spared not their soul from death, but gave their life over to the pestilence... And He led them safely, and they feared not; but the sea overwhelmed their enemies... Yet they... rebelled against God, the Most High, and kept not His testimonies; but turned back, and dealt treacherously like their fathers; they were turned aside like a deceitful bow. (Psalms, 78:4-57)

... **Let Your tender come to us quickly**... **Help us, O God of our salvation, for the sake of the glory of Your name; and deliver us, and forgive our sins, for Your name's sake**... We will give You glory forever: we will go on praising You through all generations. (Psalms, 79:8-13)

O God, restore us; and **let us see the shining of Your face**, and we shall be saved! O Lord God of hosts... let us see the shining of Your face [Your Light], and we shall be saved!... **We will not turn away from you.** Revive us, and we will call on Your name! O God, restore us; and let us see the shining of Your face, and we shall be saved! (Psalms, 80:3-19)

Sing aloud to God our strength: make a joyful noise... Take up the melody, and strike the tambourine, the sweet harp and lyre. Blow the horn at the new moon, at the full moon for our feast-day... **"You are not to give worship to any other god! I am your Lord, Who brought you up out of the land of Egypt!** (Psalms, 81:1-11)

'How long will you judge unjustly, and respect the persons of the wicked? **Judge the poor and fatherless: Do justice to the afflicted and destitute. Rescue the poor and needy; deliver them out of the hand of the wicked.** They know not, neither do they understand; they go about in darkness... (Psalms, 82:2-5)

Fill their faces with shame; that they may seek Your name, O Lord... That they may know that **You alone, Whose name is Lord, are the Most High over all the earth.** (Psalms, 83:16-18)

O Lord Almighty!... **Happy is the man whose strength is in You!**... For a day in Your courts [in holy places where God's name is uttered] is better than a thousand elsewhere; I had rather stand at the threshold of the house of my Lord [holy place where God's name is uttered], than to dwell in the tents of wickedness. For the Lord is a Sun[30], and a shield[31]. **The Lord will give grace and glory: no good will He withhold from them that walk uprightly!** (Psalms, 84:1-12)

Show us Your mercy, O Lord, and grant us Your salvation! I will hear what God will speak; for **He will speak peace unto His people, and to His saints**; but let them not turn back to folly. **Surely His salvation is near to them that fear Him**; that glory may dwell in our land. Mercy and truth are met together; righteousness and peace have kissed each other. Truth sprang out of the earth; and righteousness had looked down from heaven. Yes, **the Lord will give that which is good**; and our land shall yield her produce... (Psalms, 85:7-13)

---

30. A reference to Allah's title of "*Noor*" (Light).
31. A description by way of simile of Allah being all-Compassionate and all-Merciful.

... Please listen, Lord, and answer my prayer! I am poor and helpless. Protect me and save me, because You are my Lord. I am Your faithful servant! Be kind to me! I pray to You all day. Make my heart glad! I serve You, and my prayer is sincere. **You willingly forgive, and Your love is always for those who pray to You.** Please listen, Lord! Answer my prayer for help. **When I am in trouble, I pray, knowing You will answer**... **There is none like unto You, O Lord, and there are no works like Yours.** All nations who You have made shall come and prostrate themselves before You, O Lord; and they shall glorify Your name. **For You are great, and does wondrous things You are God alone.** Teach me, O Lord, Your way, that I may walk in Your truth; make one my heart to fear only Your name. I will thank You, O Lord my God, with my whole heart; and I will glorify Your name for evermore. **For great is Your mercy toward me; and You had delivered my soul from the lowest Hell**... But You, O Lord, are a God full of compassion and gracious... and plenteous in mercy and truth... You, O Lord, has helped me, and comforted me. (Psalms, 86:1-17)

O Lord, God of my salvation, I have been crying to You for help by day and by night... I have called upon You, O Lord every day... O Lord, do I cry, and in the morning do my prayer come to You. (Psalms, 88:1, 9-13)

I will sing of the mercies of the Lord forever; to all generations will I make known Your faithfulness with my mouth. I will declare that Your love stands firm forever, that you established your faithfulness in heaven itself... The heavens praise Your wonders, O Lord, Your faithfulness also in the assembly of the holy ones [among the true believers]... In the council of the holy ones [among the true believers] **God is greatly feared; He is more awesome than all who surround Him**... The heavens are Yours, Yours also the earth; the world and the fullness thereof, You have founded them. The north and the south, You have created them...Your arm is endued with power; Your hand is strong, and Your right hand exalted.[32] **Righteousness and justice are the foundation of Your throne [God's Glorious Authority]; mercy and truth go before You.** Happy is the people that know the joyful shout; they walk, O Lord, in the light of Your countenance. In Your name do they rejoice all the day; and through Your righteousness are they exalted. **For You are the glory of their strength; and in Your favor our strength is exalted. For Lord is our shield [God is our Protector]**... Blessed be Lord for evermore. Amen, and Amen. (Psalms, 89:1-52)

You have been our dwelling-place in all generations. Before the mountains were brought forth, or ever You have formed the earth and the world, even from everlasting to everlasting, You are God. You make mortal man to return to dust, and say, "Return, children of men." For a thousand years in Your sight are like a day that has just gone by, or like a watch in the night. You carry them away as with a flood; they are as a sleep; in the morning they are like grass which grow up. In the morning it flourish, and grow up; in the evening it is cut down, and wither... O satisfy us in the morning with Your mercy; that we may rejoice and be glad all our days. And let the graciousness of the Lord our God be upon us; establish You also upon us the work of our hands; yes, establish the work of our hands. (Psalms, 90:1-17)

---

32. The fact that Allah is the Lord of sublime might and power is described by analogy.

He who dwells in the house of the Most High [the one who remembers God in God's houses] will rest in the shadow of the Almighty [taking refuge in God].[33] I will say of Lord, Who is my refuge and my fortress, my God, in Whom I trust. That **He will deliver you from the snare of the fowler, and from the deadly pestilence. He will cover you with His wings[34], and under His wings shall you take refuge;** His truth is a shield [protector] and a rampart. **You will not fear the terror of night, nor the arrow that flies by day; nor the pestilence that stalks in the darkness, nor the plague that destroys at midday. For you have made the Lord Who is my refuge, even the Most High, your habitation** [being God's friend, seeking refuge in Him]. **No harm will befall you, no disaster will come near your tent. For He will give His angels charge over you, to keep you in all your ways**... 'Because he has set his love upon Me, therefore will I deliver him; I will set him on high [I will protect him], because he has known My name. He will call upon Me, and I will answer him; **I will be with him in trouble; I will rescue him, and bring him to honor. With long life will I satisfy him, and show him My salvation.**' (Psalms, 91:1-16)

It is a good thing to give thanks unto Your Lord, and to sing praises unto Your name, O Most High. To declare Your lovingkindness in the morning, and Your faithfulness at night. With an instrument of ten-stringed lyre, and the melody of the harp! For You, my Lord, has made me glad through Your work; I will exult in the works of Your hands. **How great are Your works, O Lord! Your thoughts are very deep!** The senseless man does not know,

---

33. A description of Allah being the Protector by way of simile.
34. A description of Allah being the Protector by way of simile.

fools do not understand... But **You, o Lord, are exalted forever. The righteous will flourish like a palm-tree; they shall grow like a cedar in Lebanon... They will still bring forth fruit in old age; they will stay fresh and green, proclaiming, "The Lord is upright; He is my strength."** (Psalms, 92:1-15)

The Lord reigns; He is clothed in majesty; the Lord is clothed, He has girded Himself with strength. The world is established, that it cannot be moved. **Your throne is established of old; You are from everlasting.** The floods have lifted up, O the Lord, the floods have lifted up their voice; the floods lift up their roaring. **Your statutes stand firm**... (Psalms, 93:1-5)

Consider, you senseless ones among the people; and you fools, when will you become wise? He that planted the ear, shall He not hear? He that formed the eye, shall He not see? He that instructed nations, shall not He correct? Even He that taught man knowledge? **The Lord knows the thoughts of man**, that they are vanity. Happy is the man whom You instruct, O Lord, and teach out of Your law!... For right shall return unto justice, and all the upright in heart shall follow it... **If I say: 'My foot slips, Your mercy, O my Lord, holds me up." When my cares are many within me, Your comforts [Your bestowing feelings of peace and security] delight my soul. But my Lord has been my high tower [my refuge, my sole helper and friend], and my God the strength in Whom I take refuge.** And He, our Lord has brought upon them their own iniquity... (Psalms, 94:8-23)

Come let us praise the Lord with joy: let us joyfully sing to God, our savior. Let us come before His presence with thanksgiving, let us shout for joy unto Him with psalms! For the Lord is great God... **In Whose hand are the depths of the earth; the heights of the mountains are His also. The sea is His, and He made it; and His hands formed the dry land.** O come, let us bow down and bend the knee; let us kneel before our Lord, our Maker. For He is our God... Harden not your heart. (Psalms, 95:1-8)

O sing unto the Lord a new song; sing unto the Lord, all the earth. Sing unto the Lord, bless His name; proclaim His salvation from day to day! Declare His glory among the nations, His marvelous works among all the peoples! **For great is the Lord, and highly to be praised; He is to be feared...** The Lord made the heavens. **Honor and majesty are before Him; strength and beauty are in His house.** Ascribe unto the Lord, you families of nations, ascribe unto the Lord glory and strength. Ascribe unto the Lord the glory due unto His name; bring an offering, and come into His courts... O worship the Lord! Tremble before Him, all the earth! Say among the nations: 'The Lord reigns.'... **He will judge the peoples with equity.** Let the heavens be glad, and let the earth rejoice; let the sea roar, and the fulness thereof! Let the field exult; and all that is therein; then shall all the trees of the wood sing for joy. (Psalms, 96:1-12)

The Lord reigns; let the earth rejoice; let the multitude of isles be glad!.. His lightnings lighted up the world; the earth saw, and trembled... The heavens declared His righteousness, and all peoples saw His glory. Ashamed be all they who worship images, that boast themselves of idols! Worship Him... **For You, my Lord, are most high above all the earth... You are exalted...** O you that love the Lord, hate evil. **He preserves the souls of His saints [His devoted servants], He delivers them out of the hand of the wicked. Light is sown for the righteous, and gladness for the upright in heart.** Be glad in the Lord, you righteous; and give thanks to His holy name! (Psalms, 97:1-12)

Oh sing unto God a new song; For **He has done marvellous things**... Shout unto the Lord, all the earth; break forth and sing for joy, you, sing praises! Sing praises unto the Lord with the harp; with the harp and the voice of melody! With trumpets and sound of the horn shout you before... the Lord. Let the sea roar, and the fulness thereof; the world, and they that dwell therein. Let the floods clap their hands; let the mountains sing for joy together. (Psalms, 98:1-9)

The Lord is great...and He is exalted over all the peoples. Let them praise Your name as great and awesome; **Holy is He.** Exalt you God, our Lord... Holy is He. Moses and Aaron among His messengers... did call upon the Lord, and He answered them... they kept His testimonies, and the statute that He gave them. O God, our Lord, You did answer them; **a forgiving God were You unto them**... Exalt our Lord, our God, and worship... for the Lord, our God is holy. (Psalms, 99:2-9)

Shout unto the Lord, all the earth! Serve the Lord with gladness; come before His presence with joyful singing. Know that the Lord is God; it is **He that has made us, and we are His**... give thanks unto Him, and bless His name. For **the Lord is good; His mercy endures for ever**... (Psalms, 100:1-5)

I will sing of mercy and justice; unto You, O Lord, will I sing praises. **I will be careful to lead a blameless life**... I will walk in my house with blameless heart **will set before my eyes no vile thing. The deeds of faithless men I hate**; they will not cling to me. **A perverse heart shall depart from me**; I will know no evil thing. **Whoever slandered his neighbour in secret, him will I destroy [in the spritiual sense]; whose is haughty of eye and proud of heart, him will I not suffer.** My eyes are upon the faithful of the land, that they may dwell with Me; he whose walk is, he will minister to Me. **No one who practices deceit will dwell in My house; no one who speaks falsely will stand in My presence**... (Psalms, 101:1-7)

... You, O my Lord... Your name is unto all generations... So **the nations will fear the name of the Lord [will have fear of God's Might and Power]**, and all the kings of the earth Your glory... **Of old You did lay the foundation of the earth; and the heavens are Your work. They will perish, but You will endure**; they will all wear out like a garment. Like clothing you will change them and they will be discarded. (Psalms, 102:12-26)

Bless the Lord, O my soul! And let all that is within me bless His holy name. Bless the Lord, O my soul, and forget not all His benefits! **Who forgives all your iniquity; Who heals all Your diseases. Who redeemed Your life from the pit; Who encompasses you with loving-kindness and tender mercies**... so that Your youth is renewed like the eagle. **The Lord executes righteousness, and acts of justice for all that are oppressed... The Lord is full of compassion and gracious... and plenteous in mercy... so great is His mercy toward them that fear Him... so has the Lord compassion upon them that fear Him...** As for man, his days are as grass; as a flower of the field, so he flourishes. For the wind passes over it, and it is gone; and the place thereof knows it no more. But **the mercy of the Lord is from everlasting to everlasting upon them that fear Him; and His righteousness unto children's children; To such as keep His covenant, and to those that remember His precepts to do them**... His kingdom rules over all. Bless the Lord, you angels of His, you mighty in strength, that fulfil His word. Praise the Lord... you His servants who do His will. Praise the Lord... praise the Lord, O my soul! (Psalms, 103:1-22)

Praise the Lord, O my soul! **You are clothed with glory and majesty... Who covers Yourself with light**...Who did establish the earth upon its foundations, that it should not be moved for ever and ever. You did cover it with the deep as with a vesture; the waters stood above the mountains... They [waters] flowed over the mountains, they went down into the valleys to the place You assigned for them. You did set a bound which they should not pass over, that they might not return to cover the earth. Who sends forth springs into the valleys; they run between the mountains. They give drink to every beast of the field, the wild don-

WISDOM AND SOUND ADVICE FROM THE TORAH

keys quench their thirst. Beside them dwell the fowl of the heaven, from among the branches they sing... He makes the grass to spring up for the cattle, and herb for the service of man; to bring forth bread out of the earth... oil to make his face shine, bread that sustains his. The trees of the Lord are well watered... Wherein the birds make their nests; as for the stork, the fir-trees are her house. The high mountains are for the wild goats; the rocks are a refuge for the conies. He appointed the Moon for seasons. The Sun knows when to set. You make darkness, and it is night, in which all the animals of the forest creep forth. The young lions roar after their prey, and seek their food from God. The Sun arises, and they are gathered together: and they lie down in their dens. Man goes forth to his work, to his labor until the evening. **O Lord, how manifold are Your works! In wisdom have You made them all: The earth is full of your riches.** So is this great and wide sea, in which are creeping animals innumerable, both small and great beasts. There the ships go to and fro... These all look unto you, that you may give their food in its season. You give it unto them, they gather it... they are satisfied with good. You send forth Your spirit [by God's leave, by His blowing from His soul], they are created; and You renew the face of the earth. May the glory of the Lord endure for ever... I will sing unto the Lord as long as I live; I will sing praise to God while I have any being. Let my musing be sweet unto Him; as for me, I will rejoice in the Lord!... Praise the Lord, my soul! Praise the Lord! (Psalms, 104:1-35)

Give thanks to the Lord, call on His name; make known among the nations what He has done. Sing to Him, sing praise to Him; tell of all His wonderful acts. Glory in His holy name; let the hearts of those who seek the Lord rejoice. **Look to the Lord and**

His strength; seek His face [approval of God] always. Remember the wonders He has done [Supreme Creation], His miracles, and the judgments He pronounced... He is the Lord our God; His judgments are in all the earth. (Psalms, 105:1-7)

Praise the Lord. O give thanks unto the Lord; for **He is good**; for **His mercy endures forever**. Who can express the mighty acts of the Lord, or fully declare his praise? **Happy are they that keep justice, that do righteousness at all times... Then believed they His words; they sang His praise.** They soon forgot His works... They believed not His word; And they murmured in their tents, they hearkened not unto the voice of the Lord. And they served their idols, which became a snare unto them; and shed innocent blood... Thus were they defiled with their works, and went astray in their doings. Many times did He deliver them; but they were rebellious in their counsel, and sank low through their iniquity. Save us, our God...

that we may give thanks to Your Holy Name and glory in Your praise. Praise be to the Lord, from everlasting to everlasting. Let all the people say, "Amen!" Praise the Lord. (Psalms, 106:1-48)

Give thanks to the Lord, for He is good; His love endures forever. Let the redeemed of the Lord say this those He redeemed from the hand of the foe, those He gathered from the lands, from east and west, from north and south. Some wandered in desert wastelands, finding no way to a city where they could settle. They were hungry and thirsty, and their lives ebbed away. Then they cried out to the Lord in their trouble, and **He delivered them from their distress**. For **He satisfies the thirsty and fills the hungry with good things**. Then they cried to the Lord in their trouble, and **He saved them from their distress. He brought them out of darkness and the deepest gloom and broke away their chains.** Let them give thanks to the Lord for His unfailing love and His wonderful deeds for men. Then they cried to the Lord in their trouble, and He saved them from their distress. Let them give thanks to the Lord for His unfailing love and His wonderful deeds for men. Let them sacrifice thank offerings and tell of his works with songs of joy. Others went out on the sea in ships; they were merchants on the mighty waters. They saw the works of the Lord, His wonderful deeds in the deep. For He spoke and stirred up a tempest that lifted high the waves. They mounted up to the heavens and went down to the depths; in their peril their courage melted away... they were at their wits' end. Then they cried out to the Lord in their trouble, and He brought them out of their distress. He stilled the storm to a whisper; the waves of the sea were hushed. They were glad when it grew calm, and He guided them to their desired haven. Let them give thanks to the Lord for His unfailing love and his wonderful deeds for men. Let them exalt Him... He turned rivers into a desert, flowing springs into thirsty ground... He turned the desert into pools of water and the parched ground into flowing springs; there He brought the hungry to live, and they founded a city where they could settle. They sowed fields and planted vineyards that yielded a fruitful harvest; the upright see and rejoice, but all the wicked shut their mouths. Whoever is wise, let Him heed these things and consider the great love of the Lord. (Psalms, 107:1-43)

I will praise You, O Lord, among the nations; I will sing of You among the peoples. For **great is Your love, higher than the heavens**; **Your faithfulness reaches to the skies**. Be exalted, O God, above the heavens, and let Your glory be over all the earth. Save us and help us with Your right hand, that those You love may be delivered. (Psalms, 108:1-12)

O God, Whom I praise... In return for my friendship they accuse me, but **I am a man of prayer**. They repay me evil for good, and hatred for my friendship... **Help me, O Lord my God; save me in accordance with Your love.** Let them know that it is Your hand, that You, O Lord, have done it. With my mouth I will greatly extol the Lord; in the great throng I will praise Him. (Psalms, 109:1-30)

Praise the Lord. I will extol the Lord with all my heart in the council of the upright and in the assembly. **Great are the works of the Lord**; they are pondered by all who delight in them. **Glorious and majestic are His deeds, and His righteousness endures forever.** He has caused His wonders to be remembered; **the Lord is gracious and compassionate. He provides food for those who fear Him... The works of His hands are faithful and just; all His precepts are trustworthy. They are steadfast for ever and** ever, done in faithfulness and uprightness... holy and awesome is His name. **The fear of the Lord is the beginning of wisdom; all who follow His precepts have good understanding.** To him belongs eternal praise. (Psalms, 111:1-10)

Praise the Lord. **Blessed is the man who fears the Lord, who finds great delight in His commands...** the generation of the upright will be blessed. **Wealth and riches are in his house, and his righteousness endures forever. Even in darkness light dawns for the upright, for the gracious and compassionate and righteous man. Good will come to him who is generous and lends freely, who conducts his affairs with justice. Surely he will never be shaken**; a righteous man will be remembered forever. **He will have no fear of bad news; his heart is steadfast, trusting in the Lord. His heart is secure, he will have no fear; in the end he will look in triumph on his foes.** He has scattered abroad his gifts to the poor, his righteousness endures forever; his horn will be lifted high in honor. The wicked man will see and be vexed, he will gnash his teeth and waste away; the longings of the wicked will come to nothing. (Psalms, 112:1-10)

Praise the Lord. Praise, O servants of the Lord, praise the name of the Lord. Let the name of the Lord be praised, both now and forevermore. From the rising of the Sun to the place where it sets, the name of the Lord is to be praised. **The Lord is exalted over all the nations, His glory above the heavens.** Who is like the Lord our God... Praise the Lord. (Psalms, 113:1-9)

But their idols are silver and gold, made by the hands of men. They have mouths, but cannot speak, eyes, but they cannot see; they have ears, but cannot hear, noses, but they cannot smell;

they have hands, but cannot feel, feet, but they cannot walk; nor can they utter a sound with their throats... trust in the Lord—He is their help and shield. **You who fear Him, trust in the Lord— He is their help and shield. He will bless those who fear the Lord— small and great alike.** May you be blessed by the Lord, the Maker of heaven and earth... Praise the Lord. (Psalms, 115: 1-18)

I love the Lord... **I will call on Him as long as I live**... I was overcome by trouble and sorrow. Then I called on the name of the Lord: "O Lord, save me!" **The Lord is gracious and righteous; our God is full of compassion. The Lord protects the simplehearted; when I was in great need, He saved me.** Be at rest once more, O my soul, for **the Lord has been good to you**. That I may walk before the Lord... I believed; therefore I said, "I am greatly afflicted." I will fulfill my vows to the Lord... Precious in the sight of the Lord is the death of His saints. O Lord, truly I am Your servant... I will sacrifice a thank offering to you and call on the name of the Lord... Praise the Lord. (Psalms, 116:1-19)

Praise the Lord, all you nations; extol Him, all you peoples. For **great is His love toward us, and the faithfulness of the Lord endures forever**. Praise the Lord. (Psalms, 117:1-2)

Give thanks to the Lord, for He is good; His love endures forever. Let those who fear the Lord say: "His love endures forever." **The Lord is with me; I will not be afraid. What can man do to me? The Lord is with me; He is my helper... It is better to take refuge in the Lord than to trust in man. It is better to take refuge in the Lord than to trust in princes...** I was pushed back and about to fall, but the Lord helped me... **He has become my salvation.** Shouts of joy and victory resound in the tents of the righteous:...

I... will proclaim what the Lord has done... This is the gate of the Lord through which the righteous may enter... I will give You thanks, for You answered me; You have become my salvation... The Lord has done this, and it is marvelous in our eyes. This is the day the Lord has made; let us rejoice and be glad in it. O Lord, save us; O Lord, grant us success. Blessed is he who comes in the name of the Lord... The Lord is God, and He has made His light shine upon us... You are my God, and I will give You thanks; You are my God, and I will exalt You. Give thanks to the Lord, for He is good; His love endures forever. (Psalms, 118:1-29)

Blessed are they whose ways are blameless, who walk according to the law of the Lord. Blessed are they who keep his statutes and seek Him with all their heart. They do nothing wrong; they walk in His ways. You have laid down precepts that are to be fully obeyed. Oh, that my ways were steadfast in obeying Your decrees! Then I would not be put to shame when I consider all Your commands. I will praise You with an upright heart as I learn Your righteous laws. I will obey Your decrees; do not utterly forsake me. How can a young man keep his way pure? By living according to Your word. I seek You with all my heart; do not let me stray from Your commands. **I have hidden Your word in my heart** that I might not sin against You. Praise be to You, O Lord; teach me Your decrees. With my lips I recount all the laws... **I rejoice in following your statutes as one rejoices in great riches.** I meditate on Your precepts and consider Your ways. I delight in Your decrees; I will not neglect Your word... Open my eyes that I may see wonderful things in Your law. I am a stranger on earth; do not hide Your commands from me [teach me the wisdom]. My soul is consumed with longing for Your laws at all times... Remove from me scorn and contempt, for I keep Your statutes. Though rulers sit together and slander me, Your servant will meditate on Your decrees. **Your statutes are my delight; they are my counselors...** Let me understand the teaching of Your precepts; then I will meditate on Your wonders... strengthen me according to Your word. Keep me from deceitful ways; be gracious to me through Your law. I have chosen the way of truth; I have set my heart on Your laws. I hold fast to Your statutes, O Lord; do not let me be put to shame. I run in the path of Your commands, for You have set my heart free. Teach me, O Lord, to follow Your decrees; then I will keep them to the end. Give me understanding, and I will keep Your law and obey it with all my heart. Direct me in the path of Your commands, for there I find delight. Turn my heart toward Your statutes and not toward selfish gain. Turn my eyes away from worthless things; preserve my life according to Your word... **Your laws are good.** How I long for your precepts! Preserve my life in Your righteousness. May Your unfailing love come to me, O Lord, Your salvation according to Your promise; then I will answer the one who taunts me, for **I trust in Your word**. Do not snatch the word of truth from my mouth, for I have put my hope in Your laws. I will always obey Your law, for ever and ever. I will walk about in freedom, for I have sought out Your precepts. I will speak of Your statutes before kings... for **I delight in Your commands because I love them**. I lift up my hands to Your commands, which I love, and **I meditate on Your decrees**... **Your promise preserves my life.** The arrogant mock me without restraint, but I do not turn from Your law. I remember Your ancient laws, O Lord, and I find comfort in them... Your decrees are the theme of my song wherever I lodge. In the night I remember Your name, O Lord, and I will keep Your law. This has been my practice: I obey Your precepts... O Lord; I have promised to obey Your words. I have sought Your face with all my heart; be gracious to me according to Your promise. I have considered my ways and have turned my steps to Your statutes. **I will hasten and not delay to obey Your commands.** Though the wicked bind me with ropes, **I will not forget Your law**. At midnight I rise to give You thanks for Your righteous laws. **I am a friend to all who fear You, to all who follow Your precepts.** The earth is filled with Your love, O Lord; teach me Your decrees. Do good to Your servant according to Your word, O Lord. Teach me knowledge and good judgment, for I believe in Your commands. Before I was afflicted I went astray, but now I obey Your word. **You are good, and what You do is good**; teach me Your decrees. Though the arrogant have smeared me with lies, I keep Your precepts with all my heart. Their hearts are callous and unfeeling, but I delight in Your law. It was good for me to be afflicted so that I might learn Your decrees... **The law... is more precious to me than thousands of pieces of silver and gold.** Your hands[35] made me and formed me; give me understanding to learn Your commands. May those who fear You rejoice when they see me, for **I have put my hope in Your word**. I know, O Lord, that **Your laws are righteous**... Let Your compassion come to me that I may live, for Your law is my delight... I will meditate on Your precepts. May those who fear You turn to me, those who understand Your statutes. May my heart be blameless toward Your decrees, that I may not be put to shame... I have put my hope in Your word... **All Your commands are trustworthy**; help me, for men persecute me without cause. They almost wiped me from the earth, but I have not forsaken Your precepts. Preserve

---

35. Allah's title of *Sani* (The Artist, He Who creates infinite beauties in His artistry) is described by use of simile.

my life according to Your love, and I will obey the statutes of Your mouth. **Your word, O Lord, is eternal**; it stands firm in the heavens. **Your faithfulness continues through all generations**; You established the earth, and it endures. Your laws endure to this day, for all things serve You. If your law had not been my delight, I would have perished in my affliction. I will never forget Your precepts, for by them You have preserved my life. Save me, for I am yours; I have sought out Your precepts. The wicked are waiting to destroy me, but **I will ponder Your statutes**. To all perfection I see a limit; but **Your commands are boundless**. Oh, how I love Your law! I meditate on it all day long. **Your commands make me wiser than my enemies**, for they are ever with me. I have more insight than all my teachers, for I meditate on Your statutes. I have more understanding than the elders, for I obey Your precepts. I have kept my feet from every evil path so that I might obey Your word. I have not departed from Your laws, for You Yourself have taught me. How sweet are Your words to my taste, sweeter than honey to my mouth! **I gain understanding from Your precepts**; therefore I hate every wrong path. **Your word is a lamp to my feet and a light for my path.** I have taken an oath and confirmed it, that I will follow Your righteous laws. I have suffered much; preserve my life, O Lord, according to Your word. Accept, O Lord, the willing praise of my mouth, and teach me Your laws. Though I constantly take my life in my hands, I will not forget Your law. The wicked have set a snare for me, but I have not strayed from Your precepts. **Your statutes are my heritage forever; they are the joy of my heart.** My heart is set on keeping Your decrees to the very end... but I love Your law. **You are my refuge and my shield**; I have put my hope in Your word. Away from me, you evildoers, that I may keep the commands of

WISDOM AND SOUND ADVICE FROM THE TORAH

my God! Sustain me according to Your promise, and I will live... Uphold me, and I will be delivered; I will always have regard for Your decrees... teach me Your decrees. I am Your servant; give me discernment that I may understand Your statutes... Because I love Your commands more than gold, more than pure gold, and because I consider all Your precepts right, I hate every wrong path. Your statutes are wonderful; therefore I obey them. **The unfolding of Your words gives light; it gives understanding to the simple.** I open my mouth and pant, longing for Your commands. Turn to me and have mercy on me, as You always do to those who love Your name. Direct my footsteps according to Your word; let no sin rule over me. Redeem me from the oppression of men, that I may obey Your precepts. Make Your face shine upon Your servant and teach me Your decrees. **Righteous are You, O Lord, and Your laws are right.** The statutes You have laid down are righteous; they are fully trustworthy... my enemies ignore Your words. Your promises have been thoroughly tested, and Your servant loves them... I do not forget Your precepts. Your righteousness is everlasting and Your law is true... Your commands are my delight. Your statutes are forever right; give me understanding that I may live. I call with all my heart; answer me, O Lord, and I will obey Your decrees. I call out to You; save me and I will keep Your statutes. I rise before dawn and cry for help; I have put my hope in Your word. My eyes stay open through the watches of the night, that I may meditate on Your promises... Those who devise wicked schemes are near, but they are far from Your law. Yet You are near, O Lord, and all Your commands are true. Long ago I learned from Your statutes that You established them to last forever... Salvation is far from the wicked, for they do not seek out Your decrees. **Your compassion is great**, O Lord; preserve my life according to Your laws. Many are the foes who persecute me, but I have not turned from Your statutes... See how I love Your precepts; preserve my life, O Lord, according to Your love. **All Your words are true; all Your righteous laws are eternal...** but my heart trembles at Your word. I rejoice in Your promise like one who finds great spoil. I hate and abhor falsehood but I love Your law... Great peace have they who love Your law, I wait for your salvation, O Lord, and I follow Your commands. **I obey your statutes, for I love them greatly.** I obey Your precepts and Your statutes, for all my ways are known to You... give me understanding according to Your word. May my supplication come before You; deliver me according to Your promise... You teach me Your decrees. May my tongue sing of Your word, for all Your commands are righteous... I long for Your salvation, O Lord, and **Your law is my delight**. Let me live that I may praise you, and may Your laws sustain me. (Psalms, 119:1-175)

I call on the Lord in my distress, Save me, O Lord, from lying lips and from deceitful tongues... **I am a man of peace**; but when I speak, they are for war. (Psalms, 120:1-2, 7)

... Where does my help come from? **My help comes from the Lord**, the Maker of heaven and earth. **He will not let your foot slip—He Who watches over you will not slumber; indeed, He... will neither slumber nor sleep. The Lord watches over you—the Lord is your shade at your right hand**[36]; the Sun will not harm you by day, nor the Moon by night. **The Lord will keep you from all harm— He will watch over your life**; the Lord will watch over your coming and going both now and forevermore. (Psalms, 121:1-8)

---

36. He is the Compassionate, the Protector.

I rejoiced with those who said to me, "Let us go to the house of the Lord." Our feet are standing in Your gates [the entrance to the holy place where God's name is remembered]... "**May those who love You be secure. May there be peace within your walls and security within your citadels.**" For the sake of my brothers and friends, I will say, "**Peace be within you.**"... **I will seek your prosperity.** (Psalms, 122:1-9)

Praise be to the Lord... **Our help is in the name of the Lord, the Maker of heaven and earth.** (Psalms, 124:6-8)

Those who trust in the Lord... cannot be shaken but endures forever. (Psalms, 125:1)

Unless the Lord builds the house, its builders labor in vain. Unless the Lord watches over the city, the watchmen stand guard in vain... toiling for food to eat—He grants sleep to those He loves. (Psalms, 127:1-2)

Blessed are all who fear the Lord, who walk in His ways. You will eat the fruit of your labor; blessings and prosperity will be yours... Thus is the man blessed who fears the Lord. (Psalms, 128:1-4)

Out of the depths I cry to you, O Lord; O Lord... If you, O Lord, kept a record of sins, O Lord, who could stand? But **with You there is forgiveness** therefore You are feared. I wait for the Lord, [I love God, I seek His approval], my soul waits, and **in His word I put my hope**. My soul waits [loves God, seeks His approval] for the Lord more than watchmen wait for the morning, more than watchmen wait for the morning... put your hope in the Lord, for **with the Lord is unfailing love and with Him is full redemption**. (Psalms, 130:1-7)

My heart is not proud, O Lord, my eyes are not haughty... I have stilled and quieted my soul... **put your hope in the Lord both now and forevermore**. (Psalms, 131:1-3)

May your priests be clothed with righteousness; may your saints sing for joy... I will clothe her priests with salvation, and her saints will ever sing for joy. (Psalms, 132:9, 16)

How good and pleasant it is when brothers live together in unity! (Psalms, 133:1)

All you servants of the Lord... praise the Lord... the Maker of heaven and earth. (Psalms, 134:1-3)

Praise the Lord. Praise the name of the Lord; praise Him, you servants of the Lord... Praise the Lord, for **the Lord is good**; sing praise to His name, for that is pleasant... I know that **the Lord is great**... **The Lord does whatever pleases Him, in the heavens and on the earth, in the seas and all their depths.** He makes clouds rise from the ends of the earth; He sends lightning with the rain and brings out the wind from His storehouses... Your name, O Lord, endures forever, Your renown, O Lord, through all generations... For **the Lord will... have compassion on His servants.** The idols of the nations are silver and gold, made by the hands of men. They have mouths, but cannot speak, eyes, but they cannot see; they have ears, but cannot hear nor is there breath in their mouths... Praise the Lord; you who fear Him, praise the Lord... Praise the Lord. (Psalms, 135:1-21)

Give thanks to the Lord, for **He is good. His love endures forever**... Give thanks... His love endures forever. Give thanks to the Lord... His love endures forever. To **Him Who alone does great**

wonders, His love endures forever. **Who by His understanding made the heavens**, His love endures forever. **Who spread out the earth upon the waters**, His love endures forever. **Who made the great lights**—His love endures forever. **The Sun to govern the day**, His love endures forever. **The Moon and stars to govern the night**; His love endures forever... and freed us from our enemies, His love endures forever. And **Who gives food to every creature**. His love endures forever. Give thanks to the God of heaven [and earth]. His love endures forever. (Psalms, 136:1-9, 24-26)

I will praise you, O Lord, with all my heart... will praise Your name for Your love and Your faithfulness... **When I called, You answered me; You made me bold and stouthearted.** May all the kings of the earth praise You, O Lord... May they sing of the ways of the Lord, for **the glory of the Lord is great**... **He looks upon [protects] the lowly**... Though I walk in the midst of trouble, You preserve my life; **The Lord will fulfill His purpose for me**; Your love, O Lord, endures forever—do not abandon the works of Your hands.[37] (Psalms, 138:1-8)

O Lord... You know when I sit and when I rise; You perceive my thought... You discern my going out and my lying down; You are familiar with all my ways. Before a word is on my tongue You know it completely, O Lord. You hem me in—behind and before; You have laid Your hand[38]... upon me... If I go up to the heavens, You are there... If I rise on the wings of the dawn, if I settle on the far side of the sea, even there Your hand will guide me, Your right hand will hold me fast.[39] If I say, "Surely the darkness

---

37. Allah's title of *Sani* (The Artist, He Who creates infinite beauties in His artistry) is described by use of simile.
38. Allah's blessings, are described by way of simile.
39. A reference to the manifestation of Allah's name of "Al-'Asim," meaning "The Protector."

will hide me and the light become night around me," even the darkness will not be dark to You; the night will shine like the day, for darkness is as light to You. For **You created my inmost being; You knit me together in my mother's womb**. I praise You because I am fearfully and wonderfully made; Your works are wonderful, I know that full well... When I was woven together in the depths of the earth, Your eyes[40] saw my unformed body. **All the days ordained for me were written in Your book before one of them came to be.** How precious to me are Your thoughts[41] O God! How vast is the sum of them! Were I to count them, they would outnumber the grains of sand. When I awake, I am still with You... lead me in the way everlasting [paradise]. (Psalms, 139:1-24)

Rescue me, O Lord, from evil men; protect me from men of violence, who devise evil plans in their hearts and stir up war every day. They make their tongues as sharp as a serpent's; the poison of vipers is on their lips. Keep me, O Lord, from the hands of the wicked; protect me from men of violence... O Lord, I say to You, "You are my God." Hear, O Lord, my cry for mercy. O Sovereign Lord, my strong deliverer... do not grant the wicked their desires, O Lord; do not let their plans succeed... I know that **the Lord secures justice for the poor**... Surely the righteous will praise Your name and **the upright will live before You**. (Psalms, 140:1-13)

O Lord, I call to You... Set a guard over my mouth [give me mercy], O Lord; keep watch over the door of my lips. Let not my heart be drawn to what is evil, to take part in wicked deeds with men who are evildoers... Let a righteous man strike me—it is a

---

40. As a manifestation of Allah's name of *al-Basir*, the One Who best sees everything at every moment.
41. Examples of His mercy, used in the sense of blessings He creates for His servants.

kindness; let him rebuke me—it is oil on my head. My head will not refuse it. Yet my prayer is ever against the deeds of evildoers. But **my eyes are fixed on You**, O Sovereign Lord; **in You I take refuge**—do not leave my soul destitute. Keep me from the snares they have laid for me, from the traps set by evildoers. Let the wicked fall into their own nets, while I pass by in safety. (Psalms, 141:1-10)

I cry aloud to the Lord; I lift up my voice to the Lord for mercy... it is You Who know my way... I cry to You, O Lord; I say, "**You are my refuge, my portion in the land of the living**." Listen to my cry, for I am in desperate need; rescue me from those who pursue me, for they are too strong for me.. (Psalms, 142:1-6)

O Lord, hear my prayer, listen to my cry for mercy; **in Your faithfulness and righteousness come to my relief**... I remember the days of long ago; I meditate on all Your works... **I spread out my hands to You; my soul thirsts for You like a parched land**... Let the morning bring me word of Your unfailing love, for **I have put my trust in You**. Show me the way I should go, for **to You I lift up my soul**. Rescue me from my enemies, O Lord, for I hide myself in You. Teach me to do Your will, for You are my God; may Your good Spirit [Your mercy and Your Light] lead me on level ground. For Your name's sake, O Lord, preserve my life; in your righteousness, bring me out of trouble. In Your unfailing love... for I am Your servant. (Psalms, 143:1-12)

... Praise be to the Lord! **He is my loving God and my fortress [protector], my stronghold and my deliverer, my shield, in Whom I take refuge**... Man is like a breath; His days are like a fleeting shadow... I will sing a new song to you,

O God; on the ten-stringed lyre I will make music to You. Deliver me and rescue me... blessed are the people whose God is the Lord! (Psalms, 144:1-15)

I will exalt You, my God, I will praise Your name for ever and ever. Every day I will praise You and extol Your name for ever and ever. **Great is the Lord and most worthy of praise; His greatness no one can fathom**. One generation will commend Your works to another; they will tell of Your mighty acts. They will speak of the glorious splendor of Your majesty, and I will meditate on Your wonderful works. They will tell of the power of Your awesome works, and I will proclaim Your great deeds. They will celebrate Your abundant goodness and joyfully sing of Your righteousness. **The Lord is gracious and compassionate... The Lord is good to all; He has compassion on all He has made.** All You have made[42] will praise You, O Lord; Your saints will extol You... **The eyes of all hope in You, and You give them their food at the proper time. You open Your hand,**[43] and satisfy the desires of every living thing. **The Lord is righteous in all His ways and loving toward all He has made. The Lord is near to all who call on Him, to all who call on Him in truth. He fulfills the desires of those who fear Him; He hears their cry and saves them. The Lord watches over all who love Him**... My mouth will speak in praise of the Lord. Let every creature praise His holy name for ever and ever. (Psalms, 145:1-21)

---

42. What is meant here is everything created by our Lord.
43. As a manifestation of Allah's attribute of al-Karim, the Benevolent.

Praise the Lord. Praise the Lord, O my soul. I will praise the Lord all my life; I will sing praise to my God as long as I live. Do not put your trust in princes, in mortal men, who cannot save. When their spirit departs, they return to the ground; on that very day their plans come to nothing. **Blessed is he whose hope is in the Lord his God, the Maker of heaven and earth, the sea, and everything in them—the Lord, Who remains faithful forever. He upholds the cause of the oppressed and gives food to the hungry. The Lord sets prisoners free, the Lord gives sight to the blind, the Lord lifts up those who are bowed down, the Lord loves the righteous. The Lord watches over the alien and sustains the fatherless and the widow**, but He frustrates the ways of the wicked... Praise the Lord. (Psalms, 146:1-10)

Praise the Lord. How good it is to sing praises to our God, how pleasant and fitting to praise Him! **He determines the number of the stars... Great is our Lord and mighty in power; His understanding has no limit. The Lord sustains the humble but casts the wicked to the ground.** Sing to the Lord with thanksgiving; make music to our God on the harp. He covers the sky with clouds; He supplies the earth with rain and makes grass grow on the hills. He provides food for the cattle and for the young ravens when they call... **The Lord delights in those who fear Him, who put their hope in His unfailing love.** Praise your God... He sends His command to the earth; His word runs swiftly. He spreads the snow like wool and scatters the frost like ashes. He hurls down His hail like pebbles. Who can withstand His icy blast? He sends His word and melts them; He stirs up His breezes, and the waters flow... Praise the Lord. (Psalms, 147:1-20)

Praise the Lord. Praise the Lord from the heavens, praise Him in the heights above. Praise Him, all His angels, praise Him... Praise Him, Sun and Moon, praise Him, all you shining stars. Praise Him, you highest heavens and you waters above the skies. Let them praise the name of the Lord, for He commanded and they were created... He gave a decree that will never pass away. Praise the Lord from the earth, you great sea creatures and all ocean depths, lightning and hail, snow and clouds, stormy winds that do His bidding, you mountains and all hills, fruit trees and all cedars, wild animals and all cattle, small creatures and flying birds, kings of the earth and all nations, you princes and all rulers on earth, young men and maidens, old men and children. Let them praise the name of the Lord, for **His name alone is exalted; His splendor is above the earth and the heavens**... Praise the Lord! (Psalms, 148:1-14)

Praise the Lord. Sing to the Lord a new song, His praise in the assembly of the saints. Let them praise His name with dancing and make music to Him with tambourine and harp... **He crowns the humble with salvation.** Let the saints rejoice in this honor and sing for joy on their beds. May the praise of God be in their mouths... Praise the Lord! (Psalms, 149:1-9)

Praise the Lord!... Praise Him in His mighty heavens. **Praise Him for His acts of power; praise Him for His surpassing greatness.** Praise Him with the sounding of the trumpet, praise Him with the harp and lyre, praise Him with tambourine and dancing, praise Him with the strings and flute, praise Him with the clash of cymbals, praise Him with resounding cymbals. Let everything that has breath praise the Lord. Praise the Lord. (Psalms, 150:1-6)

Proverbs

The proverbs of Solomon... **for attaining wisdom and discipline; for understanding words of insight; for acquiring a disciplined and prudent life, doing what is right and just and fair; for giving prudence to the simple, knowledge and discretion to the young**. Let the wise listen and add to their learning, and let the discerning get guidance... (Proverbs, 1:1-6)

The fear of the Lord is the beginning of knowledge, but fools despise wisdom and discipline... My son, **if sinners entice you, do not give in to them.** If they say, "Come along with us; let's lie in wait for someone's blood, let's waylay some harmless soul... we will get all sorts of valuable things and fill our houses with plunder; throw in your lot with us, and we will share a common purse." My son, do not go along with them, do not set foot on their paths; for their feet run to evil, they are swift to shed blood... **These men lie in wait for their own blood; they waylay only themselves! Such is the end of all who go after ill-gotten gain; it takes away the lives of those who get it.** (Proverbs, 1:7-19)

Wisdom calls aloud in the street... How long will you simple ones love your simple ways? How long will mockers delight in mockery and fools hate knowledge? If you had responded to my rebuke, I would... made My thoughts known to you. But since you rejected Me when I called and no one gave heed when I stretched out My hand, since you ignored all My advice and would not accept My rebuke [God is beyond that], since they hated knowledge and did not choose to fear the Lord, since they would not accept My advice and spurned My rebuke, they will eat the fruit of their ways and be filled with the fruit of their schemes. For the way-

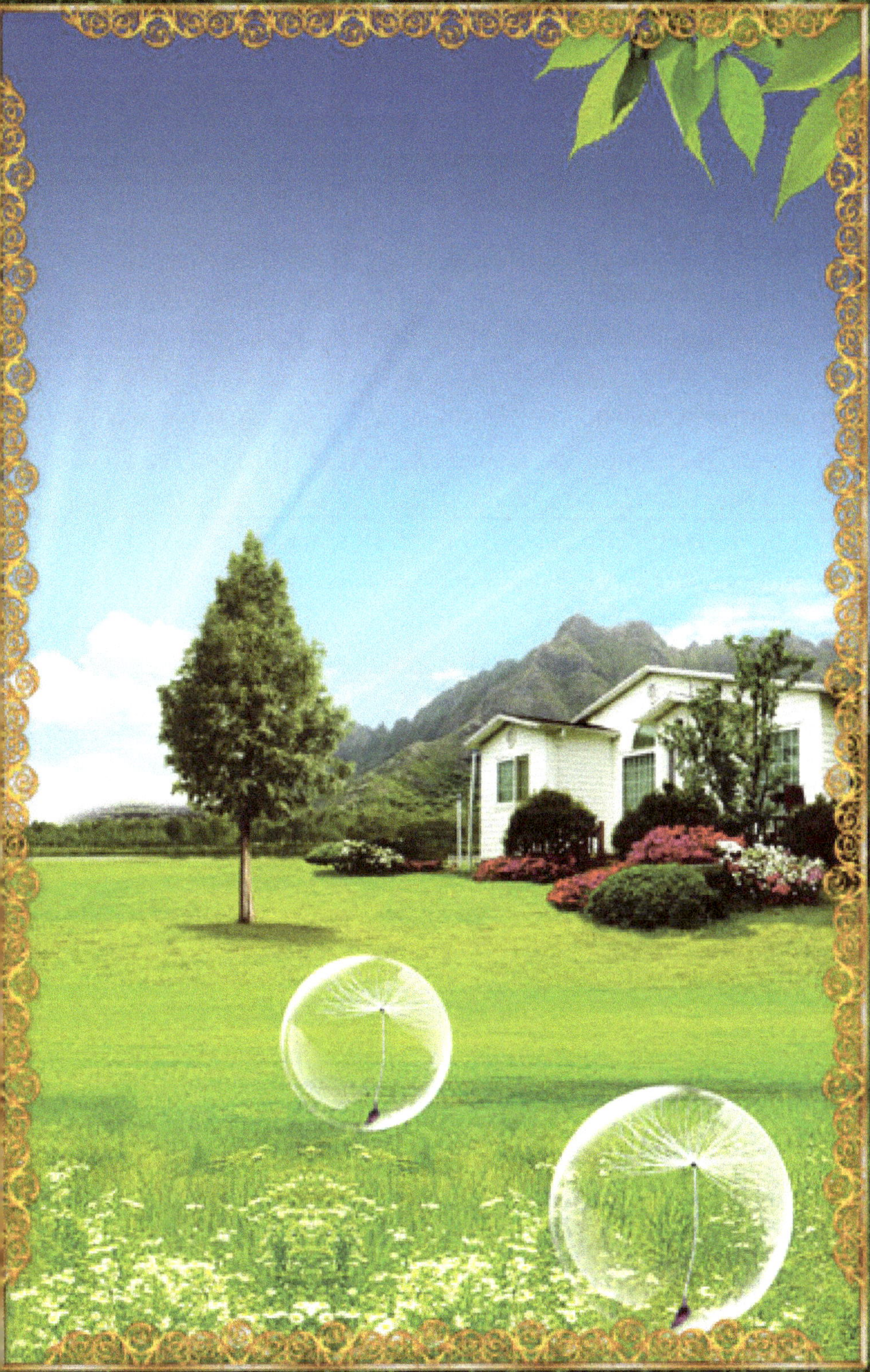

wardness of the simple will kill them, and the complacency of fools will destroy them; but **whoever listens to Me will live in safety and be at ease, without fear of harm."** (Proverbs, 1:20-33)

My son, if you accept My words and store up My commands within you, turning your ear to wisdom and applying your heart to understanding, and if you call out for insight and cry aloud for understanding, and if you look for it as for silver and search for it as for hidden treasure, then **you will understand the fear of the Lord and find the knowledge of God. For the Lord gives wisdom, and from His mouth [His words] come knowledge and understanding. He holds victory in store for the upright, He is protection to those whose walk is blameless, for He guards the course of the just and protects the way of His faithful ones.** Then you will understand what is right and just and fair—every good path. For wisdom will enter your heart, and knowledge will be pleasant to your soul. Discretion will protect you, and understanding will guard you. **Wisdom will save you** from the ways of wicked men, from men whose words are perverse, who leave the straight paths to walk in dark ways, who delight in doing wrong and rejoice in the perverseness of evil, whose paths are crooked and who are devious in their ways... **Thus you will walk in the ways of good men and keep to the paths of the righteous. For the upright will live in the land, and the blameless will remain in it; but the wicked will be cut off from the land, and the unfaithful will be torn from it.** (Proverbs, 2:1-20)

My son, do not forget my teaching, but keep my commands in your heart for they will prolong your life many years and bring you prosperity. **Let love and faithfulness never leave you; bind** them around your neck, write them on the tablet of your heart. Then you will win favor and a good name in the sight of God and man. **Trust in the Lord with all your heart and lean not on your own understanding; in all your ways acknowledge Him, and He will make your paths straight.** Do not be wise in your own eyes; fear the Lord and shun evil. Do not be wise in your own eyes; **fear the Lord and shun evil**. This will bring health to your body and nourishment to your bones. **Honor the Lord** with your wealth, with the first fruits of all your crops; then your barns will be filled to overflowing… (Proverbs, 3:1-10)

Blessed is the man who finds wisdom, the man who gains understanding, for she is more profitable than silver and yields better returns than gold. She is more precious than rubies; nothing you desire can compare with her... Her ways are pleasant ways, and all her paths are peace. She is a tree of life to those who embrace her; those who lay hold of her will be blessed... My son, preserve sound judgment and discernment, do not let them out of your sight; they will be life for you, an ornament to grace your neck. Then you will go on your way in safety, and your foot will not stumble; when you lie down, you will not be afraid; when you lie down, your sleep will be sweet. **Have no fear of sudden disaster or of the ruin that overtakes the wicked, for the Lord will be your confidence and will keep your foot from being snared.** Do not withhold good from those who deserve it, when it is in your power to act. Do not say to your neighbor, "Come back later; I'll give it tomorrow"—when you now have it with you. Do not plot harm against your neighbor, who lives trustfully near you... Do not envy a violent man or choose any of his ways, for the Lord dislikes a perverse man but takes the upright

into His confidence. The Lord's curse is on the house of the wicked but He blesses the home of the righteous. God mocks them but **gives grace to the humble.** The wise inherit honor, but fools He holds up to shame. (Proverbs, 3:13-35)

... Pay attention and gain understanding. I give you sound learning, so do not forsake my teaching... **"Lay hold of my words with all your heart...** Get wisdom, get understanding; do not forget my words or swerve from them. Do not forsake wisdom, and she will protect you [by God's will]; love her, and she will watch over you [by God's will]. The first sign of wisdom is to get wisdom; go give all you have to get true knowledge. Esteem her, and she will exalt you; embrace her, and she will honor you. She will set a garland of grace on your head and present you with a crown of splendor." Listen, my son, accept what I say, and the years of your life will be many. **I guide you in the way of wisdom and lead you along straight paths.** When you walk, your steps will not be hampered; when you run, you will not stumble. Hold on to instruction, do not let it go; guard it well, for it is your life. **Do not set foot on the path of the wicked or walk in the way of evil men. Avoid it, do not travel on it; turn from it and go on your way.** For they sleep not except they have done mischief, and their sleep is taken away unless they have caused some to fall.. They eat the bread of wickedness and drink the wine of violence. **The path of the righteous is like the first gleam of dawn, shining ever brighter till the full light of day. But the way of the wicked is like deep darkness; they do not know what makes them stumble.** My son, pay attention to what I say; listen closely to My words. Do not let them out of your sight, keep them within your heart; for they are life to those who find them and health to a man's whole body. Above all else, guard your heart, for it is the wellspring of life. **Put away perversity from your mouth; keep corrupt talk far from your lips.** Let your eyes look straight ahead, fix your gaze directly before you. Make level paths for your feet and take only ways that are firm. **Do not swerve to the right or the left; keep your foot from evil.** (Proverbs, 4:1-27)

My son, pay attention to my wisdom, listen well to my words of insight, that you may maintain discretion and your lips may preserve knowledge... Now then, my sons, listen to me; do not turn aside from what I say... **At the end of your life you will groan, when your flesh and body are spent.** You will say, "How I hated discipline! How my heart spurned correction! I would not obey my teachers or listen to my instructors... **For a man's ways are in full view of the Lord, and He examines all his paths.** The evil deeds of a wicked man ensnare him; the cords of his sin hold him fast. He will die for lack of discipline, led astray by his own great folly. (Proverbs, 5:1-23)

Go to the ant, you sluggard; consider its ways and be wise!... How long will you lie there, you sluggard? When will you get up from your sleep? A little sleep, a little slumber, a little folding of the hands to rest and poverty will come on you like a bandit and scarcity like an armed man. A scoundrel and villain, who goes about with a corrupt mouth, who winks with his eye, signals with his feet and motions with his fingers, who plots evil with deceit in his heart—he always stirs up dissension. Therefore disaster will overtake him in an instant; he will suddenly be destroyed—without remedy... **The Lord dislikes... haughty eyes, a lying tongue, hands that shed innocent blood, a heart that devises wicked schemes, feet that are quick to rush into evil, a false wit-**

ness who pours out lies and a man who stirs up dissension among brothers. (Proverbs, 6:6-19)

A man who commits adultery lacks judgment; whoever does so destroys himself... and his reproach will never be wiped away... (Proverbs, 6:32-33)

My son, keep my words and store up my commands within you. Keep my commands and you will live [live in the paradise]; guard my teachings as the apple of your eye. Bind them on your fingers; write them on the tablet of your heart. Say to wisdom, "You are my sister," and call understanding your kinsman. (Proverbs, 7:1-4)

Does not wisdom call out? Does not understanding raise her voice? On the heights along the way, where the paths meet, she takes her stand; beside the gates leading into the city, at the entrances, she cries aloud: "To you, O men, I call out; I raise my voice to all mankind. **You who are simple, gain prudence;** you who are foolish, gain understanding. Listen, for I have worthy things to say; I open my lips to speak what is right. My mouth speaks what is true, for my lips dislike wickedness. All the words of my mouth are just; none of them is crooked or perverse. To the discerning all of them are right; they are faultless to those who have knowledge. Choose my instruction instead of silver, knowledge rather than choice gold, for **wisdom is better than jewels,** and nothing you desire can compare with her. "I, wisdom, dwell together with prudence; I possess knowledge and discretion. **To fear the Lord is to hate evil; I hate pride and arrogance, evil behavior and perverse speech.** (Proverbs, 8:1-13)

I walk in the way of righteousness, along the paths of justice... I was filled with delight day after day, **rejoicing always in His presence,** rejoicing in His whole world and delighting in mankind [sincere believers]. "Now then, My sons, listen to Me; **blessed are those who keep My ways. Listen to My instruction and be wise; do not ignore it. Blessed is the man who listens to Me... For whoever finds Me finds life and receives favor from the Lord**. But whoever fails to find Me harms himself... (Proverbs, 8:20, 31-36)

... Walk in the way of understanding... Rebuke a wise man and he will love you. Instruct a wise man and he will be wiser still; teach a righteous man and he will add to his learning. "**The fear of the Lord is the beginning of wisdom, and knowledge of the Holy One [God] is understanding... If you are wise, your wisdom will reward you; if you are a mocker, you alone will suffer.**" The woman folly is loud; she is undisciplined and without knowledge. She sits at the door of her house, on a seat at the highest point of the city, calling out to those who pass by, who go straight on their way. "Let all who are simple come in here!" she says to those who lack judgment. "Stolen water is sweet; food eaten in secret is delicious!" But little do they know that the dead are there, that her guests are in the depths of the world of death [hell]. (Proverbs, 9:6-18)

Ill-gotten treasures are of no value, but righteousness delivers from death [hell]. The Lord does not let the righteous go hungry but He thwarts the craving of the wicked. Lazy hands make a man poor, but diligent hands bring wealth... Blessings crown the head of the righteous, but violence overwhelms the mouth of the wicked. The memory of the righteous will be a blessing, but the name of the wicked will rot. **The wise in heart accept commands, but a chattering fool comes to ruin. The man of integrity walks securely, but he who takes crooked paths will be found out.** He who winks maliciously causes grief, and a chattering fool comes to ruin. **The mouth of the righteous is a fountain of life,** but violence overwhelms the mouth of the wicked. **Hatred stirs up dissension, but love covers over all wrongs.** Wisdom is found on the lips of the discerning, but a rod is for the back of him who lacks judgment. Wise men store up knowledge, but the mouth of a fool invites ruin... He who heeds discipline shows the way to life, but whoever ignores correction leads others astray... whoever spreads slander is a fool. **When words are many, sin is not absent, but he who holds his tongue is wise. The tongue of the righteous is choice silver, but the heart of the wicked is of little value.** The lips of the righteous nourish many, but fools die for lack of judgment. T**he blessing of the Lord brings wealth...** A fool finds pleasure in evil conduct, but a man of understanding delights in wisdom. What the wicked dreads will overtake him; what the righteous desire will be granted... the righteous stand firm forever[1]... As vinegar to the teeth and smoke to the eyes, so is a sluggard to those who send him. **The fear of the Lord adds length to life, but the years of the wicked are cut short [unfruitful]. The prospect of the righteous is joy, but the hopes of the wicked come to nothing. The way of the Lord is a refuge for the righteous, but it is the ruin of those who do evil. The righteous will never be uprooted... The mouth of the righteous brings forth wisdom... but the mouth of the wicked only what is perverse.** (Proverbs, 10:2-32)

---

1. For those seeking Allah's approval, the good news of the existence of the eternal life of paradise is given.

The Lord abhors dishonest scales, but accurate weights are His delight. When pride comes, then comes disgrace, but with humility comes wisdom. The integrity of the upright guides them, but the unfaithful are destroyed by their duplicity. **Wealth is worthless in the day of wrath, but righteousness delivers from death [hell]. The righteousness of the blameless makes a straight way for them,** but the wicked are brought down by their own wickedness. **The righteousness of the upright delivers them, but the unfaithful are trapped by evil desires. When a wicked man dies, his hope perishes; all he expected from his power comes to nothing. The righteous man is rescued from trouble, and it comes on the wicked instead.** With his mouth the godless destroys his neighbor, but through knowledge the righteous escape. **When the righteous prosper, the city rejoices...** Through the blessing of the upright a city is exalted, but by the mouth of the wicked it is destroyed. A man who lacks judgment derides his neighbor, but a man of understanding holds his tongue. A gossip betrays a confidence, but a trustworthy man keeps a secret. For lack of guidance a nation falls, but many advisers make victory sure... **A kindhearted woman gains respect,** but ruthless men gain only wealth. A kind man benefits himself, but a cruel man brings trouble on himself. The wicked man earns deceptive wages, but he who sows righteousness reaps a sure reward. **The truly righteous man attains life [paradise], but he who pursues evil goes to his death [hell]. The Lord dislikes men of perverse heart but He delights in those whose ways are blameless. Be sure of this: The wicked will not go unpunished, but those who are righteous will go free.** Like a gold ring in a pig's snout is a beautiful woman who shows no discretion. **The desire of the righteous ends only in good, but the hope of the**

wicked only in wrath. One man gives freely, yet gains even more; another withholds unduly, but comes to poverty. A generous man will prosper; he who refreshes others will himself be refreshed. People curse the man who hoards grain, but blessing crowns him who is willing to sell. He who seeks good finds goodwill, but evil comes to him who searches for it. **Whoever trusts in his riches will fall, but the righteous will thrive like a green leaf.** (Proverbs, 11:1-31)

Whoever loves discipline loves knowledge, but he who hates correction is stupid. A good man obtains favor from the Lord, but the Lord condemns a crafty man. A **man cannot be established through wickedness,** a wife of noble character is her husband's crown... **The plans of the righteous are just, but the advice of the wicked is deceitful. The words of the wicked lie in wait for blood, but the speech of the upright rescues them. Wicked men are overthrown and are no more, but the house of the righteous stands firm.** A man is praised according to his wisdom, but men with warped minds are despised... The kindest acts of the wicked are cruel... **The wicked desire the plunder of evil men, but the root of the righteous nourishes. An evil man is trapped by his sinful talk, but a righteous man escapes trouble.** From the fruit of his lips a man is filled with good things as surely as the work of his hands rewards him. The way of a fool seems right to him, but a wise man listens to advice. A fool shows his annoyance at once, but a prudent man overlooks an insult. A truthful witness gives honest testimony, but a false witness tells lies. Reckless words pierce like a sword, but the tongue of the wise brings healing... There is deceit in the hearts of those who plot evil, but joy for those who promote peace. **No harm befalls**

the righteous, but the wicked have their fill of trouble. The Lord dislikes lying lips, but He delights in men who are truthful... An anxious heart weighs a man down, but a kind word cheers him up. A righteous man is cautious in friendship, but the way of the wicked leads them astray... **In the way of righteousness there is life; along that path is immortality**.[2] (Proverbs, 12:1-28)

A wise son heeds his father's instruction, but a mocker does not listen to rebuke. From the fruit of his lips a man enjoys good things, but the unfaithful have a craving for violence. He who guards his lips guards his life, but he who speaks rashly will come to ruin... **The righteous hate what is false, but the wicked bring shame and disgrace. Righteousness guards the man of integrity, but wickedness overthrows the sinner...** The light of the righteous shines brightly, but the lamp of the wicked is snuffed out. **Pride only breeds quarrels**, but wisdom is found in those who take advice... **He who scorns instruction will pay for it, but he who respects a command [commands of God] is rewarded.** The teaching of the wise is a fountain of life, turning a man from the snares of death.[3] **Good understanding wins favor, but the way of the unfaithful is hard.** Every prudent man acts out of knowledge, but a fool exposes his folly. A wicked messenger falls into trouble, but a trustworthy envoy brings healing. **He who ignores discipline comes to poverty and shame, but whoever heeds correction is honored...** Fools dislike turning from evil. He who walks with the wise grows wise, but a companion of fools suffers harm. Evil pursues the sinner, but prosperity is the re-

---

2. For those seeking Allah's approval, the good news of the existence of the eternal life of paradise is given.
3. Here, life and death refer to paradise and hell.

ward of the righteous... he who loves him [his son] is careful to discipline him. (Proverbs, 13:1-25)

He whose walk is upright fears the Lord... A fool's talk brings a rod to his back, but the lips of the wise protect them... A truthful witness does not deceive, but a false witness pours out lies. The mocker seeks wisdom and finds none, but knowledge comes easily to the discerning. **Stay away from a foolish man, for you will not find knowledge on his lips**. The wisdom of the prudent is to give thought to their ways, but the folly of fools is deception... goodwill is found among the upright... The tent of the upright will flourish. There is a way that seems right to a man, but in the end it leads to death [hell]... The faithless will be fully repaid for their ways, and the good man rewarded for his. A simple man believes anything, but a prudent man gives thought to his steps. **A wise man fears the Lord and shuns evil, but a fool is hotheaded and reckless.** A quick-tempered man does foolish things, and a crafty man is hated. The simple inherit folly, but the prudent are crowned with knowledge... He who despises his neighbor sins, but blessed is he who is kind to the needy. Do not those who plot evil go astray? But **those who plan what is good find love and faithfulness.** All hard work brings a profit, but mere talk leads only to poverty... the folly of fools yields folly. A truthful witness saves lives, but a false witness is deceitful. **He who fears the Lord has a secure fortress, and for his children it will be a refuge. The fear of the Lord is a fountain of life [It becomes a means for the righteous to attain paradise], turning a man from the snares of death [hell]... A patient man has great understanding, but a quick-tempered man displays folly. A heart at peace gives life to the body, but envy rots the bones...** whoever is kind to the needy honors God. When calamity comes, the wicked are brought down... Wisdom reposes in the heart of the discerning... Righteousness exalts a nation, but sin is a disgrace to any people. (Proverbs, 14:1-34)

A gentle answer turns away wrath, but a harsh word stirs up anger. **The tongue of the wise commends knowledge, but the mouth of the fool gushes folly. The eyes[4] of the Lord are everywhere, keeping watch on the wicked and the good**. The tongue that brings healing is a tree of life, but a deceitful tongue crushes the spirit. A fool spurns his father's discipline, but whoever heeds correction shows prudence. **The house of the righteous contains great treasure,** but the income of the wicked brings them trouble. The lips of the wise spread knowledge; not so the hearts of fools... **The prayer of the upright pleases Him. The Lord dislikes the way of the wicked but He loves those who pursue righteousness...** A mocker resents correction; he will not consult the wise. A happy heart makes the face cheerful, but heartache crushes the spirit. The discerning heart seeks knowledge, but the mouth of a fool feeds on folly... The cheerful heart has a continual feast. **Better a little with the fear of the Lord than great wealth with turmoil.** Better a meal of vegetables where there is love than a fattened calf with hatred. A hot-tempered man stirs up dissension, but a patient man calms a quarrel. The way of the sluggard is blocked with thorns, but the path of the upright is a highway. A wise son brings joy to his father, but a foolish man despises his mother. Folly delights a man who lacks judgment, but a man of understanding keeps a straight course. Plans fail for lack of counsel, but with many advisers they succeed. A man finds joy in giving an apt reply—and how good is a

---

4. Allah's name of al-Basir (Who best sees everything at every moment) is described by use of simile.

timely word! **The path of life [paradise] is above for the wise, that he may decline from the lowest underworld [hell].** The Lord tears down the proud man's house but He keeps the widow's boundaries intact. **The Lord dislikes the thoughts of the wicked, but those of the pure are pleasing to Him.** A greedy man brings trouble to his family, but he who hates bribes will live. The heart of the righteous weighs its answers, but the mouth of the wicked gushes evil. **The Lord is far from the wicked but He hears [respond] the prayer of the righteous.** A cheerful look brings joy to the heart, and good news gives health to the bones. He who listens to a life-giving rebuke will be at home among the wise. He who ignores discipline despises himself, but whoever heeds correction gains understanding. **The fear of the Lord teaches a man wisdom, and humility comes before honor.** (Proverbs, 15:1-33)

All a man's ways seem innocent to him, but motives are weighed by the Lord. Commit to the Lord whatever you do, and your plans will succeed. The Lord works out everything for His own ends— even the wicked for a day of disaster. The Lord dislikes all the proud of heart. Be sure of this: They will not go unpunished. Through love and faithfulness sin is atoned for; **through the fear of the Lord a man avoids evil.** When a man's ways are pleasing to the Lord, He makes even his enemies live at peace with him. **Better a little with righteousness than much gain with injustice...** His [king's] mouth should not betray justice. Honest scales and balances are from the Lord[5]; all the weights in the bag are of His making. Kings dislike wrongdoing,

---

5. Our Lord's justice and His being the best in knowing the account of everything is described by simile.

for a throne is established through righteousness. Kings take pleasure in honest lips; they value a man who speaks the truth... How much better to get wisdom than gold, to choose understanding rather than silver! **The highway of the upright avoids evil; he who guards his way guards his life. Pride goes before destruction, a haughty spirit before a fall. Better to be lowly in spirit and among the oppressed than to share plunder with the proud.** Whoever gives heed to instruction prospers, and **blessed is he who trusts in the Lord**. The wise in heart are called discerning, and pleasant words promote instruction. Understanding is a fountain of life to those who have it, but folly brings punishment to fools. A wise man's heart guides his mouth, and his lips promote instruction. Pleasant words are a honeycomb, sweet to the soul and healing to the bones. There is a way that seems right to a man, but in the end it leads to death [hell]... **A scoundrel plots evil, and his speech is like a scorching fire. A perverse man stirs up dissension, and a gossip separates close friends.** A violent man entices his neighbor and leads him down a path that is not good. **He who winks with his eye is plotting perversity; he who purses his lips is bent on evil...** Better a patient man than a warrior, a man who controls his temper than one who takes a city... **Every decision is from the Lord.** (Proverbs, 16:1-33)

Better a dry crust with peace and quiet than a house full of feasting, with strife... The crucible for silver and the furnace for gold, but the Lord tests the heart. A wicked man listens to evil lips; a liar pays attention to a malicious tongue... Arrogant lips are unsuited to a fool—how much worse lying lips to a ruler!... An evil man is bent only on rebellion... Better to meet a bear robbed of her cubs than a fool in his folly. If a man pays back evil for good, evil will never leave his house. Starting a quarrel is like breaching a dam; so drop the matter before a dispute breaks out. Acquitting the guilty and condemning the innocent—the Lord dislikes them both. Why is there money in the hand of a fool to buy wisdom, seeing he has no understanding? **A friend loves at all times, and a brother is born for adversity...** He who loves disobedience loves strife. He whose tongue is deceitful falls into trouble. To have a fool for a son brings grief... **A cheerful heart is good medicine**, but a crushed spirit dries up the bones. A wicked man accepts a bribe in secret to pervert the course of justice. **A discerning man keeps wisdom in view**, but a fool's eyes wander to the ends of the earth... **A man of knowledge uses words with restraint**, and a man of understanding is even-tempered. (Proverbs, 17:1-28)

An unfriendly man pursues selfish ends; he defies all sound judgment. A fool finds no pleasure in understanding but delights in airing his own opinions. When wickedness comes, so does contempt, and with shame comes disgrace. **The words of a man's mouth are deep waters, but the fountain of wisdom is a bubbling brook.** It is not good to be partial to the wicked or to deprive the innocent of justice. A fool's lips bring him strife... A fool's mouth is his undoing, and his lips are a snare to his soul... The wealth of the rich is their fortified city; they imagine it an unscalable wall. **Before his downfall a man's heart is proud, but humility comes before honor.** He who answers before listening—that is his folly and his shame... **The heart of the discerning** acquires knowledge; the ears of the wise seek it out... A man of many companions may come to ruin, but **there is a friend who sticks closer than a brother**. (Proverbs, 18:1-24)

Better a poor man whose walk is blameless than a fool whose lips are perverse. It is not good to have zeal without knowledge, nor to be hasty and miss the way... A false witness will not go unpunished, and he who pours out lies will not go free... **he who cherishes understanding prospers... A man's wisdom gives him patience; it is to his glory to overlook an offense...** A prudent wife is from the Lord. Laziness brings on deep sleep, and the shiftless man goes hungry. **He who obeys God's instructions guards his life [gains paradise], but he who is contemptuous of his ways will die [will be recompensed with the suffering in hell].** He who is kind to the poor lends to the Lord, and He will reward him for what he has done... **Listen to advice and accept instruction, and in the end you will be wise.** Many are the plans in a man's heart, but **it is the Lord's purpose that prevails**. What a man desires is unfailing love; better to be poor than a liar. **The fear of the Lord leads to life: Then one rests content, untouched by trouble...** rebuke a discerning man, and he will gain knowledge... Stop listening to instruction, my son, and you will stray from the words of knowledge... the mouth of the wicked gulps down evil. (Proverbs, 19:1-28)

It is to a man's honor to avoid strife, but every fool is quick to quarrel... The purposes of a man's heart are deep waters, but a man of understanding draws them out. Many a man claims to have unfailing love, but a faithful man who can find? The righteous man leads a blameless life; blessed are his children after him... **Differing weights and differing measures—the Lord dis-**

likes them both... Ears that hear and eyes that see—the Lord has made them both... Gold there is, and rubies in abundance, but lips that speak knowledge are a rare jewel... Make plans by seeking advice... Do not say, "I'll pay you back for this wrong! Wait for the Lord, and He will deliver you. The Lord dislikes differing weights, and dishonest scales do not please Him. **A man's steps are directed by the Lord...** It is a trap for a man to dedicate something rashly... A wise king winnows out the wicked... **The spirit of man is the candle of the Lord [manifestation of God's Light]**... Love and faithfulness keep a king safe; through love his throne is made secure. (Proverbs, 20:3-28)

The king's heart is in the hand of the Lord; He directs it like a watercourse wherever He pleases. All a man's ways seem right to him, but the Lord weighs the heart. **To do what is right and just is more acceptable to the Lord than sacrifice.** Haughty eyes and a proud heart, the lamp of the wicked, are sin!... A fortune made by a lying tongue is a fleeting vapor; they shall stumble upon the snares of death. The violence of the wicked will drag them away, for they refuse to do what is right. The way of the guilty is devious, but the conduct of the innocent is upright... When a wise man is instructed, he gets knowledge... If a man shuts his ears to the cry of the poor, he too will cry out and not be answered... **When justice is done, it brings joy to the righteous but terror to evildoers.** A man who strays from the path of understanding comes to rest in the company of the dead[6]. He who loves pleasure will become poor... In the house of the wise are stores of choice food and oil, but a foolish man devours all he has. **He who pur-**

---

[6]. The "death" here is an allegorical reference to the eternal suffering in hell.

sues righteousness and love finds life[7], prosperity and honor... The proud and arrogant man—"Mocker" is his name; he behaves with overweening pride. The sluggard's craving will be the death of him, because his hands refuse to work. All day long he craves for more, but the righteous give without sparing... A wicked man puts up a bold front, but an upright man gives thought to his ways. **There is no wisdom, no insight, no plan that can succeed against the Lord. The horse is made ready for the day of battle, but victory rests with the Lord.** (Proverbs, 21:1-31)

... To be esteemed is better than silver or gold. Rich and poor have this in common: The Lord is the Maker of them all... **Humility and the fear of the Lord bring wealth and honor and life.** In the paths of the wicked lie thorns and snares, but he who guards his soul stays far from them. Train a child in the way he should go, and when he is old he will not turn from it... He who sows wickedness reaps trouble, and the rod of his fury will be destroyed. **A generous man will himself be blessed, for he shares his food with the poor.** Drive out the mocker, and out goes strife; quarrels and insults are ended... The eyes of the Lord keep watch over knowledge, but He frustrates the words of the unfaithful... He who oppresses the poor to increase his wealth... will come to poverty. (Proverbs, 22:1-16)

Pay attention and listen to the sayings of the wise; apply your heart to what I teach, for it is pleasing when you keep them in your heart and have all of them ready on your lips. So that your trust may be in the Lord, I teach you today, even you. Have I not

---

7. True believers are referred to as living in blessings in this world and the Hereafter.

WISDOM AND SOUND ADVICE FROM THE TORAH

written thirty sayings for you, sayings of counsel and knowledge, teaching you true and reliable words, so that you can give sound answers to Him Who sent you? Do not exploit the poor because they are poor and do not crush the needy in court, for the Lord will take up their case... Do not make friends with a hot-tempered man, do not associate with one easily angered, or you may learn his ways and get yourself ensnared. (Proverbs, 22:17-25)

Apply your heart to instruction and your ears to words of knowledge. Do not withhold discipline from a child... My son, if your heart is wise, then my heart will be glad; my inmost being will rejoice when your lips speak what is right. **Do not let your heart envy sinners, but always be zealous for the fear of the Lord. There is surely a future hope for you, and your hope will not be cut off**. Listen, my son, and be wise, and keep your heart on the right path... **do not despise your mother when she is old. Buy the truth and do not sell it; get wisdom, discipline and understanding.** The father of a righteous man has great joy; he who has a wise son delights in him. (Proverbs, 23:12-24)

Do not envy wicked men, do not desire their company; for their hearts plot violence, and their lips talk about making trouble. By wisdom a house is built, and through understanding it is established; through knowledge its rooms are filled with rare and beautiful treasures. **A wise man has great power, and a man of knowledge increases strength**... For victory [you need] many advisers... He who plots evil will be known as a schemer... men dislike a mocker. **If you falter in times of trouble, how small is your strength!** Rescue those being led away to death; hold back those staggering toward slaughter. If you say, "But we knew nothing about this," does not He Who weighs the heart perceive it? Does not He Who guards your life know it? Will He not repay each person according to what he has done? Eat honey, my son, for it is good; honey from the comb is sweet to your taste. Know also that wisdom is sweet to your soul; if you find it, there is a future hope for you, and your hope will not be cut off. Do not lie in wait like an outlaw against a righteous man's house, do not raid his dwelling place; for though a righteous man falls seven times, he rises again, but the wicked are brought down by calamity. Do not gloat when your enemy falls; when he stumbles, do not let your heart rejoice, or the Lord will see and disapprove... Do not fret because of evil men or be envious of the wicked, for the evil man has no future hope... **Fear the Lord**... my son, and **do not join with the rebellious**... These also are sayings of the wise: To show partiality in judging is not good: Whoever says to the guilty, "You are innocent"—peoples will curse him and nations denounce him... Do not testify against your neighbor without cause, or use your lips to deceive. Do not say, "I'll do to him as he has done to me; I'll pay that man back for what he did." I went past the field of the sluggard, past the vineyard of the man who lacks judgment; thorns had come up everywhere, the ground was covered with weeds, and the stone wall was in ruins. I applied my heart to what I observed and learned a lesson from what I saw: A little sleep, a little slumber, a little folding of the hands to rest—and poverty will come on you like a bandit and scarcity like an armed man. (Proverbs, 24:1-34)

A word aptly spoken is like apples of gold in settings of silver. **Like an earring of gold or an ornament of fine gold is a wise man's rebuke to a listening ear.** Like the coolness of snow at harvest time is a trustworthy messenger to those who send him... Like clouds and wind without rain is a man who boasts of gifts he does not give. Through patience a ruler can be persuaded, and a gentle tongue can break hardness... Like a club or a sword or a sharp arrow is the man who gives false testimony against his neighbor. Like a bad tooth or a lame foot is reliance on the unfaithful in times of trouble... If your enemy is hungry, give him food to eat; if he is thirsty, give him water to drink. In doing this, you will heap burning coals on his head, and the Lord will reward you... **Like a muddied spring or a polluted well is a righteous man who gives way to the wicked... Like a city whose walls are broken down is a man who lacks self-control.** (Proverbs, 25:11-28)

Like snow in summer or rain in harvest, honor is not fitting for a fool... **Do not answer a fool according to his folly, or you will be like him yourself.** Answer a fool according to his folly, or he will be wise in his own eyes. Like cutting off one's feet... is the sending of a message by the hand of a fool. Like a lame man's legs that hang limp is a proverb in the mouth of a fool. Like tying a stone in a sling is the giving of honor to a fool. Like a thornbush in a drunkard's hand is a proverb in the mouth of a fool... Do you see a man wise in his own eyes? There is more hope for a fool than for him... As a door turns on its hinges, so a sluggard turns on his bed. The sluggard buries his hand in the dish; he is too lazy to bring it back to his mouth. The sluggard is wiser in his own eyes than seven men who answer discreetly... Without wood a fire goes out; without gossip a quarrel dies down. As charcoal to embers and as wood to fire, so is a quarrelsome man for kindling strife... Like a coating of glaze over earthenware are fervent lips with an evil heart. **A malicious man disguises himself with his**

lips, but in his heart he harbors deceit. Though his speech is charming, do not believe him, for seven abominations fill his heart. His malice may be concealed by deception, but his wickedness will be exposed in the assembly. **If a man digs a pit, he will fall into it; if a man rolls a stone, it will roll back on him.** A lying tongue hates those it hurts, and a flattering mouth works ruin. (Proverbs, 26:1-28)

Do not boast about tomorrow, for you do not know what a day may bring forth. Let another praise you, and not your own mouth; someone else, and not your own lips. Stone is heavy and sand a burden, but provocation by a fool is heavier than both. **Anger is cruel and fury overwhelming... Better is open rebuke than hidden love.** Wounds from a friend can be trusted... Perfume and incense bring joy to the heart, and **the earnest counsel of one's friend is sweet to the soul**. (Proverbs, 27:1-9)

As iron sharpens iron, so one man sharpens another... As water reflects a face, so a man's heart reflects the man. Sheol [hell] and destruction are never satisfied, and neither are the eyes of man. The crucible for silver and the furnace for gold, but **man is tested by the praise he receives**. (Proverbs, 27:17-21)

The wicked man flees though no one pursues, but **the righteous are as bold as a lion**. When a country is rebellious, it has many rulers, but a man of understanding and knowledge maintains order. A poor man who oppresses the poor is like a driving rain that leaves no crops. Those who forsake the law praise the wicked, but those who keep the law resist them. Evil men do not understand justice, but **those who seek the Lord understand it fully**. Better a poor man whose walk is blameless than a rich man whose ways are perverse. He who keeps the law[8] is a discerning son... **He who leads the upright along an evil path will fall into his own trap, but the blameless will receive a good inheritance.** A rich man may be wise in his own eyes, but a poor man who has discernment sees through him. When the righteous triumph, there is great elation... He who conceals his sins does not prosper, but **whoever confesses and renounces them finds mercy. Blessed is the man who always fears the Lord,** but he who hardens his heart falls into trouble. Like a roaring lion or a charging bear is a wicked man ruling over a helpless people. A tyrannical ruler lacks judgment, but he who hates ill-gotten gain will enjoy a long life... He whose walk is blameless is kept safe, but he whose ways are perverse will suddenly fall. He who works his land will have abundant food, but the one who chases fantasies will have his fill of poverty. **A faithful man will be richly blessed**, but one eager to get rich will not go unpunished... A stingy man is eager to get rich and is unaware that poverty awaits him... A greedy man stirs up dissension, but **he who trusts in the Lord will prosper**. He who trusts in himself is a fool, but he who walks in wisdom is kept safe. **He who gives to the poor will lack nothing**, but he who closes his eyes to them receives many curses. (Proverbs, 28:1-27)

---

8. Allah's commandments and recommendations are meant.

A man who remains stiff-necked after many rebukes will suddenly be destroyed—without remedy. **When the righteous thrive, the people rejoice;** when the wicked rule, the people groan... By justice a king gives a country stability, but one who is greedy for bribes tears it down. Whoever flatters his neighbor is spreading a net for his feet. An evil man is snared by his own sin, **but a righteous one can sing and be glad.** The righteous care about justice for the poor, but the wicked have no such concern. Mockers stir up a city, but **wise men turn away anger**. If a wise man goes to court with a fool, the fool rages and scoffs, and there is no peace. Bloodthirsty men hate a man of integrity, but the upright seek his soul. A fool gives full vent to his anger, but **a wise man keeps himself under control**... If a king judges the poor with fairness, his throne will always be secure... When the wicked thrive, so does sin, but the righteous will see their downfall. Discipline your son, and he will give you peace; he will bring delight to your soul. Where there is no revelation, the people cast off restraint; but **blessed is he who keeps the law**[9]... An angry man stirs up dissension, and a hot-tempered one commits many sins. **A man's pride brings him low, but a man of lowly spirit gains honor**... **Fear of man will prove to be a snare, but whoever trusts in the Lord is kept safe**. Many seek an audience with a ruler, but **it is from the Lord that man gets justice**. The righteous dislike the dishonest; the wicked dislike the upright. (Proverbs, 29:1-27)

Every word of God is flawless; He is a shield to those who take refuge in Him... O Lord... Keep falsehood and lies far from me... (Proverbs, 30:5-8)

---

9. Referring to Allah's commandments and advice.

WISDOM AND SOUND ADVICE FROM THE TORAH

[There are] those who are pure in their own eyes and yet are not cleansed of their filth; those whose eyes are ever so haughty, **whose glances are so disdainful**; those whose teeth are swords and whose jaws are set with knives... (Proverbs, 30:12-14)

"Four things on earth are small, yet they are extremely wise: Ants are creatures of little strength, yet they store up their food in the summer; coneys are creatures of little power, yet they make their home in the crags; locusts have no king, yet they advance together in ranks; a lizard can be caught with the hand, yet it is found in kings' palaces."... "**If you have played the fool and exalted yourself, or if you have planned evil, clap your hand over your mouth!** For as churning the milk produces butter... **so stirring up anger produces strife**." (Proverbs, 30:24-33)

"Speak up for those who cannot speak for themselves, for the rights of all who are destitute. **Speak up and judge fairly; defend the rights of the poor and needy**." A wife of noble character who can find? She is worth far more than rubies. Her husband has full confidence in her and lacks nothing of value. She brings him good, not harm, all the days of her life... **She opens her arms to the poor and extends her hands to the needy... She is clothed with strength and dignity**; she is facing the future with a smile. **She speaks with wisdom, and faithful instruction is on her tongue.** She watches over the affairs of her household and does not eat the bread of idleness... **Charm is deceptive, and beauty is fleeting; but a woman who fears the Lord is to be praised.** Give her the reward she has earned, and let her works bring her praise at the city gate. (Proverbs, 31:8-31)

Harun Yahya (Adnan Oktar)

THE DECEPTION OF EVOLUTION

Darwinism, in other words the theory of evolution, was put forward with the aim of denying the fact of Creation, but is in truth nothing but failed, unscientific nonsense. **This theory, which claims that life emerged by chance from inanimate matter, was invalidated by the scientific evidence of miraculous order in the universe and in living things, as well as by the discovery of more than 300 million fossils revealing that evolution never happened.** In this way, **science confirmed the fact that Allah created the universe and the living things in it.** The propaganda carried out today in order to keep the theory of evolution alive is based solely on the distortion of the scientific facts, biased interpretation, and lies and falsehoods disguised as science.

Yet this propaganda cannot conceal the truth. The fact that **the theory of evolution is the greatest deception in the history of science** has been expressed more and more in the scientific world over the last 20-30 years. Research carried out after the 1980s in particular has revealed that the claims of Darwinism are totally unfounded, something that has been stated by a large number of scientists. In the United States in particular, many scientists from such different fields as biology, biochemistry and paleontology recognize the invalidity of Darwinism and employ the fact of Creation to account for the origin of life.

We have examined the collapse of the theory of evolution and the proofs of Creation in great scientific detail in many of our works, and are still continuing to do so. Given the enormous importance of this subject, it will be of great benefit to summarize it here.

The Scientific Collapse of Darwinism

As **a pagan doctrine** going back as far as ancient Greece, the theory of evolution was advanced extensively in the nineteenth century. The most important development that made it the top topic of the world of science was Charles Darwin's *The Origin of Species*, published in 1859. In this book, he opposed, in his own eyes, the fact that Allah created different living species on Earth separately, for he erroneously claimed that all living beings had a common ancestor and had diversified over time through small changes. **Darwin's theory was not based on any concrete scientific finding; as he also accepted, it was just an "assumption."** Moreover, as Darwin confessed in the long chapter of his book titled **"Difficulties on Theory," the theory failed in the face of many critical questions.**

Charles Darwin

Darwin invested all of his hopes in new scientific discoveries, which he expected to solve these difficulties. However, contrary to his expectations, scientific findings expanded the dimensions of these difficulties. The defeat of Darwinism in the face of science can be reviewed under three basic topics:

1) The theory cannot explain how life originated on Earth.

2) No scientific finding shows that the "evolutionary mechanisms" proposed by the theory have any evolutionary power at all.

3) The fossil record proves the exact opposite of what the theory suggests.

In this section, we will examine these three basic points in general outlines:

The First Insurmountable Step: The Origin of Life

The theory of evolution posits that all living species evolved from a single living cell that emerged on Earth 3.8 billion years ago, supposed to have happened as a result of coincidences. How a single cell could generate millions of complex living species and, if such an evolution really occurred, why traces of it cannot be observed in the fossil record are some of the questions that the theory cannot answer. However, first and foremost, we need to ask: **How did this "first cell" originate?**

Since the theory of evolution ignorantly denies Creation, it maintains that the "first cell" originated as a product of blind coincidences within the laws of nature, without any plan or arrangement. According to the theory, inanimate matter must have produced a living cell as a result of coincidences. Such a claim, however, is inconsistent with the most unassailable rules of biology.

Life Comes From Life

In his book, Darwin never referred to the origin of life. The primitive understanding of science in his time rested on the assumption that living beings had a very simple structure. Since medieval times, spontaneous generation, which asserts that non-living materials came together to form living organisms, had been widely accepted. It was commonly believed that insects came into being from food leftovers, and mice from wheat. Interesting experiments were conducted to prove this theory. Some wheat was placed on a dirty piece of cloth, and it was believed that mice would originate from it after a while.

The French biologist Louis Pasteur

Similarly, maggots developing in rotting meat was assumed to be evidence of spontaneous generation. However, **it was later understood that worms did not appear on meat spontaneously, but were carried there by flies in the form of larvae, invisible to the naked eye.**

Even when Darwin wrote *The Origin of Species*, the belief that bacteria could come into existence from non-living matter was widely accepted in the world of science.

Russian biologist Alexander Oparin

However, **five years after the publication of Darwin's book, Louis Pasteur announced his results after long studies and experiments, that disproved spontaneous generation, a cornerstone of Darwin's theory.** In his triumphal lecture at the Sorbonne in 1864, **Pasteur said: "Never will the doctrine of spontaneous generation recover from the mortal blow struck by this simple experiment."**[62]

For a long time, advocates of the theory of evolution resisted these findings. However, as the development of science unraveled the complex structure of the cell of a living being, the idea that life could come into being coincidentally faced an even greater impasse.

Inconclusive Efforts of the Twentieth Century

The first evolutionist who took up the subject of the origin of life in the twentieth century was the renowned Russian biologist Alexander Oparin. With various theses he advanced in the 1930s, he tried to prove that a living cell could originate by coincidence. These studies, however, were doomed to failure, and Oparin had to make the following confession:

> Unfortunately, however, the problem of the origin of the cell is perhaps the most obscure point in the whole study of the evolution of organisms.[63]

Evolutionist followers of Oparin tried to carry out experiments to solve this problem. The best known experiment was carried out by the American chemist Stanley Miller in 1953. Combining the gases he alleged to have existed in the primordial Earth's atmosphere in an experiment set-up, and adding energy to the mixture, Miller synthesized several organic molecules (amino acids) present in the structure of proteins.

Barely a few years had passed before it was revealed that **this experiment, which was then presented as an important step in the name of evolution, was invalid, for the atmosphere used in the experiment was very different from the real Earth conditions.**[64]

After a long silence, **Miller confessed that the atmosphere medium he used was unrealistic**.[65]

All the evolutionists' efforts throughout the twentieth century to explain the origin of life ended in failure. The geochemist Jeffrey Bada, from the San Diego Scripps Institute accepts this fact in an article published in *Earth* magazine in 1998:

> Today as we leave the twentieth century, we still face the biggest unsolved problem that we had when we entered the twentieth century: How did life originate on Earth?[66]

The Complex Structure of Life

The primary reason why evolutionists ended up in such a great impasse regarding the origin of life is that even those living organisms Darwinists deemed to be the simplest have outstandingly complex features. The cell of a living thing is more complex than all of our man-made technological products. **Today, even in the most developed laboratories of the world, no single protein of the cell, let alone a living cell itself, can be produced by bringing organic chemicals together.**

The conditions required for the formation of a cell are too great in quantity to be explained away by coincidences.

However, there is no need to explain the situation with these details. Evolutionists are at a dead-end even before reaching the stage of the cell. That is because the probability of just a single protein, an essential building block of the cell, coming into being by chance is mathematically "0."

The main reason for this is the need for other proteins to be present if one protein is to form, and this completely eradicates the possibility of chance formation. This fact by itself is sufficient to eliminate the evolutionist claim of chance right from the outset. To summarize,

1. Protein cannot be synthesized without enzymes, and enzymes are all proteins.

2. Around 100 proteins need to be present in order for a single protein to be synthesized. There therefore need to be proteins for proteins to exist.

3. DNA manufactures the protein-synthesizing enzymes. Protein cannot be synthesized without DNA. DNA is therefore also needed in order for proteins to form.

One of the facts nullifying the theory of evolution is the incredibly complex structure of life. The DNA molecule located in the nucleus of cells of living beings is an example of this. The DNA is a sort of databank formed of the arrangement of four different molecules in different sequences. This databank contains the codes of all the physical traits of that living being. When the human DNA is put into writing, it is calculated that this would result in an encyclopedia made up of 900 volumes. Unquestionably, such extraordinary information definitively refutes the concept of coincidence.

4. All the organelles in the cell have important tasks in protein synthesis. In other words, in order for proteins to form a perfect and fully functioning cell needs to exist together with all its organelles.

The DNA molecule, which is located in the nucleus of a cell and which stores genetic information, is a magnificient databank. If the information coded in DNA were written down, it would make a giant library consisting of an estimated 900 volumes of encyclopedias consisting of 500 pages each.

A very interesting dilemma emerges at this point: DNA can replicate itself only with the help of some specialized proteins (enzymes). However, the synthesis of these enzymes can be realized only by the information coded in DNA. As they both depend on each other, they have to exist at the same time for replication. This brings the scenario that life originated by itself to a deadlock. Prof. Leslie Orgel, an evolutionist of repute from the University of San Diego, California, confesses this fact in the September 1994 issue of the *Scientific American* magazine:

> **It is extremely improbable that proteins and nucleic acids, both of which are structurally complex, arose spontaneously in the same place at the same time.** Yet it also seems impossible to have one without the other. And so, at first glance, one might have to conclude that life could never, in fact, have originated by chemical means.[67]

No doubt, if it is impossible for life to have originated spontaneously as a result of blind coincidences, then it has to be accepted that **life was created**. This fact explicitly invalidates the theory of evolution, whose main purpose is to deny Creation.

Imaginary Mechanism of Evolution

The second important point that negates Darwin's theory is that both concepts put forward by the theory as "evolutionary mechanisms" were understood to have, in reality, no evolutionary power.

Darwin based his evolution allegation entirely on the mechanism of "natural selection." The importance he placed on this mechanism was ev-

According to natural selection, the fittest living things and those best able to adapt to their environment survive, while the others die out. Evolutionists, however, maintain that natural selection evolves living things and gives rise to new species. The fact is, however, that no such consequences result from natural selection, and not a single piece of evidence supports that claim.

ident in the name of his book: *The Origin of Species, By Means of Natural Selection...*

Natural selection holds that those living things that are stronger and more suited to the natural conditions of their habitats will survive in the struggle for life. For example, in a deer herd under the threat of attack by wild animals, those that can run faster will survive. Therefore, the deer herd will be comprised of faster and stronger individuals. However, unquestionably, this mechanism will not cause deer to evolve and transform themselves into another living species, for instance, horses.

Therefore, **the mechanism of natural selection has no evolutionary power. Darwin was also aware of this fact** and had to state this in his book *The Origin of Species*:

> Natural selection can do nothing until favourable individual differences or variations occur.[68]

WISDOM AND SOUND ADVICE FROM THE TORAH

Lamarck's Impact

So, how could these "favorable variations" occur? Darwin tried to answer this question from the standpoint of the primitive understanding of science at that time. According to the French biologist Chevalier de Lamarck (1744-1829), who lived before Darwin, living creatures passed on the traits they acquired during their lifetime to the next generation. He asserted that these traits, which accumulated from one generation to another, caused new species to be formed. For instance, he claimed that giraffes evolved from antelopes; as they struggled to eat the leaves of high trees, their necks were extended from generation to generation.

Lamarck

Lamarck believed that giraffes evolved from animals resembling antelopes. In his view, these creatures' necks grew as they stretched up to eat the leaves on trees, and they gradually turned into giraffes. The laws of inheritance discovered by Mendel in 1865 proved that it was impossible for characteristics acquired during the course of life to be handed on to later generations. Thus Lamarck's just-so story was consigned to the wastebasket of history.

Darwin also gave similar examples. In his book *The Origin of Species*, for instance, he said that some bears going into water to find food transformed themselves into whales over time.[69]

However, the laws of inheritance discovered by Gregor Mendel (1822-84) and verified by the science of genetics, which flourished in the twentieth century, utterly demolished the legend that acquired traits were passed on to subsequent generations. Thus, natural selection fell out of favor as an evolutionary mechanism.

Neo-Darwinism and Mutations

In order to find a solution, Darwinists advanced the "Modern Synthetic Theory," or as it is more commonly known, Neo-Darwinism, at the end of the 1930s. Neo-Darwinism added mutations, which are distortions formed in the genes of living beings due to such external factors as radiation or replication errors, as the "cause of favorable variations" in addition to natural mutation.

Today, the model that Darwinists espouse, despite their own awareness of its scientific invalidity, is neo-Darwinism. The theory maintains that millions of living beings formed as a result of a process whereby numerous complex organs of these organisms (e.g., ears, eyes, lungs, and wings) underwent "mutations," that is, genetic disorders. Yet, there is an outright scientific fact that totally undermines this

All mutations observed in human beings are harmful. That is because living DNA has a highly complex order. Any random impact on this molecule can only be damaging to the organism. Changes caused by mutations are always death, handicaps and diseases. (side) Picture of a fruit fly subjected to mutation.

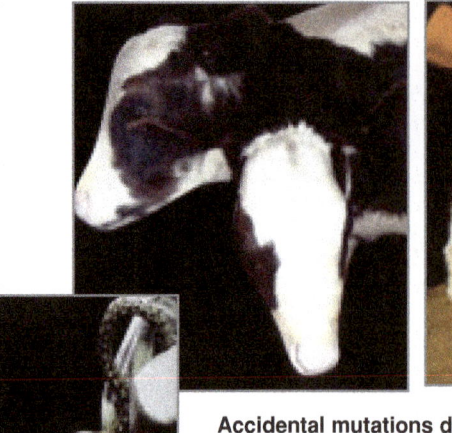

Accidental mutations develop into defects in humans as well as other living beings. The Chernobyl disaster is an eye-opener for the effects of mutations.

theory: **Mutations do not cause living beings to develop; on the contrary, they are always harmful.**

The reason for this is very simple: **DNA has a very complex structure, and random effects can only harm it.** The American geneticist B. G. Ranganathan explains this as follows:

> First, genuine mutations are very rare in nature. Secondly, most mutations are harmful since they are random, rather than orderly changes in the structure of genes; any random change in a highly ordered system will be for the worse, not for the better. For example, **if an earthquake were to shake a highly ordered structure such as a building, there would be a random change in the framework of the building which, in all probability, would not be an improvement.**[70]

Not surprisingly, no mutation example, which is useful, that is, which is observed to develop the genetic code, has been observed so far. All mutations have proved to be harmful. It was understood that mutation, which is presented as an "evolutionary mechanism," is actually a genetic occurrence that harms living things, and leaves them disabled. (The most common effect of mutation on human beings is cancer.) Of course, a destructive mechanism cannot be an "evolutionary mechanism." Natural selection, on the other hand, "can do nothing by itself," as Darwin also accepted. This fact shows us that **there is no "evolutionary mechanism" in nature**. Since no evolutionary mechanism exists, no such imaginary process called "evolution" could have taken place.

The Fossil Record: No Sign of Intermediate Forms

The clearest evidence that the scenario suggested by the theory of evolution did not take place is the fossil record.

According to the unscientific supposition of this theory, every living species has sprung from a predecessor. A previously existing species turned into something else over time and all species have come into being in this way. In other words, this transformation proceeds gradually over millions of years.

Had this been the case, numerous intermediary species should have existed and lived within this long transformation period.

For instance, some half-fish/half-reptiles should have lived in the past which had acquired some reptilian traits in addition to the fish traits they already had. Or there should have existed some reptile-birds, which acquired some bird traits in addition to the reptilian traits they already had. Since these would be in a transitional phase, they should be disabled, defective, crippled living beings. Evolutionists refer to these imaginary creatures, which they believe to have lived in the past, as "transitional forms."

If such animals ever really existed, there should be millions and even billions of them in number and variety. More importantly, the remains of these strange creatures should be present in the fossil record. In *The Origin of Species*, Darwin explained:

> If my theory be true, numberless intermediate varieties, linking most closely all of the species of the same group together must as-

LIVING FOSSILS REFUTE EVOLUTION

Fossils are proof that evolution never happened. As the fossil record reveals, living things suddenly appeared together with all the characteristics they possess, and they never undergo the slightest change so long as they remain in existence. Fish have always existed as fish, insects as insects, and reptiles as reptiles. There is no scientific validity to the claim that species emerged gradually.

Sea Urchin
Period: Paleozoic Age, Carboniferous Period
Age: 295 million years

Sun Fish
Period: Cenozoic Age, Eocene Period
Age: 54-37 million years

Crane Fly
Period: Cenozoic Age, Eocene Period
Age: 48-37 million years

Starfish
Period: Paleozoic Age, Ordovician Period
Age: 490-443 million years

Birch Tree Leaf
Period: Cenozoic Age, Eocene Period
Age: 50 million years

Cicada
Period: Mesozoic Age, Cretaceous Period
Age: 125 million years

Sequoia Leaf
Period: Cenozoic Age, Eocene Period
Age: 50 million years

suredly have existed... Consequently, evidence of their former existence could be found only amongst fossil remains.[71]

However, **Darwin was well aware that no fossils of these intermediate forms had yet been found.** He regarded this as a major difficulty for his theory. In one chapter of his book titled "Difficulties on Theory," he wrote:

> **Why,** if species have descended from other species by insensibly fine gradations, **do we not everywhere see innumerable transitional forms? Why is not all nature in confusion instead of the species being, as we see them, well defined?...** But, as by this theory innumerable transitional forms must have existed, why do we not find them embedded in countless numbers in the crust of the earth?... Why then is not every geological formation and every stratum full of such intermediate links?[72]

Darwin's Hopes Shattered

However, although evolutionists have been making strenuous efforts to find fossils since the middle of the nineteenth century all over the world, **no transitional forms have yet been uncovered.** All of the fossils, contrary to the evolutionists' expectations, show that **life appeared on Earth all of a sudden and fully-formed.**

One famous British paleontologist, Derek V. Ager, admits this fact, even though he is an evolutionist:

> The point emerges that if we examine the fossil record in detail, whether at the level of orders or of species, **we find–over and over again–not gradual evolution, but the sudden explosion of one group at the expense of another.**[73]

This means that **in the fossil record, all living species suddenly emerge as fully formed, without any intermediate forms in between.** This is just the opposite of Darwin's assumptions. Also, this is very strong evidence that **all living things are created.** The only explanation of a living species emerging suddenly and complete in every detail without any

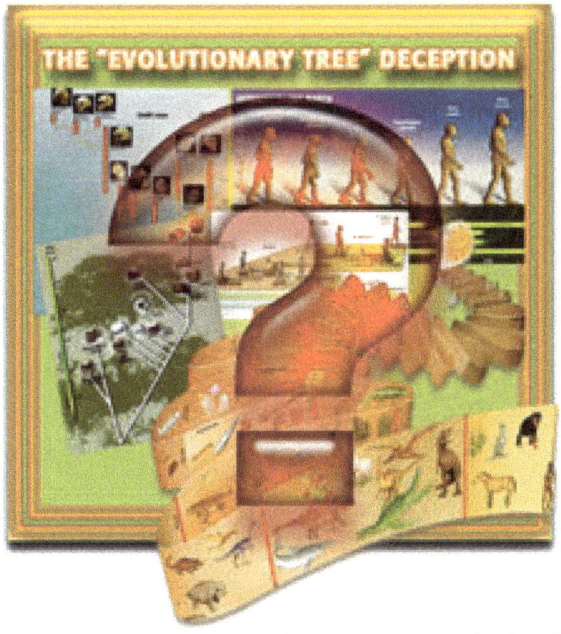

Evolutionists seek to establish a fictitious evolutionary tree by using extinct species of ape and certain human races. However, the scientific evidence allows them no opportunity of doing so.

evolutionary ancestor is that it was created. This fact is admitted also by the widely known evolutionist biologist Douglas Futuyma:

> Creation and evolution, between them, exhaust the possible explanations for the origin of living things. Organisms either appeared on the earth fully developed or they did not. If they did not, they must have developed from pre-existing species by some process of modification. If they did appear in a fully developed state, they must indeed have been created by some omnipotent intelligence.[74]

Fossils show that living beings emerged fully developed and in a perfect state on the Earth. That means that "the origin of species," contrary to Darwin's supposition, is not evolution, but Creation.

The Tale of Human Evolution

The subject most often brought up by advocates of the theory of evolution is the subject of the origin of man. The Darwinist claim holds that man evolved from so-called ape-like creatures. During this alleged evolutionary process, which is supposed to have started 4-5 million years

WISDOM AND SOUND ADVICE FROM THE TORAH

Evolutionist newspapers and magazines often print pictures of the imaginary "primitive" man. The only available source for these imaginary pictures is the imagination of the artist. However, evolutionary theory has been so dented by scientific data that today we see less and less of it in the serious press.

ago, some "transitional forms" between man and his imaginary ancestors are supposed to have existed. According to this completely imaginary scenario, four basic "categories" are listed:

1. *Australopithecus*
2. *Homo habilis*
3. *Homo erectus*
4. *Homo sapiens*

Evolutionists call man's so-called first ape-like ancestors Australopithecus, which means "South African ape." These living beings are actually nothing but an old ape species that has become extinct. Extensive research done on various Australopithecus specimens by two world famous anatomists from England and the USA, namely, Lord Solly Zuckerman and Prof. Charles Oxnard, shows that these apes belonged to an ordinary ape species that became extinct and bore no resemblance to humans.[75]

Evolutionists classify the next stage of human evolution as "homo," that is "man." According to their claim, the living beings in the Homo series are more developed than *Australopithecus*. Evolutionists devise a fanciful evolution scheme by arranging different fossils of these creatures in a particular order. This scheme is imaginary because it has never been proved that there is an evolutionary relation between these different classes. Ernst Mayr, one of the twentieth century's most important evolutionists, contends in his book *One Long Argument* that "particularly historical [puzzles] such as the origin of life or of Homo sapiens, are extremely difficult and may even resist a final, satisfying explanation."[76]

By outlining the link chain as Australopithecus > *Homo habilis* > *Homo erectus* > *Homo sapiens,* evolutionists imply that each of these species is one another's ancestor. However, recent findings of paleoanthropologists have revealed that *Australopithecus, Homo habilis,* and *Homo erectus* lived at different parts of the world at the same time.[77]

Moreover, a certain segment of humans classified as *Homo erectus* have lived up until very modern times. **Homo sapiens neandarthalensis and Homo sapiens sapiens (man) co-existed in the same region.**[78]

This situation apparently indicates the invalidity of the

Evolutionists generally interpret fossils in the light of their ideological expectations, for which reason the conclusions they arrive at are for the most part unreliable.

claim that they are ancestors of one another. Stephen Jay Gould explained this deadlock of the theory of evolution although he was himself one of the leading advocates of evolution in the twentieth century:

> What has become of our ladder if there are three coexisting lineages of hominids (A. africanus, the robust australopithecines, and H. habilis), none clearly derived from another? Moreover, none of the three display any evolutionary trends during their tenure on earth.[79]

Put briefly, the scenario of human evolution, which is "upheld" with the help of various drawings of some "half ape, half human" creatures appearing in the media and course books, that is, frankly, by means of propaganda, is nothing but **a tale with no scientific foundation.**

Lord Solly Zuckerman, one of the most famous and respected scientists in the U.K., who carried out research on this subject for years and studied *Australopithecus* fossils for 15 years, finally concluded, despite being an evolutionist himself, **that there is, in fact, no such family tree branching out from ape-like creatures to man.**

Zuckerman also made an interesting "spectrum of science" ranging from those he considered scientific to those he considered unscientific. According to Zuckerman's spectrum, the most "scientific" – that is, depending on concrete data – fields of science are chemistry and physics. After them come the biological sciences and then the social sciences. At the far end of the spectrum, which is the part considered to be most "unscientific," are "extra-sensory perception" – concepts such as telepathy and sixth sense – and finally "human evolution." Zuckerman explains his reasoning:

> We then move right off the register of objective truth into those fields of presumed biological science, like extrasensory perception or the interpretation of man's fossil history, where to the faithful [evolutionist] anything is possible – and where the ardent believer [in evolution] is sometimes able to believe several contradictory things at the same time.[80]

The tale of human evolution boils down to nothing but the prejudiced interpretations of some fossils unearthed by certain people, who blindly adhere to their theory.

Darwinian Formula!

Besides all the technical evidence we have dealt with so far, let us now for once, examine what kind of a superstition the evolutionists have with an example so simple as to be understood even by children:

The theory of evolution asserts that life is formed by chance. According to this irrational claim, lifeless and unconscious atoms came together to form the cell and then they somehow formed other living things, including man. Let us think about that. When we bring together the elements that are the building-blocks of life such as carbon, phosphorus, nitrogen and potassium, only a heap is formed. No matter what treatments it undergoes, this atomic heap cannot form even a single living being. If you like, let us formulate an "experiment" on this subject and let us examine on the behalf of evolutionists what they really claim without pronouncing loudly under the name **"Darwinian formula"**:

Let evolutionists put plenty of materials present in the composition of living things such as phosphorus, nitrogen, carbon, oxygen, iron, and magnesium into big barrels. Moreover, let them add in these barrels any material that does not exist under normal conditions, but they think as necessary. Let them add in this mixture as many amino acids and as many proteins as they like. Let them expose these mixtures to as much heat and moisture as they like. Let them stir these with whatever technologically developed device they like. Let them put the foremost scientists beside these barrels. Let these experts wait in turn beside these barrels for billions, and even trillions of years. Let them be free to use all kinds of conditions they believe to be necessary for a human's formation. **No matter what they do, they cannot produce from these barrels a human, say a professor that examines his cell structure under the electron microscope.** They cannot produce giraffes, lions, bees, canaries, horses, dolphins, roses, orchids, lilies, carnations, bananas, oranges, apples, dates, tomatoes, melons, watermelons, figs, olives, grapes, peaches, peafowls, pheasants, multicoloured butterflies, or millions of other living beings such as these. Indeed, they could not obtain even a single cell of any one of them.

Briefly, **unconscious atoms cannot form the cell by coming together.** They cannot take a new decision and divide this cell into two, then take other decisions and create the professors who first invent the electron microscope and then examine their own cell structure under that microscope. **Matter is an unconscious, lifeless heap, and it comes to life with Allah's superior Creation.**

The theory of evolution, which claims the opposite, is a total fallacy completely contrary to reason. Thinking even a little bit on the claims of evolutionists discloses this reality, just as in the above example.

Technology in the Eye and the Ear

Another subject that remains unanswered by evolutionary theory is the excellent quality of perception in the eye and the ear.

Before passing on to the subject of the eye, let us briefly answer the question of how we see. Light rays coming from an object fall oppositely on the eye's retina. Here, these light rays are transmitted into electric signals by cells and reach a tiny spot at the back of the brain, the "center of vision." These electric signals are perceived in this center as an image after a series of processes. With this technical background, let us do some thinking.

The brain is insulated from light. That means that its inside is completely dark, and that no light reaches the place where it is located. Thus, the "center of vision" is never touched by light and may even be the darkest place you have ever known. However, you observe a luminous, bright world in this pitch darkness.

The image formed in the eye is so sharp and distinct that even the technology of the twentieth century has not been able to attain it. For instance, look at the book you are reading, your hands with which you are holding it, and then lift your head and look around you. Have you ever seen such a sharp and distinct image as this one at any other place? Even the most developed television screen produced by the greatest television producer in the world cannot provide such a sharp image for you. This is a three-dimensional, colored, and extremely sharp image. For more than 100 years, thousands of engineers have been trying to achieve this sharpness. Factories, huge premises were established, much research has been done, plans and designs have been made for this purpose. Again, look at a TV screen and the book you hold in your hands. You will see that there is a big difference in sharpness and distinction. Moreover, the TV screen shows you a two-dimensional image, whereas with your eyes, you watch a three-dimensional perspective with depth.

For many years, tens of thousands of engineers have tried to make a three-dimensional TV and achieve the vision quality of the eye. Yes, they have made a three-dimensional television system, but it is not possible to watch it without putting on special 3-D glasses; moreover, it is only an artificial three-dimension. The background is more blurred, the foreground appears like a paper setting. Never has it been possible to produce a sharp and distinct vision like that of the eye. In both the camera and the television, there is a loss of image quality.

Evolutionists claim that the mechanism producing this sharp and distinct image has been formed by chance. Now, if somebody told you that the television in your room was formed as a result of chance, that all of its atoms just happened to come together and make up this device that produces an image, what would you think? How can atoms do what thousands of people cannot?

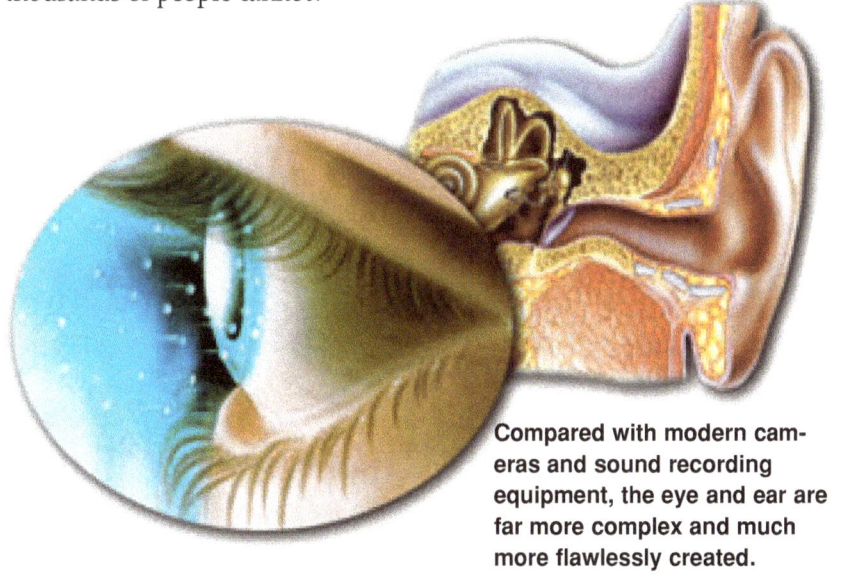

Compared with modern cameras and sound recording equipment, the eye and ear are far more complex and much more flawlessly created.

If a device producing a more primitive image than **the eye could not have been formed by chance**, then it is very evident that the eye and the image seen by the eye could not have been formed by chance. The same situation applies to the ear. The outer ear picks up the available sounds by the auricle and directs them to the middle ear, the middle ear transmits the sound vibrations by intensifying them, and the inner ear sends these vibrations to the brain by translating them into electric signals. Just as with the eye, the act of hearing finalizes in the center of hearing in the brain.

The situation in the eye is also true for the ear. That is, **the brain is insulated from sound just as it is from light.** It does not let any sound in. Therefore, no matter how noisy is the outside, the inside of the brain is completely silent. Nevertheless, the sharpest sounds are perceived in the brain. **In your completely silent brain, you listen to symphonies, and hear all of the noises in a crowded place.** However, were the sound level in your brain measured by a precise device at that moment, complete silence would be found to be prevailing there.

As is the case with imagery, decades of effort have been spent in trying to generate and reproduce sound that is faithful to the original. The results of these efforts are sound recorders, high-fidelity systems, and systems for sensing sound. Despite all of this technology and the thousands of engineers and experts who have been working on this endeavor, no sound has yet been obtained that has the same sharpness and clarity as the sound perceived by the ear. Think of the highest-quality hi-fi systems produced by the largest company in the music industry. Even in these devices, when sound is recorded some of it is lost; or when you turn on a hi-fi you always hear a hissing sound before the music starts. However, the sounds that are the products of the human body's technology are extremely sharp and clear. A human ear never perceives a sound accompanied by a hissing sound or with atmospherics as does a hi-fi; rather, it perceives sound exactly as it is, sharp and clear. This is the way it has been since **the Creation of man**.

So far, no man-made visual or recording apparatus has been as sensitive and successful in perceiving sensory data as are the eye and the ear. However, as far as seeing and hearing are concerned, a far greater truth lies beyond all this.

To Whom Does the Consciousness that Sees and Hears Within the Brain Belong?

Who watches an alluring world in the brain, listens to symphonies and the twittering of birds, and smells the rose?

The stimulations coming from a person's eyes, ears, and nose travel to the brain as electro-chemical nerve impulses. In biology, physiology, and biochemistry books, you can find many details about how this image forms in the brain. However, you will never come across the most important fact: Who perceives these electro-chemical nerve impulses as images, sounds, odors, and sensory events in the brain? **There is a consciousness in the brain that perceives all this without feeling any need for an eye, an ear, and a nose.** To whom does this consciousness belong? Of course it does not belong to the nerves, the fat layer, and neurons comprising the brain. This is why Darwinist-materialists, who believe that everything is comprised of matter, cannot answer these questions.

For this consciousness is the spirit created by Allah, which needs neither the eye to watch the images nor the ear to hear the sounds. Furthermore, it does not need the brain to think.

Everyone who reads this explicit and scientific fact should ponder on Almighty Allah, and fear and seek refuge in Him, for He squeezes the entire universe in a pitch-dark place of a few cubic centimeters in a three-dimensional, colored, shadowy, and luminous form.

A Materialist Faith

The information we have presented so far shows us that **the theory of evolution is incompatible with scientific findings.** The theory's claim regarding the origin of life is inconsistent with science, the evolutionary mechanisms it proposes have no evolutionary power, and fossils demonstrate that **the required intermediate forms have never existed.** So, it certainly follows that the theory of evolution should be pushed aside as an unscientific idea. This is how many ideas, such as the Earth-centered universe model, have been taken out of the agenda of science throughout history.

However, the theory of evolution is kept on the agenda of science. Some people even try to represent criticisms directed against it as an "attack on science." Why?

The reason is that this theory is an indispensable dogmatic belief for some circles. These circles are **blindly devoted to materialist philosophy** and adopt Darwinism because it is the only materialist explanation that can be put forward to explain the workings of nature.

Interestingly enough, they also confess this fact from time to time. A well-known geneticist and an outspoken evolutionist, Richard C. Lewontin from Harvard University, confesses that he is "first and foremost a materialist and then a scientist":

> It is not that the methods and institutions of science somehow compel us accept a material explanation of the phenomenal world, but, on the contrary, that we are forced by our a priori adherence to material causes to create an apparatus of investigation and a set of concepts that produce material explanations, no matter how counter-intuitive, no matter how mystifying to the uninitiated. Moreover, that materialism is absolute, so we cannot allow a Divine [intervention]...[81]

These are explicit statements that **Darwinism is a dogma** kept alive just for the sake of adherence to materialism. This dogma maintains that there is no being save matter. Therefore, it argues that inanimate, unconscious matter brought life into being. It insists that millions of different living species (e.g., birds, fish, giraffes, tigers, insects, trees, flowers, whales, and human beings) originated as a result of the interactions between matter such as pouring rain, lightning flashes, and so on, out of inanimate matter. This is a precept contrary both to reason and science. Yet Darwinists continue to ignorantly defend it just so as not to acknowledge, in their own eyes, the evident existence of Allah.

Anyone who does not look at the origin of living beings with a materialist prejudice sees this evident truth: **All living beings are works of a Creator**, Who is All-Powerful, All-Wise, and All-Knowing. **This Creator is Allah**, Who created the whole universe from non-existence, in the most perfect form, and fashioned all living beings.

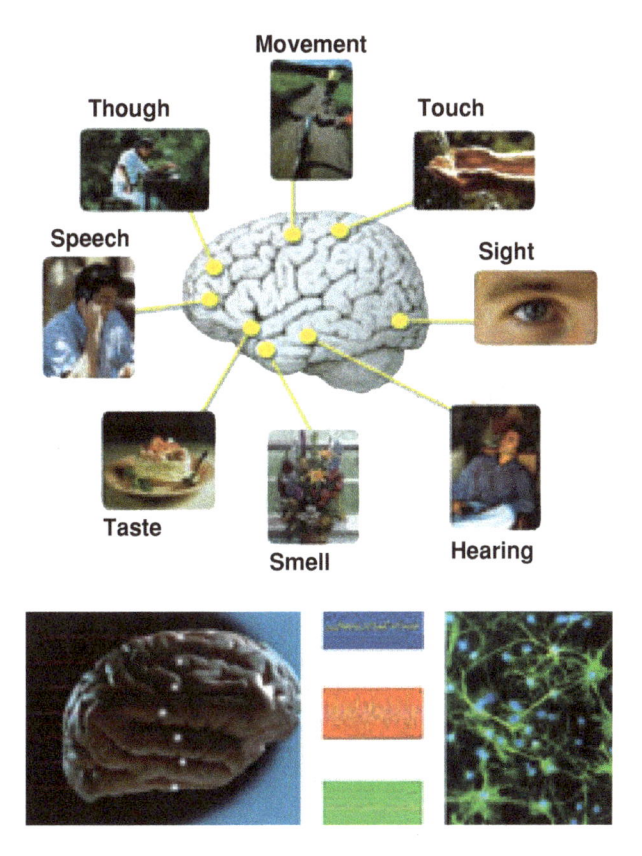

Movement
Though
Touch
Speech
Sight
Taste
Smell
Hearing

We live our whole life in our brains. People we see, flowers we smell, music we hear, fruit we taste, the moisture we feel with our hands—all these are impressions that become "reality" in the brain. But no colors, voices or pictures exist there. We live in an environment of electrical impulses. This is no theory, but the scientific explanation of how we perceive the outside world.

The Theory of Evolution: The Most Potent Spell in the World

Anyone free of prejudice and the influence of any particular ideology, who uses only his or her reason and logic, will clearly understand that belief in the theory of evolution, which brings to mind the superstitions of societies with no knowledge of science or civilization, is quite impossible.

As explained above, those who believe in the theory of evolution think that a few atoms and molecules thrown into a huge vat could produce thinking, reasoning professors and university students; such scientists as Einstein and Galileo; such artists as Humphrey Bogart, Frank Sinatra and Luciano Pavarotti; as well as antelopes, lemon trees, and carnations. Moreover, as the scientists and professors who believe in this nonsense are educated people, it is quite justifiable to speak of this theory as "the most potent spell in history." Never before has any other belief or idea so taken away peoples' powers of reason, refused to allow them to think intelligently and logically, and hidden the truth from them as if they had been blindfolded. This is an even worse and unbelievable blindness than the totem worship in some parts of Africa, the people of Saba worshipping the Sun, the tribe of the Prophet Abraham (pbuh) worshipping idols they had made with their own hands, or some among the people of the Prophet Moses (pbuh) worshipping the Golden Calf.

In fact, Allah has pointed to this lack of reason in the Qur'an. In many verses, He reveals that some peoples' minds will be closed and that they will be powerless to see the truth. Some of these verses are as follows:

As for those who do not believe, it makes no difference to them whether you warn them or do not warn them, they will not believe. Allah has sealed up their hearts and hearing and over their eyes is a blindfold. They will have a terrible punishment. (Surat al-Baqara, 6-7)

... They have hearts with which they do not understand. They have eyes with which they do not see. They have ears with which they do not hear. Such people are like cattle. No, they are even further astray! They are the unaware. (Surat al-A'raf, 179)

Even if We opened up to them a door into heaven, and they spent the day ascending through it, they would only say: "Our eyesight is befuddled! Or rather we have been put under a spell!" (Surat al-Hijr, 14-15)

Words cannot express just how astonishing it is that this spell should hold such a wide community in thrall, keep people from the truth, and not be broken for 150 years. It is understandable that one or a few people might believe in impossible scenarios and claims full of stupidity and illogicality. However, "magic" is the only possible explanation for people from all over the world believing that unconscious and lifeless atoms suddenly decided to come together and form a universe that functions with a flawless system of organization, discipline, reason, and consciousness; a planet named Earth with all of its features so perfectly suited to life; and living things full of countless complex systems.

In fact, in the Qur'an Allah relates the incident of the Prophet Moses (pbuh) and Pharaoh to show that some people who support atheistic philosophies actually influence others by magic. When Pharaoh was told about the true religion, he told the Prophet Moses (pbuh) to meet with his own magicians. When the Prophet Moses (pbuh) did so, he told them to demonstrate their abilities first. The verses continue:

> **He said: "You throw." And when they threw, they cast a spell on the people's eyes and caused them to feel great fear of them. They produced an extremely powerful magic. (Surat al-A'raf, 116)**

As we have seen, Pharaoh's magicians were able to deceive everyone, apart from the Prophet Moses (pbuh) and those who believed in him. However, his evidence broke the spell, or "swallowed up what they had forged," as revealed in the verse:

> **We revealed to Moses: "Throw down your staff." And it immediately swallowed up what they had forged. So the Truth took place and what they did was shown to be false. (Surat al-A'raf, 117-118)**

As we can see, when people realized that a spell had been cast upon them and that what they saw was just an illusion, Pharaoh's magicians lost all credibility. In the present day too, unless those who, under the influence of a similar spell, believe in these ridiculous claims under their scientific disguise and spend their lives defending them, abandon their superstitious beliefs, they also will be humiliated when the full truth emerges and the spell is broken. In fact, world-renowned British writer and philosopher Malcolm Muggeridge, who was an atheist defending evolution for some 60 years, but who subsequently realized the truth, reveals the position in which the theory of evolution would find itself in the near future in these terms:

> I myself am convinced that **the theory of evolution**, especially the extent to which it's been applied, **will be one of the great jokes in the history books in the future.** Posterity will marvel that so very flimsy and dubious an hypothesis could be accepted with the incredible credulity that it has.[82]

That future is not far off: On the contrary, people will soon see that "chance" is not a deity, and will look back on **the theory of evolution as the worst deceit and the most terrible spell in the world.** That spell is already rapidly beginning to be lifted from the shoulders of people all over the world. Many people who see its true face are wondering with amazement how they could ever have been taken in by it.

They said, "Glory be to You! We have no knowledge except what You have taught us. You are the All-Knowing, the All-Wise." (Surat al-Baqara, 32)

NOTES

1. Shamaa-il Tirmidhi; Sahih al-Bukhari.
2. al-Manaqib, vol. 1, p. 145; ed-Daaim, vol. 2, p. 207.
3. al-Makarim, vol. 1, p. 137; ad-Daim, vol. 2, p. 159.
4. Ghazali, Ihya' al-'Ulum.
5. Ghazali, Ihya' al-'Ulum.
6. al-Manaqib, vol. 1, p. 145; ad-Daim, vol. 2, p. 207.
7. al-Manaqib, vol. 1, p. 145; ad-Daim, vol. 2, p. 207.
8. al-Makarim, vol. 1, p. 118.
9. al-Manaqib, vol. 1, p. 145; ad-Daim, vol. 2, p. 207.
10. al-Manaqib, vol. 1, p. 145; ad-Daim, vol. 2, p. 207.
11. Ghazali, Ihya' al-'Ulum, vol. 2, p. 377.
12. Ghazali, Ihya' al-'Ulum.
13. Kanz al-Fuad, p. 285.
14. Falah al-Sail, p. 280.
15. al-Makarim, vol. 1.
16. Ahmad Dhiya al-Din Gumushkhanewi, Ramuz al-Ahadith, vol. 1, Gonca Publishing, Istanbul, 1997, 96/2.
17. al-Kafi, vol. 1, p. 515; al-Makarim, vol. 1, p. 44.
18. al-Makarim, vol. 1, p. 34.
19. al-Bukhari, Kitab al-Tarikh al-Kabir, vol. 1, 382, n: 1222.
20. Ahmad Cevdet Pasha, Qisas al-Anbiya, 4th Fascicle, Kanaat Press, Istanbul 1331, pp. 364-365.
21. Abu Dawud; M. Asım Köksal, Islam Tarihi (History of Islam), XI, 162 vd.
22. al-Makarim, vol. 1, p. 34.
23. M. Asim Koksal, Islam Tarihi (History of Islam), XI, 162 vd.
24. M. Asim Koksal, Islam Tarihi, (History of Islam), XI, 162 vd.
25. From Tirmidhi, Imam Ahmad and Hakim; Hujjat al-Islam Imam al-Ghazali, Ihya' al-'Ulum al-Din, vol. 2.
26. al-Mustadrak, vol. 1, p. 59; al-Makarim, vol. 1, p. 76; Qurb al-'asnad, p. 45.
27. Tuhaf al-Uqul, p. 442.
28. Shamaa-il Tirmidhi.
29. Tabarsi, Makarim al-Akhlaq, vol. 1, p. 34.
30. Ibn Adiyya al-Kamil; Hujjat al-Islam Imam al-Ghazali, Ihya' al-'Ulum al-Din, vol. 3.
31. 3131 al-Bukhari, Kitab al-Tarikh al-Kabir, vol. 1, 382, n: 1222.
32. al-Makarim, vol. 1, p. 33.
33. al-Makarim, vol. 1, p. 33.
34. Tabarsi, Makarim al-Akhlaq, vol. 1, p. 34
35. al-Makarim, vol. 1, p. 30.
36. Abu Dawud, III, 496-497, n: 3840; al-Nasa'i, VII, 207-209; Prof. Dr. Ali Yardım, Peygamberimizin Şemaili (Our Prophet's Appearance), Damla Publishing, 3rd Edition, Istanbul, 1998, p. 219.
37. al-Manaqib, vol. 1, p.145; ad-Daim, vol. 2, p. 207.
38. al-Makarim has mentioned at different places, pp. 26-29-30-31; al-Mahasin, pp. 433-459; al-Hisal; al-Kafi; al-Mustadrak; ad-Daim, vol. 2, p. 113.
39. Abu Dawud, III, 496-497, n: 3840; al-Nasa'i, VII, 207-209; Prof. Dr. Ali Yardım, Peygamberimizin Şemaili (Our Prophet's Appearance), Damla Publishing, 3rd Edition, Istanbul, 1998, p. 219.
40. Abu-Sheikh, Hujjat al-Islam Imam al-Ghazali, Ihya' al-'Ulum al-Din, vol. 2.
41. al-Makarim has mentioned at different places, pp. 26-29-30-31; al-Mahasin, pp. 433-459; al-Hisal; al-Kafi; al-Mustadrak; ad-Daim, vol. 2, p. 113.
42. Abu-Sheikh, Hujjat al-Islam Imam al-Ghazali, Ihya' al-'Ulum al-Din, vol. 2.
43. Ahmad Dhiya al-Din Gumushkhanewi, Ramuz al-Ahadith, vol. 2, Gonca Publishing, Istanbul, 1997, 552/5.
44. Ahmad Dhiya al-Din Gumushkhanewi, Ramuz al-Ahadith, vol. 2, Gonca Publishing, Istanbul, 1997, 549/1.
45. al-Kutub as-Sitta, no: 6945.
46. al-Kutub as-Sitta, no: 6946.
47. al-Kutub as-Sitta, no: 949.
48. Abu Dawud, At'ima 23, (3783).
49. Onder Cagiran, Tıbbi Nebevi (al-Tib al-Nabawi), 1st Edition, Bogazici Publishing, Istanbul 1996.
50. Onder Cagiran, Tıbbi Nebevi (al-Tib al-Nabawi), 1st Edition, Bogazici Publishing, Istanbul 1996.
51. Onder Cagiran, Tıbbi Nebevi (al-Tib al-

Nabawi), 1st Edition, Bogazici Publishing, Istanbul 1996.
52. Ahmad Dhiya al-Din Gumushkhanewi, Ramuz al-Ahadith, vol. 2, Gonca Publishing, Istanbul, 1997, 552/11.
53. Aridat al-Ahwadhi Sharh Sunan at-Tirmidhi, VIII, 89-90, Prof. Dr. Ali Yardim, Peygamberimizin Şemaili (Our Prophet's Appearance), Damla Publishing, 3rd Edition, Istanbul, 1998, p. 255.
54. Ahmad Dhiya al-Din Gumushkhanewi, Ramuz al-Ahadith, vol. 2, Gonca Publishing, Istanbul, 1997, 521/17.
55. Haydar Hatipoglu, Sünen-i İbni Mace Tercemesi ve Şerhi (Translation of Sunan Ibn Majah and Commentary), Kahraman Publishing, vol. 9, Istanbul 1983, p. 75.
56. Ahmad Dhiya al-Din Gumushkhanewi, Ramuz al-Ahadith, vol. 2, Gonca Publishing, Istanbul, 1997, 521/18.
57. al-Makarim has mentioned at different places, pp. 26-29-30-31; al-Mahasin, pp. 433-459; al-Hisal; al-Kafi; al-Mustadrak; ad-Daim, vol. 2, p. 113.
58. al-Amali, vol. 2, p. 294; al-Amali by al-Mufid, p. 114; al-Makarim, vol. 1, p. 176; al-Kafi, vol. 2, p. 138 and vol. 8, p. 168.
59. Haydar Hatipoglu, Sünen-i İbni Mace Tercemesi ve Şerhi (Translation of Sunan Ibn Majah and Commentary), Kahraman Publishing, vol. 9, Istanbul 1983, p. 73.
60. al-Ghazali, Ihya' al-'Ulum.
61. Shamaa-il Tirmidhi, vol. 1.
62. Sidney Fox, Klaus Dose, *Molecular Evolution and The Origin of Life*, W.H. Freeman and Company, San Francisco, 1972, p. 4.
63. Alexander I. Oparin, *Origin of Life*, Dover Publications, NewYork, 1936, 1953 (reprint), p. 196.
64. "New Evidence on Evolution of Early Atmosphere and Life", Bulletin of the American Meteorological Society, vol 63, November 1982, 1328-1330.
65. Stanley Miller, Molecular Evolution of Life: Current Status of the Prebiotic Synthesis of Small Molecules, 1986, p. 7.
66. Jeffrey Bada, *Earth*, February 1998, p. 40.
67. Leslie E. Orgel, "The Origin of Life on Earth", *Scientific American*, vol. 271, October 1994, p. 78.
68. Charles Darwin, *The Origin of Species by Means of Natural Selection*, The Modern Library, New York, p. 127.
69. Charles Darwin, *The Origin of Species: A Facsimile of the First Edition*, Harvard University Press, 1964, p. 184.
70. B. G. Ranganathan, *Origins?*, Pennsylvania: The Banner Of Truth Trust, 1988, p. 7.
71. Darwin, *The Origin of Species: A Facsimile of the First Edition*, p. 179.
72. Charles Darwin, *The Origin of Species*, p. 172.
723.Derek A. Ager, "The Nature of the Fossil Record," *Proceedings of the British Geological Association*, vol 87, 1976, p. 133.
74. Douglas J. Futuyma, *Science on Trial*, Pantheon Books, New York, 1983, p. 197.
75. Solly Zuckerman, *Beyond The Ivory Tower*, Toplinger Publications, New York, 1970, pp. 75-94; Charles E. Oxnard, "The Place of Australopithecines in Human Evolution: Grounds for Doubt," *Nature*, vol 258, p. 389.
76. "Could science be brought to an end by scientists' belief that they have final answers or by society's reluctance to pay the bills?" *Scientific American*, December 1992, p. 20.
77. Alan Walker, *Science*, vol. 207, 7 March 1980, p. 1103; A. J. Kelso, *Physical Antropology*, 1st ed., J. B. Lipincott Co., New York, 1970, p. 221; M. D. Leakey, *Olduvai Gorge*, vol. 03, Cambridge University Press, Cambridge, 1971, p. 272.
78. Jeffrey Kluger, "Not So Extinct After All: The Primitive Homo Erectus May Have Survived Long Enough To Coexist With Modern Humans", *Time*, 23 December 1996.
79. S. J. Gould, *Natural History*, vol. 85, 1976, p. 30.
80. Zuckerman, *Beyond The Ivory Tower*, p. 19.
81. Richard Lewontin, "The Demon-Haunted World," *The New York Review of Books*, January 9, 1997, p. 28.
82. Malcolm Muggeridge, *The End of Christendom*, Grand Rapids:Eerdmans, 1980, p. 43.

CPSIA information can be obtained
at www.ICGtesting.com
Printed in the USA
BVHW021014110621
609092BV00016B/1620